PROPERTY AND PROPHETS

PROPERTY AND PROPHETS

The Evolution of Economic Institutions and Ideologies

FIFTH EDITION

E. K. HUNT
University of Utah

HARPER & ROW, PUBLISHERS, New York
Cambridge, Philadelphia, San Francisco,
London, Mexico City, São Paulo, Singapore, Sydney

1817

Sponsoring Editor: John Greenman
Project Editor: Jo-Ann Goldfarb
Cover Design: 20/20 Services, Inc.
Production: Debra Forrest Bochner
Compositor: ComCom Division of Haddon Craftsmen, Inc.
Printer and Binder: R. R. Donnelley & Sons Company

PROPERTY AND PROPHETS

The Evolution of Economic Institutions and Ideologies, Fifth Edition

Library of Congress Cataloging in Publication Data

Hunt, E. K.
    Property and prophets.

    Includes bibliographical references and index.
     1. Capitalism—History. 2. Economic history.
3. Economics—History. I. Title.
HC21.H85   1986   330.9   85-14060
ISBN 0-06-043037-0

85 86 87 88 9 8 7 6 5 4 3 2 1

TO MY MOTHER

CONTENTS

PREFACE

This book combines a brief review of the evolution of some of the most important institutions of capitalism with analyses of recurring ideological defenses of capitalism and radical critiques of capitalism. The unique feature of the book is the method of interweaving economic history and intellectual, or ideological, history. It is my belief that neither conservative defenses of capitalism nor radical rejections of it can be adequately appreciated until one is aware of the existential context within which they arose. This book attempts to provide an introduction to the study of the relationship between economic history and intellectual history.

No methodological arguments about the nature and extent of direct causal relations between economic history and intellectual history are made. Rather, I have merely juxtaposed events and ideas in a manner which I hope will stimulate readers to ponder these issues and formulate their own conclusions.

My deep and lasting appreciation goes to all who have taught me, particularly Professors Sydney Coontz, Kiyotoshi Iwamoto, and Lawrence Nabers. Professor Howard J. Sherman has provided extensive suggestions and criticisms which have improved the book. I am also grateful to Professors William Davisson, Douglas F. Dowd, Lynn Turgeon, Thomas Weisskopf, and Stephen T. Worland, each of whom read the manuscript in its entirety and made many valuable suggestions and criticism. Valuable suggestions for the subsequent editions of this book were also received from Norris Clement, James Cypher, Clint Jenks, John Pool, Ross LaRoe, James Starkey, Howard Wachtel, and Rick Wolff.

The fifth edition has been changed in several ways. Some material from previous editions has been consolidated and rewritten. Entirely new material on Thompson and Hodgskin has been added to Chapter 5. Most of the chapters contain a number of changes that have been slight, involving only the updating or other slight alterations of the material in the earlier editions.

E. K. HUNT

PROPERTY AND PROPHETS

CHAPTER *1*

The Ideology
of Precapitalist Europe

Human beings must exist in societies in order to survive. Unlike some species of animals, whose individual members can exist fairly adequately in relative isolation, human beings are not equipped by nature with the physical prowess to provide the material requisites of life by themselves. Humans survive and indeed prosper because by living in groups they have learned to subdivide tasks and use tools. It was this division of labor and the accumulation of more and better tools (or capital) that made possible the impressive increases in human-kind's control over nature, or increases in our potential to produce the material necessities of life.

This division of labor also resulted, of necessity, in a differentiation of the roles that the different members of a society occupy. This differentiation was probably purely functional in earliest times; that is, when productivity was low, all members of society lived near the subsistence level, and social class, or hierarchical differentiation, was absent. Increasingly elaborate divisions of tasks, combined with more sophisticated tools, however, led to higher productivity, which made possible an escape from the drudgery of everyday toil for at least a small part of society.

A small leisure class could be supported because with higher per capita productivity the labor of a smaller number of people could support the entire society at its customary standard of living or at an even higher standard. When this occurred, societies began to differentiate among their members according to social class. This hierarchical class differentiation was generally economic

1

in nature. Those who worked were usually assigned to the lowest classes; those who escaped the burdens of ordinary labor were of higher class standing. Although these higher-class people were no longer directly connected with the production of everyday necessities, they often performed rites, rituals, or extensive duties, some of which were undoubtedly beneficial to society.

Such a system would not have been able to exist for long if the majority of its members did not share common feelings about the proper way of conducting economic and social affairs. These common feelings and values, which generally stemmed from a common world view, or system of metaphysics, justified both the division of productive tasks and the class differentiation that existed. These common feelings and values were expressed in ideologies.

An *ideology,* as the term is used in this book, refers to ideas and beliefs that tend to provide moral justification for a society's social and economic relationships. Most members of a society internalize the ideology and thus believe that their functional role as well as those of others is morally correct and that the method by which society divides its produce is fair. This common belief gives society its cohesiveness and viability. Lack of it creates turmoil and strife—and ultimately revolution, if the differences are deep enough.

This book is concerned primarily with our present economic system, capitalism. We sketch the broad outlines of the evolution of this system. In doing so, we focus on conflicts and social antagonisms and examine the ideologies with which the capitalist system attempted to mitigate these conflicts and to promote social cohesiveness. By way of background we begin with the economic systems and ideologies of precapitalist Europe.

ANCIENT GREEK AND ROMAN SLAVERY

In ancient Greece and Rome as much as 80 percent of the people were slaves. The slaves did all the manual work and even much of the clerical, bureaucratic, and artistic work of these societies. They were given just enough food and clothing for bare subsistence. The slave owners owned and utilized the entire surplus produced by the slaves above their own subsistence. Most of the economy was agricultural, aside from a few cities where the central government was located. On each agricultural plantation the slave owner was king and lived in splendid luxury—though he might also have a villa in Athens or Rome. In addition to his wife, who was treated as a valuable piece of property, he sexually exploited his slave women.

What sort of economic ideology existed? There were a few treatises, especially in the Roman period, on the best ways to plant crops, the best agricultural implements to use, and the best ways to supervise, control, and punish slaves. In addition, there were a large number of justifications of slavery. Even such brilliant philosophers as Plato and Aristotle argued that slavery was "natural," was the only possible system, and would exist forever; they argued that some men and women were born to be slaves and were inherently inferior, while others were born superior and were meant to be slave owners. Plato and Aristotle were not apologists; this was the dominant ideology and they simply took it for granted.

Slavery had many limitations, although it did result in many great public works and the advance of science and culture. One limitation was the fact that slaves could not be given complex or delicate machinery of any sort; they would break it up and would often use it for weapons to revolt. Moreover, agricultural organization had to be very simple, usually limited to one crop tilled with crude implements. As a result, much land was totally ruined and the agricultural product limited. Another effect of slavery was the view that all work was demeaning. Because this attitude spread even to invention, the Roman period saw little technological advance and the economy stagnated.

Its economic weaknesses—and accompanying political and social weaknesses—made the Roman Empire vulnerable to attack by the primitive Germanic and Slav tribes. The empire collapsed in the West, and out of the chaos eventually arose the system of feudalism. The kings of the feudal states were mostly former chiefs of the primitive tribes that invaded the area.

FEUDALISM

The decline of the western part of the old Roman Empire left Europe without the laws and protection the empire had provided. The vacuum was filled by the creation of a feudal hierarchy. In this hierarchy, the serf, or peasant, was protected by the lord of the manor, who, in turn, owed allegiance to and was protected by a higher overlord. And so the system went, ending eventually with the king. The strong protected the weak, but they exacted a high price. In return for payments of money, food, labor or military allegiance, overlords granted the fief, or feudum—a hereditary right to use land—to their vassals. At the bottom was the serf, a peasant who tilled the land. The vast majority of the population raised crops for food or clothing or tended sheep for wool and clothing.[1]

Custom and tradition are the keys to understanding medieval relationships. In place of laws as we know them today, the custom of the manor governed. There was no strong central authority in the Middle Ages that could have enforced a system of laws. The entire medieval organization was based on a system of mutual obligations and services up and down the hierarchy. Possession or use of the land obligated one to certain customary services or payments in return for protection. The lord was as obligated to protect the serf as the serf was to turn over a portion of the crop to or perform extensive labor for the lord.

Customs were broken, of course; no system always operates in fact as it is designed to operate in theory. One should not, however, underestimate the

[1]For a more complete discussion of the medieval economic and social system, see J. H. Claphan and Eileen E. Power, eds., *The Agrarian Life of the Middle Ages,* 2d ed., *The Cambridge Economic History of Europe,* vol. I (London: Cambridge University Press, 1966).

strength of custom and tradition in determining the lives and ideas of medieval people. Disputes between serfs were decided in the lord's court according to both the special circumstances of each case and the general customs of the manor for such cases. Of course, a dispute between a serf and a lord would usually be decided by the lord in his own favor. Even in this circumstance, however, especially in England, an overlord would impose sanctions or punishments on a lord who, as his vassal, had persistently violated the customs in his treatment of serfs. This rule by the custom of the manor stands in sharp contrast to the legal and judicial system of capitalism. The capitalist system is based on the enforcement of contracts and universally binding laws, which are softened only rarely by the possible mitigating circumstances and customs that often swayed the lord's judgment in medieval times.

The extent to which the lords could enforce their "rights" varied greatly from time to time and from place to place. It was the strengthening of these obligations and the nobleman's ability to enforce them through a long hierarchy of vassals and over a wide area that eventually led to the emergence of the modern nation-states. This process occurred during the period of transition from feudalism to capitalism. Throughout most of the Middle Ages, however, many of these claims were very weak because political control was fragmented.

The basic economic institution of medieval rural life was the manor, which contained within it two separate and distinct classes: noblemen, or lords of the manors, and serfs (from the Latin word *servus,* "slave"). Serfs were not really slaves however. Unlike slaves, who were simply property to be bought and sold at will, serfs could not be parted from either their families or their land. If their lord transferred possession of the manor to another nobleman, the serfs simply had another lord. In varying degrees, however, obligations were placed upon the serfs that were sometimes very onerous and from which there was often no escape. Usually, they were far from being "free."

The lord lived off the labor of the serfs who farmed his fields and paid taxes in kind and money according to the custom of the manor. Similarly, the lord gave protection, supervision, and administration of justice according to the custom of the manor. It must be added that although the system did rest on reciprocal obligations, the concentration of economic and political power in the hands of the lord led to a system in which, by any standard, the serf was exploited in the extreme.

The Catholic church was by far the largest owner of land during the Middle Ages. Although bishops and abbots occupied much the same place as counts and dukes in the feudal hierarchy, there was one important difference between religious and secular lords. Dukes and counts might shift their loyalty from one overlord to another, depending on the circumstances and the balance of power involved, but bishops and abbots always had (in principle at least) a primary loyalty to the church in Rome. This was also an age during which the religious teaching of the church had a very strong and pervasive influence throughout western Europe. These factors combined to make the church the closest thing to a strong central government throughout this period.

Thus the manor might be secular or religious (many times secular lords had religious overlords and vice versa), but the essential relationships between lord and serfs were not significantly affected by this distinction. There is little evidence that serfs were treated any less harshly by religious lords than by secular ones. The religious lords and the secular nobility were the joint ruling classes; they controlled the land and the power that went with it. In return for very onerous appropriations of the serf's labor, produce, and money, the nobility provided military protection and the church provided spiritual aid.

In addition to manors, medieval Europe had many towns, which were important centers of manufacturing. Manufactured goods were sold to manors and, sometimes, traded in long-distance commerce. The dominant economic institutions in the towns were the guilds—craft, professional, and trade associations that had existed as far back as the Roman Empire. If anyone wanted to produce or sell any good or service, it was necessary to join a guild.

The guilds were as involved with social and religious questions as with economic ones. They regulated their members' conduct in all their activities: personal, social, religious, and economic. Although the guilds did regulate very carefully the production and sale of commodities, they were less concerned with making profits than with saving their members' souls. Salvation demanded that the individual lead an orderly life based on church teachings and custom. Thus the guilds exerted a powerful influence as conservators of the status quo in the medieval towns.

THE CHRISTIAN PATERNALIST ETHIC

The feudal lords, secular as well as religious, needed an ideology that would reflect and justify the feudal status quo. This ideology, which provided the moral cement holding feudal Europe together and protecting its rulers, was the medieval version of the Judeo-Christian tradition. This tradition evolved a moral code sometimes called the Christian corporate ethic, reflecting the fact that all of society was considered a single entity or corporation. To emphasize another feature of it, the Judeo-Christian moral code, as interpreted in the medieval period, will be called the *Christian paternalist ethic* in this book. It can be understood most easily by comparing society with a family. Those with positions of power and wealth can be likened to the father or keeper of the family. They have strong paternalistic obligations toward the common people—the poor or, in our analogy, the children. The common person, however, is expected to accept his or her place in society and to be willingly subordinate to the leadership of the wealthy and the powerful in much the same way that a child accepts the authority of his or her father.

The Old Testament Jews quite literally regarded themselves as the children of one God.[2] This relationship meant that all Jews were brothers; the

[2]This account relies on Alexander Gray, *The Socialist Tradition* (London: Longmans, 1963), chap. 2.

Mosaic law was intended to maintain this feeling of membership in one big family. This brotherhood was one of grown children who acknowledged their mutual obligations, even though they no longer shared possessions.

From the confused mass of duties and regulations governing the early Jews, the most salient feature is the large number of provisions made for the prevention and relief of poverty. Their humane treatment of debtors was also notable. Each Jew was to be his brother's keeper; indeed, his obligations extended to caring for his neighbor's animals should they wander his way.[3] The first duty of all, however, and particularly of the wealthy, was to care for the poor. "Thou shalt open thine hand wide unto my brother, to the poor, and to the needy, in the land."[4] An important element in this paternalistic code was the sanction against taking a worker's tools as a means of satisfying a debt: "No man shall take the nether or the upper millstone to pledge: for he taketh a man's life to pledge."[5] The same point was made elsewhwere in the Old Testament: "He that taketh away his neighbor's living slayeth him."[6]

All Jews did not, of course, live up to these lofty professions. Great extremes of wealth and poverty existed that would have been impossible had the Mosaic law been strictly observed. Many of the prophets, who were often radical champions of the poor, eloquently denounced the rich for their abuse of their wealth, for their wicked, slothful luxury, and for their general unrighteousness. The important point is not that they failed to live up to the code but that the moral code of this small tribe left so important an imprint on much of the subsequent history.

The teachings of Christ in the New Testament carry on part of the Mosaic tradition relevant to economic ideology. He taught the necessity of being concerned with the welfare of one's brother, the importance of charity and almsgiving, and the evil of selfish acquisitiveness and covetousness. His emphasis on the special responsibilities and obligations of the rich is even more pronounced than that of the earlier Jewish writers. In fact, on the basis of a reading of the Gospel of Luke, one might conclude that Christ condemned the rich simply because they were rich and praised the poor simply because they were poor: "Woe unto you that are rich! . . . Woe unto you that are full! for ye shall hunger. Woe unto you that laugh now! for ye shall mourn and weep."[7] However, on examining the other gospels, it must be concluded that this is probably Luke speaking, not Christ. Luke must be seen as the radical "leveller among the apostles."[8]

In the other gospels there are warnings that wealth may be a stumbling block in getting to heaven, but there is no condemnation of wealth as such. The most important passages in this regard deal with the wealthy young man

---

[3]Deut. 22:1–4.
[4]Deut. 15:7–11.
[5]Deut. 24:6.
[6]Eccles. 34:22.
[7]Quoted in Gray, *The Socialist Tradition*, p. 41.
[8]Ibid., p. 42.

who wants to know what he must do to attain eternal life.[9] Christ's first answer amounts to nothing more than a brief statement of the Ten Commandments. It is only after being pressed further that Christ goes beyond the binding, universal moral requirements to a counsel of perfection. "If thou wilt be perfect"[10] begins the statement in which he tells the young man to sell whatever he has and give to the poor.

The Christian paternalist ethic, with its parental obligations of the wealthy toward the poor, was developed more specifically and elaborately by most of the Christian fathers. The writings of Clement of Alexandria are a reasonably good reflection of the traditional attitudes of the early church. He emphasized the dangers of greed, love of material things, and acquisition of wealth. Those who had wealth were under a special obligation to treat it as a gift from God and to use it wisely in the promotion of the general well-being of others.

Clement's *The Rich Man's Salvation* was written in order to free the rich of the "unfounded despair" they might have acquired from reading passages in the gospels like those found in Luke. Clement began by asserting that, contrary to anything one might find in Luke, "it is no great or enviable thing to be simply without riches." Those who were poor would not for that reason alone find god's blessedness. In order to seek salvation, the rich man need not renounce his wealth but need merely "banish from the soul its opinions about riches, its attachment to them, its excessive desire, its morbid excitement over them, its anxious cares, the thorns of our earthly existence which choke the seed of the true life."[11]

Not the possession of wealth but the way in which it was used was important to Clement. The wealthy were given the responsibility of administering their wealth, on God's behalf, to alleviate the suffering and promote the general welfare of their brothers. In decreeing that the hungry should be fed and the naked clothed, God certainly had not willed a situation in which no one could carry out these commandments for lack of sufficient material prerequisites. It followed, thus, that God had willed that some men should have wealth but had given them the important functions of paternalistically caring for the well-being of the rest of society.

In a similar vein, Ambrose wrote that "riches themselves are not blamable" as long as they are used righteously. In order to use wealth righteously, "we ought to be of mutual help one to the other, and to vie with each other in doing duties, to lay all advantages . . . before all, and . . . to bring help one to the other."[12]

The list of Christian fathers who wrote lengthy passages to the same effect could be expanded greatly. Suffice it to say that by the early feudal period the Christian paternalist ethic was thoroughly entrenched in western Euro-

[9]Matt. 19:16–26; Mark 10:17–27; Luke 18.
[10]Matt. 19.
[11]Quoted in Gray, *The Socialist Tradition,* p. 48.
[12]Ibid., p. 49.

pean culture. Greed, avarice, materialistic self-seeking, the desire to accumulate wealth—all such individualistic and materialistic motives—were sharply condemned. The acquisitive, individualistic person was considered the very antithesis of the good man, who concerned himself with the well-being of all his brothers. The wealthy man had the potential to do either great good or great evil with his wealth and power, and the worst evil resulted when wealth was used either exclusively for self-gratification or as a means of continually acquiring more wealth and power for its own sake. The righteously wealthy were those who realized that their wealth and power were God's gift, that they were morally obligated to act as paternalistic stewards, and that they were to administrate their worldly affairs in order to promote the welfare of all.

THE ANTICAPITALIST NATURE OF FEUDAL IDEOLOGY

The philosophical and religious assumptions on which medieval people acted were extensions of the Christian paternalist ethic. The many particular additions to the ethic were profoundly conservative in purpose and content. Both the continuity in and conservative modifications of this ethic can be seen in the writings of Thomas Aquinas, the preeminent spokesman of the Middle Ages.

Tradition was upheld in his insistence that private property could be justified morally only because it was a necessary condition for almsgiving. The rich, he asserted, must always be "ready to distribute, . . . [and] willing to communicate."[13] Aquinas believed, with the earlier fathers, that "the rich man, if he does not give alms, is a thief."[14] The rich man held wealth and power for God and for all society. He administered his wealth for God and for the common good of mankind. Wealth that was not properly used and administered could no longer be religiously and morally justified, in which case the wealthy man was to be considered a common thief.

Aquinas's and, indeed, most of the medieval church fathers' profoundly conservative addition to the Christian paternalist ethic was their insistence that the economic and social relationships of the medieval manorial system reflected a natural and eternal ordering of these relationships—indeed, that these relationships were ordained by God. They stressed the importance of a division of labor and effort, with different tasks assigned to the different classes, and insisted that the social and economic distinctions between the classes were necessary to accommodate this specialization.

If one occupied the position of a lord, secular or religious, it was necessary to have an abundance of material wealth in order to do well the tasks providence had assigned. Of course, it took little wealth to perform the tasks expected of a serf. It was every person's duty to labor unquestioningly at the task providence had assigned, to accept the station into which one was born,

---

[13]Ibid., p. 57.
[14]Ibid.

and to accept the rights of others to have and do the things appropriate to their stations in life. Thus the Christian paternalist ethic could be, and was, used to defend as natural and just the great inequities and intense exploitation that flowed from the concentration of wealth and power in the hands of the Church and nobility.

Any account of medieval social and economic thought must also stress the great disdain with which people viewed trade and commerce and the commercial spirit. The medieval way of life was based on custom and tradition; its viability depended on the acceptance by the members of society of that tradition and their place within it. Where the capitalist commercial ethic prevails, greed, selfishness, covetousness, and the desire to better oneself materially or socially are accepted by most people as innate qualities. Yet they were uniformly denounced and reviled in the Middle Ages. The serfs (and sometimes the lower nobility) tended to be dissatisfied with the traditions and customs of medieval society and thus threatened the stability of the feudal system. It is not surprising, therefore, to find pervasive moral sanctions designed to repress or to mitigate the effects of these motives.

One of the most important of such sanctions, repeated over and over throughout this period, was the insistence that it was the moral duty of merchants and traders to transact all trade or exchanges at the just price. This notion illustrates the role played by paternalistic social control in the feudal era. A *just price* was one that would compensate the seller for his efforts in transporting the good and in finding the buyer at a rate that was just sufficient to maintain the seller at his *customary* or *traditional* station in life. Prices above the just price would, of course, lead to profits, which would be accumulated as material wealth.

It was the lust for wealth that the Christian paternalist ethic consistently condemned. The doctrine of the just price was intended as a curb on such acquisitive and socially disruptive behavior. Then as now, accumulation of material wealth was a passport to greater power and upward social mobility. This social mobility was eventually to prove totally destructive to the medieval system because it put an end to the status relationships that were the backbone of medieval society.

Another example of this condemnation of acquisitive behavior was the prohibition of usury, or the lending of money at interest. A "bill against usury" passed in England reflected the attitudes of most of the people of those times. It read in part,

But forasmuch as usury is by the word of God utterly prohibited, as a vice most odious and detestable . . . which thing, by no godly teachings and persuasions can sink in to the hearts of divers greedy, uncharitable and covetous persons of this Realm . . . be it enacted . . . that . . . no person or persons of what Estate, degree, quality or condition so ever he or they be, by any corrupt, colorable or deceitful conveyance, sleight or engine, or by any way or mean, shall lend, give, set out, deliver or forbear any sum or sums

of money . . . to or for any manner of usury, increase, lucre, gain or interest to be had, received or hoped for, over and above the sum or sums so
lent . . . as also of the usury . . . upon pain of imprisonment.[15]

The church believed usury was the worst sort of acquisitive behavior
because most loans on which interest was charged were granted to poor
farmers or peasants after a bad crop or some other tragedy had befallen them.
Thus, interest was a gain made at the expense of one's brother at a time when
he was most in need of help and charity. Of course, the Christian ethic strongly
condemned such rapacious exploitation of a needy brother.

Many historians have pointed out that bishops and abbots as well as
dukes, counts, and kings often flagrantly violated these sanctions. They themselves granted loans at interest, even while they were punishing others for
doing so. We are more interested, however, in the values and motives of the
period than in the bending or breaking of the rules. The values of the feudal
system stand in stark, antithetical contrast to those that were shortly to prevail
under a capitalist system. The desire to maximize monetary gain, accumulate
material wealth, and advance oneself socially and economically through acquisitive behavior was to become the dominant motive force in the capitalist
system.

The sins that were most strongly denounced within the context of the
Christian paternalist ethic were to become the behavioral assumptions on
which the capitalist market economy was to be based. It is obvious that such
a radical change would render the Christian ethic, at least in its medieval
version, inadequate as the basis of a moral justification of the new capitalist
system. The ethic would have to be modified drastically or rejected completely
in order to elaborate a defense for the new system. Attempts to do both are
explored in later chapters.

SUMMARY

Economic systems organize human effort to transform the resources given in
nature into usable articles, or economic goods. Ideologies are systems of ideas
and beliefs that are used to provide moral justification for the economic and
social relationships within an economic system.

The Christian paternalist ethic was used to justify the feudal economy
and its attendant social and economic relationships. This ideology contained
elements that were antithetical to the functioning of a capitalist market system.
In later chapters we examine the ways in which men attempted to substitute
new ideologies for the older Christian paternalist ethic or to modify this ethic
in such a way that it could be used to provide a moral justification of a capitalist
market economic system.

[15]Quoted in Leo Huberman, *Man's Worldly Goods* (New York: Monthly Review Press,
1961), p. 39.

CHAPTER 2

The Transition to Early Capitalism and the Beginnings of the Mercantilist View

Medieval society was an agrarian society. The social hierarchy was based on individuals' ties to the land, and the entire social system rested on an agricultural base. Yet, ironically, increases in agricultural productivity were the original impetus to a series of profound changes. These changes, occurring over several centuries, resulted in the dissolution of medieval feudalism and the beginnings of capitalism.

CHANGES IN TECHNOLOGY

The most important technological advance in the Middle Ages was the replacement of the two-field system of crop rotation with the three-field system. Although there is evidence that the three-field system was introduced into Europe as early as the eighth century, its use was probably not widespread until around the eleventh century.

Yearly sowing of the same land would deplete the land and eventually make it unusable. Consequently, in the two-field system half of the land was always allowed to lie fallow in order to recover from the previous year's planting.

With the three-field system, arable land was divided into three equal fields. Rye or winter wheat would be planted in the fall in the first field. Oats, beans, or peas would be planted in the spring in the second, and the third would lie fallow. In each subsequent year there was a rotation of these posi-

11

tions. Any given piece of land would have a spring planting one year, a fall planting the next year, and none the third year.

A dramatic increase in agricultural output resulted from this seemingly simple change in agricultural technology. With the same amount of arable land, the three-field system could increase the amount under cultivation at any particular time by as much as 50 percent.[1]

The three-field system led to other important changes. Spring sowing of oats and other fodder crops enabled the people to support more horses, which began to replace oxen as the principal source of power in agriculture. Horses were much faster than oxen, and consequently the region under cultivation could be extended. An increase in the area under cultivation enabled the countryside to support more concentrated population centers. Transportation of people, commodities, and equipment was much more efficient with horses. Greater efficiency was also attained in plowing: A team of oxen required three people to do the plowing; a horse-drawn plow could be operated by one person. The costs of transporting agricultural products were substantially reduced in the thirteenth century, when the four-wheeled wagon with a pivoted front axle replaced the two-wheeled cart.

These improvements in agriculture and transportation cotributed to two important and far-reaching changes. First, they made possible a rapid increase in population growth. The best historical estimates are that the population of Europe doubled between 1000 and 1300.[2] Second, closely related to the expansion of population was a rapid increase in urban concentration. Before the year 1000, most of Europe, except for a few Mediterranean trade centers, consisted of only manors, villages, and a few small towns. By 1300, there were many thriving cities and larger towns.

The growth of towns and cities led to a growth of rural-urban specialization. With urban workers severing all ties to the soil, the output of manufactured goods increased impressively. Along with increased manufacturing and increased economic specialization came many additional gains in human productivity. Interregional, long-distance trade and commerce was another very important result of this increased specialization.

THE INCREASE IN LONG-DISTANCE TRADE

Many historians have argued that the spread of trade and commerce was the single most important force leading to the disintegration of medieval society. The importance of trade cannot be doubted, but it must be emphasized that this trade did not arise by accident or by factors completely external to the European economy, such as increased contact with the Arabs. On the contrary, it was shown in the previous section that this upsurge in trade was prepared for by the internal economic evolution of Europe itself. The growth

[1]Lynn White, Jr., *Medieval Technology and Social Change* (Oxford: Clarendon,1962), pp. 71–72.
  [2]Harry A. Miskimin, *The Economy of Early Renaissance Europe, 1300–1460* (Englewood Cliffs, N.J.: Prentice-Hall, 1969), p. 20.

of agricultural productivity meant that a surplus of food and handicrafts was available for local and international markets. The improvements in power and transportation meant that it was possible and profitable to concentrate industry in towns, to produce on a mass scale, and to sell the goods over a widespread, long-distance market. Thus the basic agricultural and industrial developments were necessary prerequisites for the spread of trade and commerce, which in turn further encouraged industry and town expansion.

The expansion of trade, particularly long-distance trade in the early period, led to the establishment of commercial and industrial towns that serviced this trade. And the growth of these cities and towns, as well as their increased domination by merchant capitalists, led to important changes in both industry and agriculture. Each of these areas of change, particularly the latter, brought about a weakening and ultimately a complete dissolving of the traditional ties that held together the feudal economic and social structure.

From the earliest part of the medieval period, some long-distance trade had been carried on throughout many parts of Europe. This trade was very important in southern Europe, on the Mediterranean and Adriatic seas, and in northern Europe, on the North and Baltic seas. Between these two centers of commercialism, however, the feudal manorial system in most of the rest of Europe was relatively unaffected by commerce and trade until the later Middle Ages.

From about the eleventh century onward, the Christian Crusades gave the impetus to a marked expansion of commerce. Yet the Crusades themselves cannot be viewed as an accidental or external factor to European development. The Crusades were not undertaken for religious reasons, nor were they the result of Turkish molestation of pilgrims, for the Turks continued the Moslem policy of tolerance. Developments on the Moslem side did lead to increased attacks on Byzantium, but the West would normally have sent only token aid since it had no great love for Byzantium. The basic reasons for the Crusades may be seen in the internal developments of France, where they had their most powerful backing. France had been growing stronger, it had more trade relations with and interest in the East, and it needed an outlet for social unrest at home. Additional propaganda for the Crusades came from the oligarchy of Venice, which wanted to expand its own Eastern trade and influence.

The development of trade with the Arabs—and with the Vikings in the North—led to increased production for export and to the great trade fairs that flourished from the twelfth through the late fourteenth centuries. Held annually in the principal European trading cities, these fairs usually lasted for one to several weeks. Northern European merchants exchanged their grain, fish, wool, cloth, timber, pitch, tar, salt, and iron for the spices, silks, brocades, wines, fruits, and gold and silver that were the dominant items in southern European commerce.[3]

---

[3]For a more complete discussion of the rise of trade and commerce, see Dudley Dillard, *Economic Development of the North Atlantic Community* (Englewood Cliffs, N.J.: Prentice-Hall, 1967), pp. 3–178.

By the fifteenth century the fairs were being replaced by commercial cities where year-round markets thrived. The trade and commerce of these cities were incompatible with restrictive feudal customs and traditions. Generally the cities were successful in gaining independence from church and feudal lords. Within these commercial centers there arose complex systems of currency exchange, debt-clearing, and credit facilities, and modern business instruments like bills of exchange came into widespread use. New systems of commercial law developed. Unlike the system of paternalistic adjudication based on custom and tradition that prevailed in the manor, the commercial law was fixed by precise code. Hence it became the basis of the modern capitalistic law of contracts, negotiable instruments, agency sales, and auctions.

In the manorial handicraft industry, the producer (the master craftsman) was also the seller. The industries that burgeoned in the new cities, however, were primarily export industries—that is, the producer was distant from the final buyer. Craftsmen sold their goods wholesale to merchants, who, in turn, transported and resold them. Another important difference was that the manorial craftsman was also generally a farmer. The new city craftsman gave up farming and became devoted to a craft, with which money could be obtained to satisfy other needs.

THE PUTTING-OUT SYSTEM AND THE BIRTH
OF CAPITALIST INDUSTRY

As trade and commerce thrived and expanded, the need for more manufactured goods and greater reliability of supply led to increasing control of the productive process by the merchant-capitalist. By the sixteenth century the handicraft type of industry, in which the craftsman owned his workshop, tools, and raw materials and functioned as an independent, small-scale entrepreneur, had been largely replaced in the exporting industries by the *putting-out system*. In the earliest period of the putting-out system, the merchant-capitalist would furnish an independent craftsman with raw materials and pay the latter a fee to work the materials into finished products. In his way the capitalist owned the product throughout all stages of production, although the work was done in independent workshops. In the later period of the putting-out system, the merchant-capitalist owned the tools and machinery and often the building in which the production took place. The merchant-capitalist hired workers to use these tools, furnished them with the raw materials, and took the finished products.

The worker no longer sold a finished product to the merchant. Rather, the worker sold only the worker's own labor power. The textile industries were among the first in which the putting-out system developed. Weavers, spinners, fullers, and dyers found themselves in a situation where their employment, and hence their ability to support themselves and their families, depended on the merchant-capitalists, who had to sell what the workers produced at a price that was high enough to pay wages and other costs and still make a profit.

Capitalists' control was, then, extended into the process of production.

At the same time, a labor force was created that owned little or no capital and had nothing to sell but its labor power. These two features mark the appearance of the economic system of capitalism. Some writers and historians have defined capitalism as existing when trade, commerce, and the commercial spirit expanded and became more important in Europe. Trade and commerce, however, had existed throughout the feudal era. Yet as long as feudal tradition remained the organizing principle in production, trade and commerce were really outside the social and economic system. The market and the search for money profits replaced custom and tradition in determining who would perform what task, how that task would be performed, and whether a given worker could find work to support himself. When this occurred, the capitalist system was created.[4]

Capitalism became dominant with the extension to most lines of production of the relationship that existed between capitalists and workers in the sixteenth-century export industries. For such a system to evolve, the economic self-sufficiency of the feudal manor had to be broken down and manorial customs and traditions undermined or destroyed. Agriculture had to become a capitalistic venture in which workers would sell their labor power to capitalists, and capitalists would buy labor only if they expected to make a profit in the process.

A capitalist textile industry existed in Flanders in the thirteenth century. When for various reasons its prosperity began to decline, the wealth and poverty it had created led to a long series of violent class wars, starting around 1280, that almost completely destroyed the industry. In the fourteenth century a capitalist textile industry flourished in Florence. There as in Flanders, adverse business conditions led to tensions between a poverty-stricken working class and their affluent capitalist employers. The results of these tensions were violent rebellions in 1379 and 1382. Failure to resolve these class antagonisms significantly worsened the precipitous decline in the Florentine textile industry, as it had earlier in Flanders.

In the fifteenth century England dominated the world textile market. Its capitalist textile industry solved the problem of class conflict by ruralizing the industry. Whereas the earlier capitalist textile industries of Flanders and Florence had been centered in the densely populated cities, where the workers were thrown together and organized resistance was easy to initiate, the English fulling mills were scattered about the countryside. This meant that the workers were isolated from all but a small handful of other workers, and effective organized resistance did not develop.

The later system, however, in which wealthy owners of capital employed propertyless craftsmen, was usually a phenomenon of the city rather than of the countryside. From the beginning, these capitalistic enterprises sought monopolistic positions from which to exploit the demand for their products. The rise of livery guilds, or associations of merchant-capitalist employers,

[4]See Maurice H. Dobb, *Studies in the Development of Capitalism* (London: Routledge & Kegan Paul, 1946), particularly chap. 4.

created a host of barriers to protect their position. Different types of apprenticeships, with special privileges and exemptions for the sons of the wealthy, excessively high membership fees, and other barriers, prevented ambitious poorer craftsmen from competing with or entering the new capitalist class. Indeed, these barriers generally resulted in the transformation of poorer craftsmen and their sons into a new urban working class that lived exclusively by selling its labor power.

THE DECLINE OF THE MANORIAL SYSTEM

Before a complete system of capitalism could emerge, however, the force of capitalist market relations had to invade the rural manor, the bastion of feudalism. This was accomplished as a result of the vast increase of population in the new trading cities. Large urban populations depended on the rural countryside for food and much of the raw materials for export industries. These needs fostered a rural-urban specialization and a large flow of trade between the rural manor and the city. The lords of the manors began to depend on the cities for manufactured goods and increasingly came to desire luxury goods that merchants could sell to them.

The peasants on the manor also found that they could exchange surpluses for money at the local grain markets; the money could be used by the peasants to purchase commutation of their labor services.[5] Commutation often resulted in a situation in which the peasant became very nearly an independent small businessman. He might rent the land from the lord, sell the product to cover the rents, and retain the remaining revenues himself. This system gave peasants a higher incentive to produce and thereby increased their surplus marketings, which led to more commutations, more subsequent marketings, and so forth. The cumulative effect was a very gradual breaking down of the traditional ties of the manor and a substitution of the market and the search for profits as the organizing principle of production. By the middle of the fourteenth century, money rents exceeded the value of labor services in many parts of Europe.

Another force that brought the market into the countryside and was closely related to commutation was the alienation of the lords' demesnes. The lords who needed cash to exchange for manufactured goods and luxuries began to rent their own lands to peasant farmers rather than having them farmed directly with labor service obligations. This process led increasingly to a situation in which the lord of the manor was simply a landlord in the modern sense of that term. In fact, he very often became an absentee landlord, as many lords chose to move to the cities or were away fighting battles.

The breakup of the manorial system, however, stemmed more directly from a series of catastrophes in the late fourteenth and fifteenth centuries. The

[5]Commutation involved the substitution of money rents for the labor services required of the serf.

Hundred Years' War between France and England (1337–1453) created general disorder and unrest in those countries. The Black Death was even more devastating. On the eve of the plague of 1348–1349, England's population stood at 4 million. By the early fifteenth century, after the effects of the wars and the plague, England had a population of a scant 2.5 million. This was fairly typical of trends in other European countries. The depopulation led to a desperate labor shortage, and wages for all types of labor rose abruptly. Land, now relatively more plentiful, began to rent for less.

These facts led the feudal nobility to attempt to revoke the commutations they had granted and to reestablish the labor service obligations of the serfs and peasants (peasants were former serfs who had attained some degree of independence and freedom from feudal restrictions). They found, however, that the clock could not be turned back. The market had been extended into the countryside, and with it had come greater freedom, independence, and prosperity for the peasants. They bitterly resisted efforts to reinstate the old obligations, and their resistance did not go unchallenged.

The result was the famous peasant revolts that broke out all over Europe from the late fourteenth through the early sixteenth centuries. These rebellions were extreme in their cruelty and ferocity. A contemporary French writer described a band of peasants who killed a "knight and putting him on a broach, roasted him over a fire in the sight of his wife and children. Ten or twelve of them ravished the wife and then forced her to eat of her husband's flesh. Then they killed her and her children. Wherever these ungracious people went they destroyed good houses and strong castles."[6] Rebellious peasants were ultimately slaughtered with equal or greater cruelty and ferocity by the nobility.

England experienced a series of such revolts in the late fourteenth and fifteenth centuries. But the revolts that occurred in Germany in the early sixteenth century were probably the bloodiest of all. The peasant rebellion in 1524–1525 was crushed by the imperial troops of the Holy Roman emperor, who slaughtered peasants by the tens of thousands. Over 100,000 persons probably were killed in Germany alone.

These revolts are mentioned here to illustrate the fact that fundamental changes in the economic and political structure of a social system are often achieved only after traumatic and violent social conflict. Any economic system generates a class or classes whose privileges are dependent on the continuation of that system. Quite naturally, these classes go to great lengths to resist change and to protect their positions. The feudal nobility fought a savage rearguard action against the emerging capitalist market system, but the forces of change ultimately swept them aside. Although the important changes were brought about by aspiring merchants and minor noblemen, the peasants were the pathetic victims of the consequent social upheavals. Ironically, they were usually struggling to protect the status quo.

[6]N. S. B. Gras, *A History of Agriculture in Europe and America* (New York: Appleton, 1940), p. 108.

THE CREATION OF THE WORKING CLASS

The early sixteenth century is a watershed in European history. It marks the vague dividing line between the old, decaying feudal order and the rising capitalist system. After 1500, important social and economic changes began to occur with increasing frequency, each reinforcing the other and together ushering in the system of capitalism. Among the most important of these changes were those creating a working class that was systematically stripped of any control over the production process and forced into a situation in which the sale of its labor power was its only means of survival. The population of western Europe, which had been relatively stagnant for a century and a half, increased by nearly one-third in the sixteenth century and stood at about 70 million in 1600.

The increase in population was accompanied by the enclosure movement, which had begun in England as early as the thirteenth century. The feudal nobility, in ever-increasing need of cash, fenced off or enclosed lands that had formerly been used for communal grazing, using the lands to graze sheep to satisfy the booming English wool and textile industries' demand for wool. The sheep brought good prices, and a minimal amount of labor was needed to herd them.

The enclosure movement reached its peak in the late fifteenth and sixteenth centuries, when in some areas as many as three-fourths to nine-tenths of the tenants were forced out of the countryside and into the cities to try to support themselves. Subsequent waves of enclosure continued until well into the nineteenth century. The enclosures and the increasing population further destroyed the remaining feudal ties, creating a large new labor force—a labor force without land, without any tools or instruments of production, and with only labor power to sell. This migration to the cities meant more labor for the capitalist industries, more men for the armies and navies, more men to colonize new lands, and more potential consumers, or buyers of products.

But the enclosures and the increase in population were by no means the sole source of the new working class. Innumerable peasants, yeomen, and minor nobility were bankrupted by exorbitant increases in monetary rents. Mounting debts that could not be repaid ruined countless others. In the cities and towns the guilds came to be more and more concerned with the income levels of their members. It was obvious to the craftsmen and merchants in the guilds that steps taken to minimize their number would serve to monopolize their crafts and to increase their incomes. Increasing numbers of urban producers came to be denied any means of independent production as the guilds became more exclusive. Thus a considerable portion of the new working class was created within the towns and cities.

Many of the farmers and craftsmen who were thus uprooted and denied access to their former means of production became vagabonds and beggars. Even more attempted to secure a subsistence by squatting on marginal, unused lands where they could grow crops for their own use. Harshly repressive laws were passed against such farming and against being an unemployed vag-abond.[7] Thus when force, fraud, and starvation were insufficient to create the new working class, criminal statutes and government repression were used.

OTHER FORCES IN THE TRANSITION TO CAPITALISM

Other sources of change were also instrumental in the transition to capitalism. Among these was the intellectual awakening of the sixteenth century, which fostered scientific progress that was promptly put to practical use in naviga-tion. The telescope and the compass enabled men to navigate much more accurately for much greater distances. Hence the "Age of Exploration." Within a short period, Europeans had charted sea routes to India, Africa, and the Americas. These discoveries had a twofold importance: First, they resulted in a rapid and large flow of precious metals into Europe; and second, they ushered in a period of colonization.

Between 1300 and 1500, European gold and silver production had stag-nated. The rapidly expanding capitalist trade and the extension of the market system into city and countryside had led to an acute shortage of money. Because money consisted primarily of gold and silver coin, the need for these metals was critical. Beginning around 1450, this situation was alleviated some-what when the Portuguese began extracting metals from the African Gold Coast, but the general shortage continued until the middle of the sixteenth century. After that date there occurred such a large inflow of gold and silver from the Americas that Europe experienced the most rapid and long-lasting inflation in history.

During the sixteenth century prices rose in Europe between 150 and 400 percent, depending on the country or region chosen. Prices of manufactured goods rose much more rapidly than either rents or wages. In fact, the disparity between prices and wages continued until late in the seventeenth century. This meant that the landlord class (or feudal nobility) and the working class both suffered, because their incomes rose less rapidly than their expenses. The capitalist class was the great beneficiary of the price revolution. It received larger and larger profits as it paid lower real wages and bought materials that appreciated greatly as it held the materials as inventories.

These larger profits were accumulated as capital. Capital refers to the materials that are necessary for production, trade, and commerce, and consists of all tools, equipment, factories, raw materials, goods in process, means of transporting goods, and money. There are physical means of production in every kind of economic system, but they can become capital only in a social context in which the social relationships exist that are necessary for commod-ity production and private ownership. Thus capital refers to more than simply physical objects; it refers to a complex set of social relations as well. In our earlier discussion we saw that one of the defining features of the capitalist

[7]See Dobb, *Development of Capitalism*, chap. 6.

system is the existence of a class of capitalists who own the capital stock. It is by virtue of their ownership of this capital that they derive their profits. These profits are then reinvested, or used to augment the capital stock. The further accumulation of capital leads to more profits, which leads to more accumulation, and the system continues in an upward spiral.

The term *capitalism* describes this system of profit seeking and accumulation very well. Ownership of capital is the source of profits and hence the source of further accumulation of capital. But this chicken-egg process had to have a beginning. The substantial initial accumulation, or primitive accumulation, of capital took place in the period under consideration. The four most important sources of the initial accumulation of capital were (1) the rapidly growing volume of trade and commerce, (2) the putting-out system of industry, (3) the enclosure movement, and (4) the great price inflation. There were several other sources of initial accumulations, some of which were somewhat less respectable and often forgotten—for example, colonial plunder, piracy, and the slave trade.

During the sixteenth and seventeenth centuries the putting-out system was extended until it was common in most types of manufacturing. Although this was not yet the modern type of factory production, the system's increased degree of specialization led to significant increases in productivity. Technical improvements in shipbuilding and navigation also lowered transportation costs. Capitalist production and trade and commerce were thus able to grow very rapidly during this period. The new capitalist class (or middle class or bourgeoisie) slowly but inexorably replaced the nobility as the class that dominated the economic and social system.

The emergence of the new nation-states signaled the beginning of the transition to a new dominant class. The new monarchs usually drew on the bourgeois capitalist class for support in their efforts to defeat feudal rivals and unify the state under one central power. This unification freed the merchants from the feudal maze of different rules, regulations, laws, weights and measures, and moneys; consolidated many markets; and provided military protection for commercial ventures. In return, the monarch relied on the capitalists for much needed sources of revenues.

Although England was nominally unified much earlier, it was not until Henry VII (1485–1509) founded the line of Tudor monarchs that England was unified in fact. Henry VIII (1509–1547) and Elizabeth I (1558–1603) were able to complete the work of nation building only because they had the support of Parliament, which represented the middle classes of the shires and boroughs. In the revolutions of 1648 and 1688, the supremacy of Parliament, or of the bourgeois middle classes, was finally established.

The other important early capitalist nation-states also came into existence during this period. In France, Louis XI (1461–1483) was the first king to unify France effectively since the time of Charlemagne. The marriage in 1469 of Ferdinand of Aragon and Isabella of Castile, and their subsequent defeat of the Moors, led to the unification of Spain. The Dutch republic, the fourth of the important early nation-states, did not win its independence until 1690, when it finally expelled its Spanish oppressors.

By the late sixteenth and early seventeenth centuries, most of the large cities in England, France, Spain, and the Low Countries (Belgium and Holland) had been transformed into thriving capitalist economies dominated by the merchant-capitalists, who controlled not only commerce but also much of the manufacturing. In the modern nation-states, coalitions of monarchs and capitalists had wrested effective power from the feudal nobility in many important areas, especially those related to production and commerce. This period of early capitalism is generally referred to as mercantilism.

MERCANTILISM: FEUDAL PATERNALISM
IN EARLY CAPITALISM

The earliest phase of mercantilism, usually called *bullionism,* originated in the period (discussed earlier) during which Europe was experiencing an acute shortage of gold and silver bullion and hence did not have enough money to service the rapidly expanding volume of trade. Bullionist policies were designed to attract a flow of gold and silver into a country and to keep them there by prohibiting their export. These restrictions lasted from the late Middle Ages into the sixteenth and seventeenth centuries.

Spain, the country into which most of the gold from the Americas flowed, applied bullionist restrictions over the longest period and imposed the most severe penalty for the export of gold and silver—death. Yet the needs of trade were so pressing and such large profits could be made by importing foreign commodities that even in Spain merchant-capitalists succeeded in bribing corrupt officials or smuggling large quantities of bullion out of the country. Spanish bullion rapidly found its way all over Europe and was, to a large extent, responsible for the long period of inflation described above. Spain did not legalize the export of gold and silver until long after the bullionist restrictions had been removed in England and Holland in the middle of the sixteenth century.

After the bullionist period, the mercantilists' desire to maximize the gold and silver within a country took the form of attempts by the government to create a favorable balance of trade. To them a *favorable balance of trade* meant that money payments into the country would be greater than money flowing out of the country. Thus exports of goods as well as such things as shipping and insuring when they were performed by compatriots and paid for by foreigners were encouraged, and imports of goods and shipping and insurance charges paid to foreigners were discouraged. A favorable balance of trade would ensure the augmentation of the country's treasure. Even though some gold and silver would be paid out in the process, more would come in than would leave.

One of the most important types of policies designed to increase the value of exports and decrease that of imports was the creation of trade monopolies.

A country like England could buy most cheaply (from a backward area, for example) if only one English merchant bargained with the foreigners involved rather than having several competing English merchants bidding the price up in an effort to capture the business. Similarly, English merchants could sell their goods to foreigners for much higher prices if there was only one seller rather than several sellers bidding the price down to attract each other's customers.

The English government could prohibit English merchants from competing in an area where such a monopoly had been established. It was much more difficult, however, to keep out French, Dutch, or Spanish merchants. Various governments attempted to exclude such rival foreign merchants by establishing colonial empires that could be controlled by the mother country to ensure a monopoly of trade. Colonial possessions could thereby furnish cheap raw materials to the mother country and purchase expensive manufactured goods in return.

In addition to the creation of monopolies, all the western European countries (with the exception of Holland) applied extensive regulations to the businesses of exporting and importing. These regulations were probably most comprehensive in England, where exporters who found it difficult to compete with foreigners were given tax refunds or, if that were not enough, subsidized. Export duties were placed on a long list of raw materials to keep them within England. Thus the price English merchant-manufacturers would have to pay for these raw materials would be minimized. Sometimes, when these items were in short supply for British manufacturers, the state would completely prohibit their export. The English prohibited the export of most raw materials and semifinished products, such as sheep, wool, yarn, and worsted, which were used by the textile industry.

Measures aimed at discouraging imports were also widespread. The importation of some commodities was prohibited, and other commodities had such high duties that they were nearly eliminated from trade. Special emphasis was placed on protecting England's principal export industries from foreign competitors attempting to cut into the export industries' domestic markets.

Of course these restrictions profited some capitalists and harmed others. As would be expected, coalitions of special interest groups were always working to maintain the restrictions or to extend them into different areas in different ways. Attempts such as the English Navigation Acts of 1651 and 1660 were made to promote the use of British ships (both British-made and British-manned) in both import and export trade. All these regulations of foreign trade and shipping were designed to augment the flow of money into the country while decreasing the outflow. Needless to say, many of the measures also stemmed from appeals and pressures by special interest groups.

In addition to these restrictions on foreign trade, there was a maze of restrictions and regulations aimed at controlling domestic production. Besides the tax exemptions, subsidies, and other privileges used to encourage larger output by industries that were important exporters, the state also engaged in extensive regulation of production methods and of the quality of produced goods. In France, the regime of Louis XIV codified, centralized, and extended the older decentralized guild controls. Specific techniques of production were made mandatory, and extensive quality control measures were enacted, with inspectors appointed in Paris charged with enforcing these laws at the local level. Jean Baptiste Colbert, Louis XIV's famous minister and economic advisor, was responsible for the establishment of extensive and minute regulations. In the textile industry, for example, the width of a piece of cloth and the precise number of threads contained within it were rigidly specified by the government.

In England, the Statute of Artificers (1563) effectively transferred to the state the function of the old craft guilds. It led to central control over the training of industrial workers, over conditions of employment, and over allocation of the labor force among different types of occupations. Regulation of wages, of the quality of many goods, and of other details of domestic production was also tried in England during this period.

What was the source of this extensive control of trade, commerce, and domestic production? It might seem at first glance that the state was merely using its powers to promote the special interests of the capitalists. This view is reinforced by the fact that most of the important writers of this period who dealt with economic issues were either merchants or employees of merchants. Undoubtedly many of the particular statutes and regulatory measures were backed by special interest groups that benefited handsomely from these measures.

However, the rising new middle class of merchant and industrial capitalists were often constrained in their pursuit of profits by the maze of state regulations. Therefore, throughout the period one finds extensive arguments advanced by these capitalists and their spokesmen for greater freedom from state controls. Economic regulation increasingly became anathema to the capitalists and their spokesmen. In fact, the mercantilist period represents an era in which an outdated economic ideology, the medieval version of the Christian corporate ethic, came into increasingly sharp conflict with a new social and economic order with which it was incompatible. Chapter 3 is concerned with this conflict.

SUMMARY

A series of profound changes resulted in the decline of feudalism and the rise of a new market-oriented economy. Perhaps the most important of these changes were the improvements in agricultural technology that occurred between the eleventh century and the end of the thirteenth century. These improvements in farming techniques were the original force that set into motion a centuries-long chain of events that ushered in capitalism.

The rapid growth of population and increase in urban concentration led to a resurgence of long-distance trade. In the cities the putting-out system was created to produce items that were sold in this trade. This practice, in turn, led to an urban-rural specialization that could be accomplished only by the monetization of economic tasks and productive activities. The transformation of feudal social relationships into market cash relations destroyed the social base of feudalism. Attempts to preserve the feudal system resulted in peasant revolts—and their ruthless suppression.

The new capitalist market system was ushered in by the enclosure movement, an intellectual awakening, world exploration, the discovery of large quantities of precious metals, the price inflation of the sixteenth and seventeenth centuries, and the creation of the new nation-states.

In the early stages of capitalism, mercantilist policies resulted in extensive government intervention into market processes, particularly those related to international commerce. These policies were generally aimed at securing high profits for the great merchant trading companies, raising revenues for national governments, and, more generally, bringing a maximum of precious metals into the country concerned.

CHAPTER 3

The Conflict in Mercantilist Thought

The Christian paternalist ethic, with its condemnation of acquisitive behavior, conflicted with the interests of merchants throughout the feudal period. As the importance of trade and commerce grew, the intensity of the conflict grew. There were two principal themes underlying the development of English mercantilism.[1] "One was the biblical injunction to promote the general welfare and common good of God's corporate world and its creatures. The second was the growing propensity to define God's estate as the civil society in which the Christian resided."[2] During this period the state began to take over the role of the church in interpreting and enforcing the Christian paternalist ethic. The basic issue for the earliest formulators of mercantilist policies was whether the growing merchant class was to be allowed to pursue its profits recklessly, regardless of the social and economic consequences of that pursuit. The Christian ethic demanded that the activities of the merchants be checked and controlled in the interest of the welfare of the entire community.

[1]We concentrate primarily on English mercantilism in this chapter because industrial capitalism developed first in England and because most of the ideas in the capitalist ideology that we discuss in Chapter 4 were developed in England.

[2]William Appleman Williams, *The Contours of American History* (New York: Quadrangle, 1966), p. 33.

THE MEDIEVAL ORIGINS OF MERCANTILIST POLICIES

The first indications of a mercantilistic type of economic policy can be traced to Edward I (1272–1307), who evicted several foreign economic enterprises from England, established the English wool trade in Antwerp, and made various attempts to control commerce within England. A short time later, Edward III significantly extended these policies of economic control. The long war with France (1333–1360) led him to attempt to mitigate the harsh effects of wartime inflation on the laborers. He did this by fixing wages and prices in a ratio that was more favorable to the laborers. In return for this aid, Edward required all men to work at whatever jobs were available. "As this quid pro quo indicates, mercantilism was grounded in the idea of a mutual, corporate responsibility. God's way was based on such reciprocal respect and obligation, and Jerusalem provided the example to be followed."[3]

Richard II (1377–1399) extended and systematized his predecessors' policies. The principal problems facing England during his reign were the social and economic conflict that led to the Peasants' Rebellion of 1381 (see Chapter 2) and the necessity of countering foreign competition more effectively. The latter led to the Navigation Act of 1381, which was designed to favor English shippers and traders and to bring gold and silver into England. This money was needed for his program of building England into a "well and rightly governed kingdom" in which greater economic security for all would mitigate the social tensions that existed.

Henry VII (1485–1509) renewed these policies. He commissioned numerous voyages of explorers and adventurers and attempted in various ways to secure legislation and negotiate treaties advantageous to English merchants. At the same time he subjected merchants to many controls and regulations imposed by the Crown, for he believed that the unlimited pursuit of self-interest in the quest for profits was often harmful to general social interests and harmony.

Henry was still balancing feudal and capitalist interests; neither was dominant enough to persuade him to favor one over the other. The rapid growth of mining and wool raising during his reign led to an unfortunate neglect of food production. Moreover, the general excesses of the merchants had alienated both the peasants and the agrarian aristocracy. The merchants seemed to understand these problems and accepted a relationship in which, in return for Crown policies that would benefit them in foreign dealings, they submitted to domestic regulation of manufacturing and commerce.

THE SECULARIZATION OF CHURCH FUNCTIONS

During the reign of Henry VIII, England broke with Roman Catholicism. This event was significant because it marked the final secularization (in England at least) of the functions of the medieval church. Under Henry, "the state in the

---

[3] Ibid., p. 34. The following several pages draw heavily on Williams's excellent book.

form of God's monarchy assumed the role and the functions of the old universal church. What Henry had done in his own blunt way was to sanctify the processes of this world."[4] During his reign, as well as the reigns of Elizabeth I, James I, and Charles I (1558–1649), there was widespread social unrest. The cause of this unrest was poverty, and the cause of much of the poverty was unemployment.

The enclosure movements (discussed in Chapter 2) were responsible for much of the unemployment. Another factor, however, was the decline in the export of woolens in the second half of the sixteenth century, which created a great deal of unemployment in England's most important manufacturing industry. There were also frequent commercial crises similar to, but without the regularity of, the depression phase of later business cycles. In addition to these factors, seasonal unemployment put many workers out of work for as many as 4 months of the year.

The people could no longer look to the Catholic church for relief from widespread unemployment and poverty. Destruction of the power of the church had eliminated the organized system of charity. The state attempted to assume responsibility for the general welfare of society. In order to do this, "England's leaders undertook a general, coordinated program to reorganize and rationalize . . . industry by establishing specifications of standards of production and marketing."[5] All these measures were designed to stimulate English trade and alleviate the unemployment problem.

In fact, it appears that the desire to achieve full employment is the unifying theme of most policy measures advocated by mercantilist writers. The mercantilists preferred measures designed to stimulate foreign rather than domestic trade "because they believed it contributed more to employment, to the nation's wealth and to national power. The writers after 1600 stressed the inflationary effect of an excess of exports over imports and the consequent increase in employment which inflation produced."[6]

Among the other measures taken to encourage industry during this period was the issuance of patents of monopoly. The first important patent was granted in 1561, during the reign of Elizabeth I. Monopoly rights were given in order to encourage inventions and to establish new industries. These rights were severely abused, as might be expected. Moreover, they led to a complex system of special privileges and patronage and a host of other evils, which outraged most mercantilist writers every bit as much as similar abuses outraged late nineteenth-century American reformers. The evils of monopoly led to the Statute of Monopolies of 1624, which outlawed all monopolies except those that involved genuine inventions or would be instrumental in promoting a favorable balance of payments. Of course these loopholes were large, and abuses continued almost unchecked.

The Statute of Artificers (1563) specified conditions of employment and

[4]Ibid., p. 36.
[5]Ibid., p. 40.
[6]William D. Grampp, *Economic Liberalism*, vol. 1 (New York: Random House, 1965), p. 59.

length of apprenticeships, provided for periodic wage assessments and established maximum rates that could be paid to laborers. The statute is important because it illustrates the fact that the Crown's paternalistic ethic never led to any attempt to elevate the status of the laboring classes. Monarchs of this period felt obliged to protect the working classes but, like their predecessors in the Middle Ages, believed those classes should be kept in their proper place. Maximum wage rates were designed to protect the capitalists, and furthermore, the justices who set these maximums and enforced the statute generally belonged to the employing class themselves. It is probable that these maximums reduced the real wages of laborers because prices generally rose faster than wages during the succeeding years.

Poor laws passed in 1531 and 1536 attempted to deal with the problems of unemployment, poverty, and misery then widespread in England. The first sought to distinguish between "deserving" and "undeserving" poor. Only the deserving poor were allowed to beg. The second decreed that each individual parish throughout England was responsible for its poor and that the parish should, through voluntary contributions, maintain a poor fund. This proved completely inadequate, and the "pauper problem" grew increasingly severe.

Finally, in 1572 the state accepted the principle that the poor would have to be supported by tax funds and enacted a compulsory "poor rate." And in 1576 "houses of correction" for "incorrigible vagrants" were authorized and provisions made for the parish to purchase raw materials to be worked up by the more tractable paupers and vagrants. Between that time and the close of the sixteenth century, several other poor-law statutes were passed.

The Poor Law of 1601 was the Tudor attempt to integrate these laws into one consistent framework. Its main provisions included formal recognition of the right of the poor to receive relief, imposition of compulsory poor rates at the parish level, and provision for differential treatment for various classes of the poor. The aged and the sick could receive help in their homes; pauper children who were too young to be apprenticed in a trade were to be boarded out; the deserving poor and unemployed were to be given work as provided for in the act of 1576; and incorrigible vagrants were to be sent to houses of correction and prisons.[7]

From the preceding discussion it is possible to conclude that the period of English mercantilism was characterized by acceptance, in the spirit of the Christian paternalist ethic, of the idea that "the state had an obligation to serve society by accepting and discharging the responsibility for the general welfare."[8] The various statutes passed during this period "were predicated upon the idea that poverty, instead of being a personal sin, was a function of the economic system."[9] They acknowledged that those who were the victims of the

[7]For an extension of this discussion of the poor laws, see Arthur Birnie, *An Economic History of the British Isles* (London: Methuen, 1936), chaps. 12 and 18.
[8]Williams, *Contours of American History,* p. 41.
[9]Ibid., p. 44.

deficiencies of the economic system should be cared for by those who benefited from the system.

THE RISE OF INDIVIDUALISM

After the civil war of 1648–1660 and the Glorious Revolution of 1688, the English government was dominated by the gentry and the middle-class capitalists. The medieval world view that underlay the Christian paternalist ethic was eclipsed. A fundamental shift in the philosophy of the role of the state in society took place over the next 100 years. In 1776, with the publication of Adam Smith's *The Wealth of Nations,* a new individualistic philosophy— classical liberalism[10]—had definitely gained the ascendancy in England. This individualistic philosophy had existed throughout the mercantilist period, struggling to break the hold of the older paternalist world view. In the end the new classical liberalism prevailed because it—and not the older, essentially medieval world view—reflected the needs of the new capitalist order.

In condemning greed, acquisitive behavior, and the desire to accumulate wealth, the medieval Christian paternalist ethic condemned what had become the capitalist order's dominant motive force. The capitalist market economy, which had been extended by the late eighteenth century to almost every phase of production, demanded self-seeking, acquisitive behavior to function successfully. In this context new theories about human behavior began to emerge. Writers began to assert that selfish, egoistic motives were the primary if not the only ones that moved people to action.

This interpretation of humankind's behavior is expressed in the writings of many important thinkers of the period. Many philosophers and social theorists began to assert that every human act was related to self-preservation and hence was egoistic in the most fundamental sense. The English nobleman Sir Robert Filmer was greatly alarmed by the large number of people who spoke of "the natural freedom of mankind, a new, plausible and dangerous opinion" with anarchistic implications.[11] Thomas Hobbes' *Leviathan,* published in 1651, trenchantly articulated a widely held opinion—that all human motives stem from a desire for whatever promotes the "vital motion" of the human organism. Hobbes believed that everyone's motives, even compassion, were merely so many disguised species of self-interest: "Grief for the calamity of another is *pity,* and ariseth from the imagination that the like calamity may befall himself; and therefore is called . . . *compassion,* and . . . fellow-feeling."[12]

Except for the few special interest groups that benefited from the exten-

---

[10]We use the adjective *classical* to differentiate the traditional liberal world view from what is called liberalism in the twentieth century. This distinction is clarified further in Chapter 4.

[11]Lee Cameron McDonald, *Western Political Theory: The Modern Age* (New York: Harcourt Brace Jovanovich, 1962), p. 29.

[12]Quoted in Harry K. Girvetz, *The Evolution of Liberalism* (New York: Colliers, 1963), pp. 28–29.

sive restrictions and regulations of commerce and manufacturing during this period, most capitalists felt constrained and inhibited by state regulations in their quest for profits. The individualistic and egoistic doctrines were eagerly embraced by such people. This view began to dominate economic thinking, even among the mercantilists. One careful history asserts that "most of the mercantilist . . . policy assumed that self-interest governs individual conduct."[13]

The majority of mercantilist writers were either capitalists or employees of the great capitalist trading companies. It was quite natural for them to perceive the motives of the capitalists as universal. From the capitalists' views of the nature of humans, and their need to be free from the extensive economic restrictions that inhibited them in the conduct of their everyday business, grew the philosophy of individualism that provided the basis of classical liberalism. Against the well-ordered, paternalistic view Europe had inherited from the feudal society, they asserted "the view that the human person ought to be independent, self-directing, autonomous, free—ought to be, that is, an individual, a unit distinguished from the social mass rather than submerged in it."[14]

PROTESTANTISM AND THE INDIVIDUALIST ETHIC

One of the most important examples of this individualistic and middle-class philosophy was the Protestant theology that emerged from the Reformation. The new middle-class capitalists wanted to be free not only from economic restrictions that encumbered manufacturing and commerce but also from the moral opprobrium the Catholic church had heaped upon their motives and activities. Protestantism not only freed them from religious condemnation but eventually made virtues of the selfish, egoistic, and acquisitive motives the medieval church had so despised.[15]

The principal originators of the Protestant movement were quite close to the Catholic position on such questions as usury and the just price. On most social issues they were deeply conservative. During the German peasant revolt of 1524, Luther wrote a virulent pamphlet, *Against the Murdering Hordes of Peasants,* in which he said princes should "knock down, strangle and stab . . . Such wonderful times are these that a prince can merit heaven better with bloodshed than another with prayer." His advice contributed to the general atmosphere in which the slaughter of over 100,000 peasants was carried out with an air of religious righteousness.

Yet despite the conservatism of the founders of Protestantism, this religious outlook contributed to the growing influence of the new individualistic philosophy. The basic tenet of Protestantism, which laid the groundwork for

---

[13]Grampp, *Economic Liberalism,* p. 69.
[14]McDonald, *Western Political Theory,* p. 16.
[15]The classic studies of the relationship between Protestantism and capitalism are Max Weber, *The Protestant Ethic and the Spirit of Capitalism* (New York: Scribner, 1958), and Richard H. Tawney, *Religion and the Rise of Capitalism* (New York: Mentor Books, 1954).

religious attitudes that were to sanction middle-class business practices, was the doctrine that human beings were justified by faith rather than by works. The Catholic church had taught that humans were justified by *works,* which generally meant ceremonies and rituals. In the Catholic view no one could be justified on merit alone. "Justification by works . . . did not mean that an individual could save himself: it meant that he could be saved through the Church. Hence the power of the clergy. Compulsory confession, the imposition of penance on the whole population . . . together with the possibility of withholding absolution, gave the priests a terrifying power."[16] These powers also created a situation in which the medieval doctrines of the Catholic church were not easily abandoned and in which the individual was still subordinated to society (as represented by the church).

The Protestant doctrine of justification by faith asserted that motives were more important than specific acts or rituals. Faith was "nothing else but the truth of the heart."[17] Each person had to search his or her own heart to discover if acts stemmed from a pure heart and faith in God. Each man and woman had to judge for himself and herself. This individualistic reliance on each person's private conscience appealed strongly to the new middle-class artisans and small merchants. "When the businessman of sixteenth and seventeenth century Geneva, Amsterdam or London looked into his inmost heart, he found that God had planted there a deep respect for the principle of private property . . . Such men felt quite genuinely and strongly that their economic practices, though they might conflict with the traditional law of the old church, were not offensive to God. On the contrary: they glorified God."[18]

It was through this insistence on the individual's own interpretation of God's will that the "Puritans tried to spiritualize [the new] economic processes" and eventually came to believe that "God instituted the market and exchange."[19] It was only a matter of time before the Protestants expounded dogma that they expected everyone to accept. But the new dogma was radically different from medieval doctrines. The new doctrines stressed the necessity of doing well at one's earthly calling as the best way to please God, and emphasized diligence and hard work.

The older Christian distrust of riches was "translated" into a condemnation of extravagance and needless dissipation of wealth. Thus the Protestant ethic stressed the importance of asceticism and abstemious frugality. A theologian who has studied the connection between religion and capitalism sums up the relationship in this way: "The religious value set upon constant, systematic, efficient work in one's calling as the readiest means of securing the certainty of salvation and of glorifying God became a most powerful agency in economic expansion. The rigid limitations of consumption on the one hand

---

[16]Christopher Hill, "Protestantism and the Rise of Capitalism," in D. S. Landes, ed., *The Rise of Capitalism* (New York: Macmillan, 1966), p. 43.
[17]Ibid.
[18]Ibid., pp. 46–47.
[19]Ibid., p. 49.

and the methodical intensification of production on the other could have but one result—the accumulation of capital."[20] Thus, although neither Calvin nor Luther was a spokesman for the new middle-class capitalist, within the context of the new religious individualism the capitalists found a religion in which, over time, "profits . . . [came to be] looked upon as willed by God, as a mark of his favor and a proof of success in one's calling."[21]

THE ECONOMIC POLICIES OF INDIVIDUALISM

Throughout the mercantilist period this new individualism led to innumerable protests against the subordination of economic affairs to the will of the state. From the middle of the seventeenth century, almost all mercantilist writers condemned state-granted monopolies and other forms of protection and favoritism in the internal economy (as opposed to international commerce). Many believed that in a competitive market that pitted buyer against buyer, seller against seller, and buyer against seller, society would benefit most greatly if the price were left free to fluctuate and find its proper (market-equilibrating) level. One of the earliest mercantilist writers of importance, John Hales, argued that agricultural productivity could best be improved if husbandmen were allowed to

> have more profit by it than they have, and liberty to sell it at all times, and to all places, as freely as men may do their other things. But then no doubt, the price of corn would rise, specially at the first more than at length; yet that price would evoke every man to set plough in the ground, to husband waste grounds, yes to turn the lands which be enclosed from pasture to arable land; for every man will gladder follow that wherein they see the more profit and gains, and thereby must need ensure both plenty of corn, and also much treasure should be brought into this realm by occasion thereof; and besides that plenty of other victuals increased among us.[22]

This belief—that restrictions on production and trade within a nation were harmful to the interests of everyone concerned—became increasingly widespread in the late seventeenth and early eighteenth centuries. Numerous statements of this view can be found in the works of such writers as Malynes, Petty, North, Law, and Child.[23] Of these men, perhaps Sir Dudley North (1641–1691) was the earliest clear spokesman for the individualistic ethic that was to become the basis for classical liberalism. North believed that all men were motivated primarily by self-interest and should be left alone to compete in a free market if the public welfare were to be maximized. He argued that

[20]Kemper Fullerton, "Calvinism and Capitalism; an Explanation of the Weber Thesis," in Robert W. Green, ed., *Protestantism and Capitalism: The Weber Thesis and Its Critics* (Lexington, Mass.: Heath, 1959), p. 19.
[21]Ibid., p. 18.
[22]Quoted in Grampp, *Economic Liberalism,* p. 78.
[23]Ibid., pp. 77–81.

whenever merchants or capitalists advocated special laws to regulate production or commerce, "they usually esteem the immediate interest of their own to be the common Measure of Good and Evil. And there are many, who to gain a little in their own Trades, care not how much others suffer; and each man strives that all others may be forced in their dealings to act subserviently for his Profit, but under the cover of the Publick."[24] The public welfare would best be served, North believed, if most of the restrictive laws that bestowed special privileges were entirely removed.

In 1714 Bernard Mandeville published *The Fable of the Bees: or Private Vices, Publick Benefits,* in which he put forth the seemingly strange paradox that the vices most despised in the older moral code, if practiced by all, would result in the greatest public good. Selfishness, greed, and acquisitive behavior, he maintained, all tended to contribute to industriousness and a thriving economy. The answer to the paradox was, of course, that what had been vices in the eyes of the medieval moralists were the very motive forces that propelled the new capitalist system. And in the view of the new religious, moral, and economic philosophies of the capitalist period these motives were no longer vices.

The capitalists had struggled throughout the mercantilist period to free themselves from all restrictions in their quest for profits. These restrictions had resulted from the paternalistic laws that were the remnants of the feudal version of the Christian paternalist ethic. Such an ethic simply was not compatible with the new economic system that functioned on the basis of strict contractual obligations between people rather than on traditional personal ties. Merchants and capitalists who invested large sums in market ventures could not depend on the forces of custom to protect their investments.

Profit seeking could be effective only in a society based on the protection of property rights and the enforcement of impersonal contractual commitments between individuals. The new ideology that was firmly taking root in the late seventeenth and eighteenth centuries justified these motives and relationships between individuals. It is to a consideration of this new individualistic philosophy of classical liberalism that we turn in Chapter 4.

SUMMARY

There is a basic continuity between medieval and mercantilist social thought. State intervention in economic processes was originally justified in terms of the medieval Christian notion that those to whom God had given power were obligated to use this power to promote the general welfare and common good of all society. In early capitalism the state began to assume many of the roles formerly held by the church.

The Christian paternalist ethic, however, had thoroughly condemned the

---

[24]Quoted in Robert Lekachman, ed., *The Varieties of Economics,* vol. I (New York: Meridian, 1962), p. 185.

acquisitive behavior that was to become the dominant motive force of the new capitalist system. It was therefore necessary to create a new philosophical and ideological point of view that morally justified individualization, greed, and profit seeking.

Protestantism and the new philosophies of individualism furnished the bases for the new ideology. The economic writings of the later mercantilists reflected the new individualism. The new point of view emphasized the need for greater freedom for capitalists to seek profits and hence the need for less government intervention in the market. Thus the presence of two fundamentally different general points of view in mercantilist writings created an intellectual conflict that was not resolved until the classical liberal philosophy, including classical economics, effectively ferreted out all remnants of the medieval Christian paternalist ethic.

CHAPTER *4*

Classical Liberalism and the Triumph of Industrial Capitalism

A single theme runs through the works of the later mercantilist writers (considered in the latter part of Chapter 3) that distinguished them from the later classical liberal writers. They argued for a minimum of internal restriction and regulation, but they favored an active government policy designed to further England's commerce in the international trading markets. The classical liberals, however, advocated free trade internationally as well as domestically. In this chapter we examine the changes in England's commercial position that encouraged its economists to favor free trade.

THE INDUSTRIAL REVOLUTION

Between 1700 and 1770 the foreign markets for English goods grew much faster than did England's domestic markets. During the period 1700–1750, output of domestic industries increased by 7 percent, while that of export industries increased by 76 percent. For the period of 1750–1770, the figures are 7 percent and 80 percent, respectively. This rapidly increasing foreign demand for English manufactures was the single most important cause of the most fundamental transformation of human life in history: the Industrial Revolution.

Eighteenth-century England was an economy with a well-developed market and one in which the traditional anticapitalist and antimarket biases in attitudes and ideology had been greatly weakened. In this England, larger

35

outputs of manufactured goods produced at lower prices meant ever-increasing profits. Thus profit seeking was the motive that, stimulated by increasing foreign demand, accounted for the virtual explosion of technological innovations that occurred in the late eighteenth and early nineteenth centuries, radically transforming all England and eventually most of the world.

The textile industry was the most important in the early Industrial Revolution. In 1700 the woolen industry had persuaded the government to ban the import of Indian-made "calicoes" (cotton) and thus had secured a protected home market for domestic producers. As outlined earlier, rising foreign demand spurred mechanization of the industry.

More specifically, an imbalance between the spinning and weaving processes led to many of the innovations. The spinning wheel was not as productive as the hand loom, especially after the 1730s, when the flying shuttle was invented and the weaving process was speeded up considerably. This imbalance led to three inventions that reversed it: the spinning jenny, developed in the 1760s, with which one person could spin several threads simultaneously; the water frame, invented in 1768, which improved spinning by using both rollers and spindles in the process; and the mule, developed in the 1780s, which combined features of the other two and permitted the application of steam power. These new inventions could be used most economically in factories located near sources of water power (and later steam power). Richard Arkwright, who claimed to be the inventor of the water frame, raised sufficient capital to put a great many factories into operation, each employing anywhere from 150 to 600 people. Others followed his example, and textile manufacturing in England was rapidly transformed from a cottage to a factory industry.

The iron industry was also very important in the early drive to mechanized factory production. In the early eighteenth century England's iron industry was quite inconsequential. Charcoal was still used for smelting, as it had been since prehistoric times. By this time, however, the forests surrounding the iron mines were almost completely depleted. England was forced to import pig iron from its colonies, as well as from Sweden, Germany, and Spain. In 1709, Abraham Darby developed a process for making coke from coal for use in the smelting process.

Despite the relative abundance of coal near the iron mines, it was not until the latter part of the eighteenth century (when military demands on the arms and munitions industries were very great) that the iron industry began using coke extensively. This increased demand led to the development of the puddling process, which eliminated the excess carbon left by the coke. A whole series of innovations followed, including the rolling mill, the blast furnace, the steam hammer, and metal-turning lathes. All these inventions led to a very rapid expansion of the iron and coal-mining industries, which permitted the increasingly widespread use of machines made of iron in a great variety of industries.

Entrepreneurs in many other industries saw the possibilities for larger profits if they could increase output and lower costs. In this period there was a "veritable outburst of inventive activity":

During the second half of the eighteenth century, interest in technical innovations became unusually intensive. For a hundred years prior to 1760, the number of patents issued during each decade had reached 102 only once, and had otherwise fluctuated between a low of 22 (1700–1709) and a high of 92 (1750–1759). During the following thirty-year period (1760–1789), the average number of patents issued increased from 205 in the 1760s to 294 in the 1770s and 477 in the 1780s.[1]

Undoubtedly the most important of these innovations was the development of the steam engine. Industrial steam engines had been introduced in the early 1700s, but mechanical difficulties had limited their use to the pumping of water in mines. In 1769 James Watt designed an engine with such accurate specifications that the straight thrust of a piston could be translated into rotary motion. A Birmingham manufacturer named Boulton formed a partnership with Watt, and with Boulton's financial resources they were able to go into large-scale production of steam engines. By the turn of the century steam was rapidly replacing water as the chief source of power in manufacturing. The development of steam power led to profound economic and social changes.

With this new great event, the invention of the steam engine, the final and most decisive stage of the industrial revolution opened. By liberating it from its last shackles, steam enabled the immense and rapid development of large-scale industry to take place. For the use of steam was not, like that of water, dependent on geographical position and local resources. Whenever coal could be brought at a reasonable price a steam engine could be erected. England had plenty of coal, and by the end of the eighteenth century it was already applied to many different uses, while a network of waterways, made on purpose, enabled it to be carried everywhere very cheaply; the whole country became a privileged land, suitable above all others for the growth of industry. Factories were now no longer bound to the valleys, where they had grown up in solitude by the side of rapid-flowing streams. It became possible to bring them nearer the markets where their raw materials were bought and their finished products sold, and nearer the centers of population where their labor was recruited. They sprang up near one another and thus, huddled together, gave rise to those huge black industrial cities which the steam engine surrounded with a perpetual cloud of smoke.[2]

The growth in the major manufacturing cities was truly spectacular. For example, the population of Manchester rose from 17,000 in 1760 to 237,000 in 1831 and 400,000 in 1851. Output of manufactured goods approximately doubled in the second half of the eighteenth century and grew even more rapidly in the early nineteenth century. By 1801 nearly 30 percent of the English work force was employed in manufacturing and mining; by 1831 this

[1]Reinhard Bendix, *Work and Authority in Industry* (New York: Harper & Row, Torchbooks, 1963), p. 27

[2]Paul Mantoux, *The Industrial Revolution in the Eighteenth Century* (New York: Harcourt Brace Jovanovich, 1927), pp. 344–345.

figure had risen to more than 40 percent. Thus the Industrial Revolution transformed England into a country of large urban manufacturing centers, where the factory system was dominant. The result was a very rapid growth of productivity that vaulted England into the position of the greatest economic and political power of the nineteenth century. The effects of the Industrial Revolution on the lives of the English people are discussed in Chapter 5.

THE RISE OF CLASSICAL LIBERALISM

It was during this period of industrialization that the individualistic world view of classical liberalism became the dominant ideology of capitalism.[3] Many of the ideas of classical liberalism had taken root and even gained wide acceptance in the mercantilist period, but it was in the late eighteenth and nineteenth centuries that classical liberalism most completely dominated social, political, and economic thought in England. The Christian paternalist ethic was still advanced in the writings of many of the nobility and their allies as well as many socialists, but in this era these expressions were, by and large, dissident minority views.

The Psychological Creed

Classical liberalism's psychological creed was based on four assumptions about human nature. People were believed to be egoistic, coldly calculating, essentially inert, and atomistic. (See Chapter 3 for a discussion of the egoistic theory of human nature.) The egoism argued by Hobbes furnished the basis for this view, and in the works of later liberals, especially Jeremy Bentham, it was blended with psychological hedonism: the view that all actions are motivated by the desire to achieve pleasure and avoid pain.

"Nature," Bentham wrote, "has placed mankind under the governance of two sovereign masters, *pain* and *pleasure*. . . . They govern us in all we do, in all we say, in all we think."[4] Pleasures differed in intensity, Bentham believed, but there were no qualitative differences. He argued that "quantity of pleasure being equal, pushpin is as good as poetry." This theory of human motivation as purely selfish is found in the writings of many of the most eminent thinkers of the period, including John Locke, Bernard Mandeville, David Hartley, Abraham Tucker, and Adam Smith. Smith's ideas are examined in some detail later in this chapter.

The rational intellect played a significant role in the classical liberal's scheme of things. Although all motives stemmed from pursuit of pleasure and avoidance of pain, the decisions people made about what pleasures or pains to seek or avoid were based on a cool, dispassionate, and rational assessment of the situation. Reason would dictate that all alternatives in a situation be

[3]This account of classical liberalism relies heavily on Harry K. Girvetz, *The Evolution of Liberalism* (New York: Collier, 1963), pp. 1–149.

[4]Jeremy Bentham, "An Introduction to the Principles of Morals and Legislation," in A. I. Meiden, ed., *Ethical Theories* (Englewood Cliffs, N.J.: Prentice-Hall, 1955), p. 341.

weighed in order to choose that which would maximize pleasure or minimize pain. It is this emphasis on the importance of rational measurement of pleasures and pains (with a corresponding deemphasis of caprice, instinct, habit, custom, or convention) that forms the calculating, intellectual side of the classical liberal's theory of psychology.

The view that individuals were essentially inert stemmed from the notion that pleasure or the avoidance of pain were people's only motives. If people could see no activities leading to pleasurable conclusions or feared no pain, then they would be inert, motionless, or, in simpler terms, just plain lazy. Any kind of exertion or work was viewed as painful and therefore would not be undertaken without the promise of greater pleasure or the avoidance of greater pain. "Aversion," wrote Bentham, "is the emotion—the only emotion—which labor, taken by itself, is qualified to produce: of any such emotion as *love* or *desire, ease,* which is the *negative* or *absence* of *labor*—ease not labor—is the object."[5]

The practical outcome of this doctrine (or perhaps the reason for it) was the widespread belief of the time that laborers were incurably lazy. Thus only a large reward or the fear of starvation and deprivation could force them to work. The Reverend Joseph Townsend put this view very succinctly: "Hunger is not only peaceable, silent and unremitted pressure, but, as the most natural motive to industry and labor, it calls forth the most powerful exertions." Townsend believed that "only the experience of hunger would goad them [laborers] to labor."[6]

This view differed radically from the older, paternalistic ethic that had led to the passage of the Elizabethan Poor Relief Act of 1601. The paternalistic concern for the poor had lasted for two centuries and had culminated in 1795 in the *Speenhamland system,* which guaranteed everyone, able-bodied or not, working or not, a minimal subsistence to be paid by public taxes. It was against this system that the classical liberals railed. They eventually succeeded in passing the Poor Law of 1834, the object of which, according to Dicey, "was in reality to save the property of hard-working men from destruction by putting an end to the monstrous system under which laggards who would not toil for their support lived at the expense of their industrious neighbors."[7]

Classical liberals were persuaded, however, that the "higher ranks" of individuals were motivated by ambition. This differentiation of people into different ranks betrayed an implicit elitism in their individualistic doctrines. In order to ensure ample effort on the part of the "elite," the classical liberals believed the state should put the highest priority on the protection of private property. Although the argument began "as an argument for guaranteeing to the worker the fruits of his toil, it has become one of the chief apologies for the institution of private property in general."[8]

[5]Quoted in Girvetz, *Evolution of Liberalism,* p. 38.
[6]Bendix, *Work and Authority,* p. 74.
[7]Albert V. Dicey, *Law and Public Opinion in England,* 2d ed. (London: Macmillan, 1926), p. 203.
[8]Girvetz, *Evolution of Liberalism,* p. 50.

The last of the four tenets was atomism, which held that the individual was a more fundamental reality than the group or society. "Priority . . . [was] . . . assigned to the ultimate components out of which an aggregate or whole . . . [was] composed; they constituted the fundamental reality."[9] With this notion the classical liberals rejected the concept, implicit in the Christian paternalist ethic, that society was like a family and that the whole and the relationships that made up the whole were more important than any individual. The liberals' individualistic beliefs were inconsistent with the personal and human ties envisioned in the Christian paternalist ethic. The group was no more than the additive total of the individuals that constituted it. They believed that restrictions placed on the individual by society were generally evil and should be tolerated only when an even worse evil would result without them.

This atomistic psychology can be contrasted with a more socially oriented psychology that would lead to the conclusion that most of the characteristics, habits, ways of perceiving and thinking about life processes, and general personality patterns of the individual are significantly influenced, if not determined, by the social institutions and relationships of which he or she is a part. Atomistic psychology, however, sees the makeup of the individual as somehow independently given. It therefore regards social institutions as both tools for and the handiwork of these individuals. In this view society exists only because it is useful, and if it were not for this usefulness each individual could go his or her own way, discarding society much as he or she would discard a tool that no longer served its purpose.

The Economic Creed

Several explanations are necessary for an understanding of why the classical liberals thought society so useful. For example, they talked about the "natural gregariousness of men," the need for collective security, and the economic benefits of the division of labor, which society makes possible. The latter was the foundation of the economic creed of classical liberalism, and the creed was crucial to classical liberalism because this philosophy contained what appear to be two contradictory or conflicting assumptions.

On the one hand, the assumption of the individual's innate egoism had led Hobbes to assert that, in the absence of restraints, people's selfish motives would lead to a "natural state" of war, with each individual pitted against all others. In this state of nature, Hobbes believed, the life of a person was "solitary, poor, nasty, brutish, and short." The only escape from brutal combat was the establishment of some source of absolute power—a central government—to which each individual submitted in return for protection from all other individuals.[10]

On the other hand, one of the cardinal tenets of classical liberalism was that individuals (or, more particularly, businessmen) should be free to give

[9]Ibid., p. 41.
[10]Hobbes, *Leviathan,* reprinted in Melden, ed., *Ethical Theories,* pp. 192–205.

vent to their egoistic drives with a minimum of control or restraint imposed by society. This apparent contradiction was bridged by the liberal economic creed, which asserted that if the competitiveness and rivalry of unrestrained egoism existed in a capitalist market setting, then this competition would benefit the individuals involved and all society as well. This view was put forth in the most profound single intellectual achievement of classical liberalism: Adam Smith's *The Wealth of Nations,* published in 1776.

Smith believed that "every individual . . . [is] continually exerting himself to find out the most advantageous employment for whatever capital he can command."[11] Those without capital were always searching for the employment at which the monetary return for their labor would be maximized. If both capitalists and laborers were left alone, self-interest would guide them to use their capital and labor where they were most productive. The search for profits would ensure that what was produced would be what people wanted most and were willing to pay for. Thus Smith and classical liberals in general were opposed to having some authority or law determine what should be produced. "It is not from the benevolence of the butcher, the brewer, or the baker, that we expect our dinner, but from their regard to their own interest,"[12] wrote Smith. Producers of various goods must compete in the market for the dollars of consumers. The producer who offered a better-quality product would attract more consumers. Self-interest would, therefore, lead to constant improvement of the quality of the product. The producer could also increase profits by cutting the cost of production to a minimum.

Thus a *free market,* in which producers competed for consumers' money in an egoistic quest for more profits, would guarantee the direction of capital and labor to their most productive uses and ensure production of the goods consumers wanted and needed most (as measured by their ability and willingness to pay for them). Moreover, the market would lead to a constant striving to improve the quality of products and to organize production in the most efficient and least costly manner possible. All these beneficial actions would stem directly from the competition of egoistical individuals, each pursuing his or her self-interest.

What a far cry from the "solitary, poor, nasty, brutish" world Hobbes thought would result from human competitiveness. The wonderful social institution that could make all this possible was the free and unrestrained market, the forces of supply and demand. The market, Smith believed, would act as an "invisible hand," channeling selfish, egoistic motives into mutually consistent and complementary activities that would best promote the welfare of all society. And the greatest beauty of it was the complete lack of any need for paternalistic guidance, direction, or restrictions. Freedom from coercion in a capitalist market economy was compatible with a natural orderliness in which the welfare of each, as well as the welfare of all society (which was, after all, only the aggregate of the individuals that constituted it), would be maximized. In Smith's words, each producer

---

[11]Adam Smith, *The Wealth of Nations* (New York: Modern Library, 1937), p. 421.
[12]Ibid., p. 14.

intends only his own security; and by directing that industry in such a manner as its produce may be of the greatest value, he intends only his own gain, and he is in this, as in many other cases, led by an invisible hand to promote an end which was no part of his intention. Nor is it always the worse for the society that it was not a part of it. By pursuing his own interest he frequently promotes that of society more effectually than when he really intends to promote it. I have never known much good done by those who affected to trade for the public good. It is an affectation, indeed, not very common among merchants, and very few words need be employed in dissuading them from it.[13]

With this statement it is evident that Smith had a philosophy totally antithetical to the paternalism of the Christian paternalist ethic. The Christian notion of the rich promoting the security and well-being of the poor through paternalistic control and almsgiving contrasts sharply with Smith's picture of a capitalist who is concerned only with "his own advantage, indeed, and not that of the society. . . . But the study of his own advantage naturally, or rather necessarily leads them to prefer that employment which is most advantageous to the society."[14]

Not only would the free and unfettered market channel productive energies and resources into their most valuable uses, but it would also lead to continual economic progress. Economic well-being depended on the capacity of an economy to produce. Productive capacity depended, in turn, on accumulation of capital and division of labor. When one man produced everything he needed for himself and his family, production was very inefficient. But if men subdivided tasks, each producing only the commodity for which his own abilities best suited him, productivity increased. For such a subdivision of tasks a market was necessary in order to exchange goods. In the market each person could get all the items he needed but did not produce.

This increase in productivity could be extended further if the production of each commodity were broken down into many steps or stages. Each person would then work on only one stage of the production of one commodity. In order to achieve a division of labor of this degree, it was necessary to have many specialized tools and other equipment. It was also necessary that all the stages of production for a particular commodity be brought together and coordinated, as, for example, in a factory. Thus an increasingly fine division of labor required accumulation of capital in the form of tools, equipment, factories, and money. This capital would also provide wages to maintain workers during the period of production before their coordinated efforts were brought to fruition and sold on the market.

The source of this capital accumulation was, of course, the profits of production. As long as demand was brisk and more could be sold than was being produced, capitalists would invest their profits in order to expand their capital, which would lead to an increasingly intricate division of labor. The increased division of labor would lead to greater productivity, higher wages,

[13]Ibid., p. 423.
[14]Ibid., p. 421.

higher profits, more capital accumulation, and so forth, in a never-ending, upward-moving escalator of social progress. The process would be brought to a halt only when there was no longer sufficient demand for the products to warrant further accumulation and more extensive division of labor. Government regulation of economic affairs, or any restriction on the freedom of market behavior, could only decrease the extent of demand and bring the beneficial process of capital accumulation to a halt before it would have ended otherwise. So here again there was no room for paternalistic government meddling in economic affairs.

The Theory of Population

Thomas Robert Malthus's population theory was an important and integral part of classical liberal economic and social doctrines. He believed most human beings were driven by an insatiable desire for sexual pleasure and that consequently natural rates of human reproduction, *when unchecked,* would lead to geometric increases in population—that is, the population would increase each generation at the ratio of 1, 2, 4, 8, 16, and so forth. But food production, at the very best, increases at an arithmetic rate—that is, with each generation it can increase only at a rate such as 1, 2, 3, 4, 5, and so on.

Obviously, something would have to hold the population in check. The food supply could not support a population that was growing at a geometric rate. Malthus believed there were two general kinds of checks that limited population growth: preventive checks and positive checks. Preventive checks reduced the birthrate, whereas positive checks increased the death rate.

Moral restraint, vice, and birth control were the primary preventive checks. Moral restraint was the means by which the higher ranks of humans limited their family size in order not to dissipate their wealth among larger and larger numbers of heirs. For the lower ranks of humans, vice and birth control were the preventive checks; but they were grossly insufficient to curb the vast numbers of the poor.

Famine, misery, plague, and war were the positive checks. The fact that preventive checks did not succeed in limiting the numbers of lower-class people made these positive checks inevitable. Finally, if the positive checks were somehow overcome, the growing population would press upon the food supply until starvation—the ultimate and unavoidable check—succeeded in holding the population down.

Before starvation set in, Malthus advised that steps be taken to help the positive checks do their work:

> It is an evident truth that, whatever may be the rate of increase in the means of subsistence, the increase in population must be limited by it, at least after the food has once been divided into the smallest shares that will support life. All the children born, beyond what would be required to keep up the population to this level, must necessarily perish, unless room be made for them by the deaths of grown persons. . . . To act consistently therefore, we should facilitate, instead of foolishly and vainly endeavouring to impede, the opera-

tion of nature in producing this mortality; and if we dread the too frequent visitation of the horrid form of famine, we should sedulously encourage the other forms of destruction, which we compel nature to use. Instead of recommending cleanliness to the poor, we should encourage contrary habits. In our towns we should make the streets narrower, crowd more people into the houses, and court the return of the plague. In the country, we should build our villages near stagnant pools, and particularly encourage settlements in all marshy and unwholesome situations. But above all, we should reprobate specific remedies for ravaging diseases; and those benevolent, but much mistaken men, who have thought they were doing a service to mankind by projecting schemes for the total extirpation of particular disorders. If by these and similar means the annual mortality were increased . . . we might probably every one of us marry at the age of puberty, and yet few be absolutely starved.[15]

The masses, in Malthus's opinion, were incapable of exercising moral restraint, which was the only real remedy for the population problem. They were therefore doomed to live perpetually at a bare subsistence level. If all income and wealth were distributed among them, it would be totally dissipated within one generation because of profligate behavior and population growth, and they would be as poor and destitute as ever.

Paternalistic attempts to aid the poor were thus doomed to failure. Furthermore, they were a positive evil because they drained wealth and income from the higher (more moral) ranks of human beings. These higher-class individuals were responsible, either in person or by supporting others, for all the great achievements of society. Art, music, philosophy, literature, and the other splendid cultural attainments of Western civilization owed their existence to the good taste and generosity of the higher classes of men. Taking money from them would dry up the source of such achievement; using the money to alleviate the conditions of the poor was a futile, foredoomed exercise.

It is obvious that the Malthusian population theory and the liberal economic theories led to the same conclusion: Paternalistic government should avoid any attempt to intervene in the economy on behalf of the poor. Malthusian views—that poverty is the fault of the poor, who have too many babies, and that nothing can be done to end poverty—are still held by many people today.

The Political Creed

The economic and population doctrines of classical liberalism gave rise quite naturally to a political creed that rejected the state, or government, as an evil to be tolerated only when it was the sole means of avoiding a worse evil. Much of this antipathy stemmed directly from the many corrupt, despotic, capricious, and tyrannical actions of several European kings, as well as from the actions of the English Parliament, which was notoriously unrepresentative and

[15]Thomas Robert Malthus, *Essay on the Principle of Population,* vol. 2 (New York: Dutton, 1961), pp. 179–180.

often despotic. The liberal creed was not put forward as an objection against particular governments, however, but against governments in general. Thomas Paine reflected the sentiment of classical liberals when he wrote: "Society in every state is a blessing, but government, even in its best state, is but a necessary evil; in its worst state an intolerable one."[16]

What were the functions that classical liberals thought should be given to governments? In *The Wealth of Nations* Adam Smith listed three: protection of the country against foreign invaders, protection of citizens against "injustices" suffered at the hands of other citizens, and the "duty . . . of erecting and maintaining those public institutions and those public works, which, though they may be in the highest degree advantageous to a great society, are, however, of such a nature, that the profit could never repay the expense to any individual or small number of individuals, and which it therefore cannot be expected that any individual or small number of individuals should erect and maintain."[17]

This list is very general, and almost any kind of government action could be justified under one of these three functions. In order to understand the specific functions the liberals believed government should have, it is necessary to deal first with an objection that is frequently raised when the writings of Adam Smith are said to comprise part of an ideology justifying capitalism. It is often pointed out not only that Smith was not a spokesman for the capitalists of his day but also that many of his passages show that he was in general suspicious and distrustful of capitalists.[18] This contention is certainly true. Nevertheless capitalists used the arguments put forward by Smith to justify their attempts to eliminate the last vestiges of paternalistic government when these stood in the way of their quest for profits. It was Smith's rationale that enabled them to quiet their consciences when their actions created widespread hardship and suffering. After all, they were only following his advice and pursuing their own profits; and this was the way they should act if they wished to be of the greatest service to society.

Finally, most classical liberals interpreted Smith's theory of the three general governmental functions in a way that showed they were not hesitant about endorsing a paternalistic government when they, the capitalists, were the beneficiaries of paternalism. Thus "the original doctrine of laissez faire . . . passed, for the most part, from the care of intellectuals like Adam Smith . . . into the custodianship of businessmen and industrialists and their hired spokesmen."[19]

First, the requirement that the government protect the country from external threats was often extended in the late nineteenth century to a protection or even enlargement of foreign markets through armed coercion. Second, protection of citizens against "injustices" committed by other citizens was

[16]Quoted in Girvetz, *Evolution of Liberalism,* p. 66.

[17]Smith, *Wealth of Nations,* p. 681.

[18]For a statement of this view, as well as a scholarly inquiry into classical economics from a viewpoint that differs from the one presented in this book, see Lionel Robbins, *The Theory of Economic Policy in English Classical Political Economy* (London: Macmillan, 1953).

[19]Girvetz, *Evolution of Liberalism,* p. 81.

usually defined to mean protection of private property, enforcement of contracts, and preservation of internal order. Protection of private property, especially ownership of factories and capital equipment, is of course tantamount to protection of the sine qua non of capitalism. It was their ownership of the means of production that gave the capitalists their economic and political power. Giving the government the function of protecting property relations meant giving the government the job of protecting the source of power of the economically and politically dominant class: the capitalists.

Contract enforcement was also essential for the successful functioning of capitalism. The complex division of labor and the necessity of complex organization and coordination in production, as well as the colossal capital investments necessary in many commercial ventures, meant that capitalists had to be able to depend on people to meet contractual commitments. The medieval notion that custom and the special circumstances of a case defined an individual's obligations was just not compatible with capitalism. Therefore the duty to enforce contracts amounted to governmental coercion of a type necessary for capitalism to function.

The preservation of internal order was (and is) always necessary. In the late eighteenth and early nineteenth centuries, however, it often meant brutally crushing labor union movements or the English Chartist movement, which capitalists considered threats to their profit-making activities.

Finally, the function of "erecting and maintaining those public institutions and those of public works" that were in the public interest generally was interpreted to mean the creation and maintenance of institutions that fostered profitable production and exchange. These included the provision of a stable and uniform currency, standard weights and measures, and the physical means necessary for conducting business. Roads, canals, harbors, railroads, the postal services, and other forms of communication were among the prerequisites of business. Although these were often privately owned, most capitalist governments were extensively involved in their erection and maintenance either through financial subsidies to private businesses or through the government's direct undertaking of these projects.

Thus it may be concluded that the classical liberals' philosophy of laissez-faire was opposed to government interference in economic affairs only if such interference were harmful to the interests of capitalists. They welcomed and even fought for any paternalistic interferences in economic affairs that stabilized business or made larger profits possible.[20]

CLASSICAL LIBERALISM AND INDUSTRIALIZATION

The Industrial Revolution and the triumph of the classical liberal capitalist ideology occurred together during the late eighteenth and early nineteenth centuries. Liberalism was the philosophy of the new industrial capitalism, and

[20]Considerable evidence for this assertion can be found in Warren J. Samuels, *The Classical Theory of Economic Policy* (New York: World Publishing, 1966).

the new liberal ideas created a political and intellectual atmosphere in eighteenth-century England that fostered the growth of the factory system.

In its medieval version the Christian paternalist ethic had led to a pervasive system of restrictions on the behavior of capitalists during the mercantilist period. Capitalists and their spokesmen opposed most of these restrictions with a new individualistic philosophy that advocated greater freedom for the capitalist to seek profits in a market free of encumbrances and restrictions. It is not surprising that the triumph of this philosophy should coincide with the greatest achievement of the capitalist class: the Industrial Revolution. The Industrial Revolution vaulted the capitalist class into a position of economic and political dominance, and this fact goes far toward explaining the triumph of classical liberalism as the ideology of the new age of industrial capitalism.

SUMMARY

The pressure of rapidly increasing demand and the prospect of larger profits led to a "veritable outburst of inventive activity" in the late eighteenth and early nineteenth centuries. This period of widespread innovation—the Industrial Revolution—transformed England (and later western Europe and North America) into urban societies dominated by great manufacturing cities in which large numbers of workers were subjected to the dehumanizing discipline of factory production.

During this period the classical liberal ideology of capitalism came to dominate social and economic thinking. The new ideology pictured individuals as egoistic, coldly calculating, lazy, and generally independent of the society of which they were a part. Adam Smith's analysis of the market as an "invisible hand" that channeled egoistic drives into the most socially useful activities supported a doctrine of laissez-faire. The only functions this philosophy assigned to the government were those that would support and encourage profit-making activities.

Finally, the Malthusian theory of population taught that social action designed to mitigate the suffering of the poor was not only useless but even had socially deleterious effects. Acceptance of this view necessitated complete abandonment of the Christian paternalist ethic.

CHAPTER 5

Socialist Protest Amid the Industrial Revolution

The Industrial Revolution brought about increases in human productivity without precedent in history. The widespread construction of factories and extensive use of machinery represented the mechanical basis of this increase. In order to channel the economy's productive capacity into the creation of capital goods, however, it was necessary to devote a relatively much smaller part of this capacity to the manufacture of consumer goods. Capital goods had to be purchased at a social cost of mass deprivation.

THE SOCIAL COSTS OF THE INDUSTRIAL REVOLUTION

Historically, in all cases in which society has had to force a bare subsistence existence on some of its members it has always been those with the least economic and political power who have made the sacrifices. So it was in the Industrial Revolution in England. The working class lived near the subsistence level in 1750, and their standard of living (measured in terms of the purchasing power of wages) deteriorated during the second half of the eighteenth century. The trend of working-class living standards in the first several decades of the nineteenth century is a subject of dispute among historians. Many eminent scholars find sufficient evidence to argue that the living standard failed to increase, or even decreased, so one can conclude that any increase during this period was slight at best.

Throughout the period of the Industrial Revolution, there is no doubt that the standard of living of the poor fell precipitously in relative terms. A detailed analysis shows that "relatively the poor grew poorer, simply because the country, and its rich and middle class, so obviously grew wealthier. The very moment when the poor were at the end of their tether . . . was the moment when the middle class dripped with excess capital, to be wildly invested in railways and spent on the bulging opulent household furnishings displayed at the Great Exhibition of 1851, and on palatial municipal constructions . . . in the smoky northern cities."[1] There can be no doubt about which class paid the social costs in terms of the sacrificed consumption that was necessary for industrialization.

Yet decreased consumption was by no means the only, and perhaps not even the worst, of the hardships forced upon the laboring class by the Industrial Revolution. The new factory system completely destroyed the laborers' traditional way of life, throwing them into a nightmare world with which they were completely unprepared to cope. They lost the pride of workmanship and close personal relationships that had existed in handicraft industries. Under the new system their only relationships with their employers was through the impersonal market, or *cash nexus*. They lost direct access to the means of production and were reduced to mere sellers of labor power totally dependent on market conditions for their livelihoods.

Perhaps worse still was the monotonous, mechanical regularity imposed on the worker by the factory system. In preindustrial Europe the worker's tasks were not so specialized. The worker went from one task to another, and the work was interrupted by variations in the seasons or the weather. When the worker felt like resting or playing or changing the pace of the work routine, there was a certain amount of freedom to do so. Factory employment brought the tyranny of the clock. Production was mechanized. Absolute regularity was necessary to coordinate the complex interaction of processes and to maximize the use of new, expensive machinery. The pace of work was no longer decided by the worker but by the machine.

The machine, which had formerly been an appendage to the worker, was now the focal point of the productive process. The worker became a mere appendage to the cold, implacable, pace-setting machine. During the late eighteenth and early nineteenth centuries, in a spontaneous revolt against the new factory system, bands of workers smashed and destroyed machines and factories, which they blamed for their plight. These revolts, called the Luddite revolts, ended in 1813 when large numbers of workers were hanged or deported for their activities.

The extensive division of labor in the factory made much of the work so routine and simple that untrained women and children could do it as well as men, and because in many cases entire families had to work in order to earn enough to eat, women and children were employed widely. Many factory

---

[1]E. J. Hobsbawm, *Industry and Empire: An Economic History of Britain Since 1750* (London: Weidenfeld & Nicolson, 1968), p. 72. Several of Hobsbawm's ideas appear in this chapter.

owners preferred women and children because they could be reduced to a state of passive obedience more easily than men. The widespread ideology in this period that the only good woman is a submissive woman was a great help to their employers.

Children were bound to factories by indentures of apprenticeship for 7 years, or until they were 21 years old. In these cases almost nothing was given the children in return for long hours of work under the most horrendous conditions. Poor-law authorities could indenture the children of paupers. This led to "regular bargains . . . [where] children . . . were dealt with as mere merchandise . . . between the spinners on the one hand and the Poor Law authorities on the other. Lots of fifty, eighty or a hundred children were supplied and sent like cattle to the factory, where they remained imprisoned for many years."[2]

These children endured the cruelest servitude. They were totally isolated from anyone who might take pity on them and were thus at the mercy of the capitalists or their hired managers, whose main concern was the challenge of competitive factories. The children's workday was from 14 to 18 hours, or until they dropped from complete exhaustion. The foremen were paid according to how much the children produced and therefore pushed them mercilessly. In most factories the children had hardly more than 20 minutes a day for their main (and often only) meal. "Accidents were very common, especially towards the end of the overlong day, when the exhausted children almost fell asleep at their work. The tale never ended of fingers cut off and limbs crushed in the wheels."[3] The children were disciplined in such savage and brutal ways that a recitation of the methods used would appear completely incredible to the reader of today.

Women were mistreated almost as badly. Work in a factory was long, arduous, and monotonous. Discipline was harsh. Many times the price of factory employment was submission to the sexual advances of employers and foremen.[4] Women in the mines toiled from 14 to 16 hours a day, stripped naked to the waist, working with men and doing the work of men. There were reports of women who came out of the mines to bear children and were back in the mines within days after the birth. Many accounts have been written of the fantastically cruel and dehumanizing working conditions for women during this period. Of course, workingmen were not much better off than the women or their children. Industrialization was stern, harsh, and cruel in the extreme for men as well as for women and children.

Another important consideration in assessing the living standard of the working class during the period of capitalist industrialization was the rapid urbanization that took place at that time. In 1750, only two cities in Britain

[2]Paul Mantoux, *The Industrial Revolution in the Eighteenth Century* (New York: Harcourt Brace Jovanovich, 1927), pp. 410–411.
[3]Ibid., p. 413.
[4]Ibid., p. 416.

had populations over 50,000. In 1850, there were 29. By the latter date nearly one person in three lived in a city with more than 50,000 inhabitants.

Conditions in the cities of this period were terrible:

> And what cities! It was not merely that smoke hung over them and filth impregnated them, that the elementary public services—water-supply, sanitation, street-cleaning, open spaces, etc.—could not keep pace with the mass migration of men into the cities, thus producing, especially after 1830, epidemics of cholera, typhoid and an appalling constant toll of the two great groups of nineteenth-century urban killers—air pollution and water pollution, or respiratory and intestinal disease. . . . The new city populations . . . [were] pressed into overcrowded and bleak slums, whose very sight froze the heart of the observer. "Civilization works its miracles" wrote the great French liberal de Tocqueville of Manchester, "and civilized man is turned back almost into a savage."[5]

Included in these slums was a district of Glasgow that, according to a report of a government commissioner, housed

> a fluctuating population of between 15,000 and 30,000 persons. This district is composed of many narrow streets and square courts and in the middle of each court there is a dunghill. Although the outward appearance of these places was revolting, I was nevertheless quite unprepared for the filth and misery that were to be found inside. In some bedrooms we visited at night, we found a whole mass of humanity stretched on the floor. There were often 15 to 20 men and women huddled together, some being clothed and others naked. There was hardly any furniture there and the only thing which gave these holes the appearance of a dwelling was fire burning on the hearth. Thieving and prostitution are the main sources of income of these people.[6]

The total destruction of the laborers' traditional way of life and the harsh discipline of the new factory system, combined with deplorable living conditions in the cities, generated social, economic, and political unrest. Chain reactions of social upheaval, riots, and rebellion occurred in the years 1811–1813, 1815–1817, 1819, 1826, 1829–1835, 1838–1842, 1843–1844, and 1846–1848. In many areas these were purely spontaneous and primarily economic in character. In 1816 one rioter from the Fens exclaimed: "Here I am between Earth and Sky, so help me God. I would sooner lose my life than go home as I am. Bread I want and bread I will have."[7] In 1845 an American named Colman reported that the working people of Manchester were "wretched,

[5]Hobsbawm, *Industry and Empire*, pp. 67–68.
[6]Quoted in Friedrich Engels, *The Condition of the Working Class in England in 1844* (New York: Macmillan, 1958), p. 46.
[7]Quoted in Hobsbawm, *Industry and Empire*, p. 74.

defrauded, oppressed, crushed human nature lying in bleeding fragments all over the face of society."[8]

There can be no doubt that industrial capitalism was erected on the base of the wretched suffering of a laboring class denied access to the fruits of the rapidly expanding economy and subjected to the most degrading of excesses in order to increase the capitalists' profits. The basic cause of the great evils of this period was "the absolute and uncontrolled power of the capitalist. In this, the heroic age of great undertakings, it was acknowledged, admitted and even proclaimed with brutal candor. It was the employer's own business, he did as he chose and did not consider that any other justification of his conduct was necessary. He owed his employees wages and once those were paid the men had no further claim on him."[9]

LIBERAL SOCIAL LEGISLATION

From the time that factory production was first introduced into the textile industries, workers tried to band together to protect their interests collectively. In 1787, during a period of high unemployment, the Glasgow muslin manufacturers attempted to lower the piece rates they were paying. The workers resisted collectively, refusing to work below a certain minimum rate. The struggle led to open rioting and shooting, but the workers proved to have a strong and well-disciplined group, and they built a strong union. In 1792, a union of weavers forced a collective agreement upon Bolton and Bury Manufacturers.

Labor organizations spread rapidly in the 1790s. As a result of this and the concurrent growth of social and economic discontent, the upper classes became very uneasy. The memory of the French Revolution was fresh in their minds, and they feared the power of the united workers. The result was the Combination Act of 1799, which outlawed any combination of workers whose purpose was to obtain higher wages, shorter hours, or the introduction of any regulation constraining the free action of their employers. Proponents couched their arguments in terms of the necessity of free competition and the evils of monopoly—cardinal tenets of classical liberalism—but did not mention combinations of employers or monopolistic practices of capitalists. The effects of this legislation have been summarized as follows:

The Combination Laws were considered as absolutely necessary to prevent ruinous extortions of workmen, which, if not thus restrained, would destroy the whole of the trade, manufactures, commerce and agriculture of the nation. . . . So thoroughly was this false notion entertained, that whenever men were prosecuted to conviction for having combined to regulate their wages or the hours of working, however heavy the sentence passed upon them was, and however rigorously it was inflicted, not the slightest feeling of compassion was manifested by anybody for the unfortunate sufferers.

[8]Ibid., p. 75.
[9]Mantoux, *Industrial Revolution*, p. 417.

Justice was entirely out of the question: They could seldom obtain a hearing before a magistrate, never without impatience or insult. . . . An accurate account . . . of proceedings, or hearings before magistrates, trials at sessions and in the Court of King's Bench, the gross injustice, the foul invective, and terrible punishments inflicted would not, after a few years have passed away, be credited to any but the best evidence.[10]

Another cause for which the classical liberals campaigned vigorously was the abolition of the Speenhamland system of poor relief that had come into existence in 1795. This system was (continuing in the tradition of the Elizabethan Statute of Artificers) the result of the Christian paternalist ethic. It held that unfortunates would be entitled to a certain minimum living standard whether employed or not. To be sure, the system had serious drawbacks: It actually depressed wages below the relief level in many cases (with the parish taxes making up the difference) and severely limited labor mobility at a time when greater mobility was needed.

The important issue, however, is not the deficiencies of the Speenhamland system but rather the type of legislation the liberals enacted in its place when they succeeded in abolishing it in 1834. The view of the classical liberals was that workers should accept any job the market offered, regardless of the conditions or pay involved. Any person who would not or could not do so should be given just enough to prevent physical starvation. His dole should be substantially lower than the lowest wage offered in the market, and his general situation should stigmatize him sufficiently to motivate him to seek gainful employment. Thus the new law

was an engine of degradation and oppression more than a means of material relief. There have been few more inhuman statutes than the Poor Law Act of 1834, which made all relief "less eligible" than the lowest wage outside, confined it to the jail-like workhouse, forcibly separated husbands, wives and children in order to punish the poor for their destitution, and discourage them from the dangerous temptation of procreating further paupers.[11]

SOCIALISM WITHIN THE CLASSICAL LIBERAL TRADITION

Socialism had it origins in England in the late eighteenth and early nineteenth century. It was a protest against the inequality of capitalism and the social evils resulting from this inequality. This inequality, in the opinion of all socialists from the earliest times to the present, resulted inevitably from the institution of private property in the means of production. Hence socialism's most cardinal tenet is that social justice requires the abolition of private ownership of capital. Socialists have never accepted unanimously any particular social philosophy or body of doctrines. On nearly any given issue one can find differences

[10]Ibid., p. 449.
[11]Hobsbawm, *Industry and Empire,* pp. 69–70.

of opinion among socialists. The essential and defining feature of socialism, and the one idea that all socialists accept, is that private ownership of capital necessarily involves inequality and a host of other evils and that such ownership must be abolished if we are ever to achieve a just society.

Although there are today many schools of socialism, if we go back to the early 1800s we find that socialists can be divided into two groups, each having a distinctly different general social philosophy. The two traditions can be labeled *classical liberal individualistic socialism* and *cooperative socialism.* As we saw in Chapter 4, as well as the preceding section of this chapter, classical liberalism most generally functioned as an ideology justifying the new capitalist order and its many economically oppressive laws. In order for classical liberalism to function in this manner, however, people had to accept without question the institution of private ownership of capital.

There were many classical liberals who did not accept the institution. Particularly influential among these liberals was Thomas Hodgskin (1787–1869), who for most of his life received a naval disability pension that enabled him to devote most of his time to writing. In 1825 Hodgskin wrote a book entitled *Labour Defended Against the Claims of Capital,* in which he attempted to refute the principal intellectual justification for the private ownership of capital—the argument that capital is productive.

Hodgskin's refutation of the notion that capital was productive showed that the production usually attributed to capital was actually the production of interdependent workers. If we observe, for example, a fisherman catching fish with the aid of a net, then it appears to the conservative defender of capitalism that part of the fish are caught by the labor of the fisherman and part are caught by aid of the net. Therefore, it appears that the net is productive and that the capitalist owner of the net *deserves* a profit due to the productivity of his net. The real productivity, said Hodgskin, is that of interdependent workers. The fisherman was able to catch so many fish because other *workers* are making nets. The fish are caught through the joint labors of *both* the fisherman *and* the net makers. But since at the point at which the catch takes place the net making laborers are not present then it may appear that their share of the productive endeavor of fishing is actually performed by the product they have created—the net. Thus, while in capitalism it may appear that a worker (e.g., a fisherman) depends on the productivity of capital (e.g., the net) and hence depends on the capitalists (e.g., the capitalist owner of the net), this appearance is false. The worker depends, solely on the co-existing labor being performed by other workers. Hodgskin concluded that the productive

> effects usually attributed to a stock of commodities are caused by co-existing labour, and that it is by the command the capitalist possesses over the *labour of some men,* not by possessing a stock of commodities, that he is enabled to *support* and consequently employ other labourers.[12]

---

[12]Thomas Hodgskin, *Labour Defended Against the Claims of Capital* (London: Labour Publishing, 1922), pp. 51–52.

Hodgskin argued that labor is interdependent in all societies. But only in capitalist economies does private ownership of the means of production transform this universal interdependence into "capital." Then, the strange theory that things "produce" obscures the true essence of what capital really is. "Capital is a sort of cabalistic word, like Church or State, or any other of those general terms which are invented by those who fleece the rest of mankind to conceal the hand that shears them."[13]

With the exception of rejecting private ownership of capital by capitalists who do not produce, Hodgskin accepted all of the tenets of classical liberalism. It is not surprising, therefore, that his intellectual defense of economic greed and the unrestrained operation of the free market was nearly identical to that of the classical liberals. He was the first advocate of what today we call free market socialism. He took Adam Smith's notion of the invisible hand a giant step beyond the conservative classical liberals.

Hodgskin's arguments that capital is not productive and that private ownership of capital is the source of the worst inequities of capitalism remains the basis for the advocacy of market socialism to this day. Most market socialists, like Hodgskin, accept the tenets of classical liberalism and believe that a competitive market will indeed function like a benevolent invisible hand *if and only if* social ownership of the means of production is substituted for private ownership of these means.

WILLIAM THOMPSON AND THE REJECTION
OF CLASSICAL LIBERALISM

Most socialists, however, have rejected many of the individualistic tenets of classical liberalism as well as the notion that the market should allocate resources in a socialist society. Perhaps the most influential of the early socialists in this regard was William Thompson. Writing in the 1820s, he agreed with Hodgskin that if one had to live in a competitive market society, then market socialism was certainly preferable to capitalism. He argued, however, that the individualistic pursuit of wealth within a competitive market, whether that market be in a capitalist or a socialist society, led inevitably to five evils. These evils were "inherent in the *very principle* of competition."[14]

The first evil of competitive, market socialism was that every "labourer, artisan and trader [saw] a competitor, a rival in every other." Moreover, each saw "a second competition, a second rivalship between . . . [his or her profession] and the public."[15] Hence, the "principle of selfishness necessarily . . . [dominated] in all ordinary affairs of life."[16] For example, under competitive, market socialism, it would be "in the interest of all medical men that diseases

---

[13]Ibid., p. 60.

[14]William Thompson, *An Inquiry into the Principles of the Distribution of Wealth Most Conducive to Human Happiness* (London: Wm. S. Orr & Co., 1850 [first published 1824]) p. 258.

[15]Ibid., p. 259.

[16]Ibid., p. 257.

should exist and prevail, or their trade would be decreased ten, or one hundred, fold."[17]

The second evil inherent in the individualistic pursuit of wealth even in a market socialist economy was the systematic oppression of women. This oppression was an evil in itself, and it also led to enormous economic waste. The individualistic pursuit of wealth, Thompson believed, was compatible only with individual nuclear families. Within an individual family "all the little items of domestic drudgery" must be "done at stated hours." Women could be relieved of this drudgery if "numbers of families adjoining each other . . . [formed] a common fund for preparing their food and educating their children."[18]

The third evil of market competition—whether capitalistic or socialistic—was the economic instability caused by the anarchy of the market. Although socialism would eliminate the capriciousness of the luxurious tastes of the capitalists as a source of crises and depressions, as long as the competitive market allocated resources, economic instability, unemployment, waste, and social suffering would result.[19]

The fourth evil of competitive, market socialism was that it would not eliminate many of the insecurities of capitalism—insecurities that came from reliance on the market. The selfishness and egoism fostered by a competitive market society would create a situation in which there would be "no adequate . . . resource for malformation, sickness, or old age, or for numerous accidents incident to human life."[20]

The fifth evil of market competition was that it retarded the advance and dissemination of knowledge by making the acquisition of knowledge subsidiary to greed and personal gain. "Concealment, therefore, of what is new or excellent from competitors, must accompany individual competition . . . because the strongest personal interest is by it opposed to the principle of benevolence."[21]

Thus, Thompson concluded that while competitive, market socialism would be a dramatic improvement over capitalism, the reliance on the market would still involve numerous social evils. The best form of society, he argued, would be a planned cooperative socialist society. Such a society would consist of mutually coordinated, self-governing, cooperative communities, each having from 500 to 2000 members.

In such communities, people could freely obtain the necessities of life from a common store. Children would be cared for communally and sleep in common dormitories, while adults would live in small apartments. There would be common kitchen facilities for everyone. There would be no sexual division of labor—cooking, child rearing, and other forms of women's drudg-

[17]Ibid., p. 259.
[18]Ibid., p. 260.
[19]Ibid., pp. 261–263.
[20]Ibid., p. 263.
[21]Ibid., p. 267.

ery would be shared by everyone on a rotational basis. All persons would become skilled in a variety of occupations and would regularly alternate employments in order to eliminate the monotony of work. Every adult member of each community would participate regularly in the necessary coordinating or governing bodies. The finest education would be freely available to everyone. Absolute political, intellectual, and religious freedom would be guaranteed. Finally, all wealth would be communally controlled and shared so that no invidious distinctions could result from the distribution of material wealth.[22] Thompson's view of a cooperative, socialist community reflected, in general, the views of most of the people in the Owenite movement of his era (discussed in the next section). Throughout the history of that movement, he was its most influential spokesman after Robert Owen. Thompson's description of a planned, cooperative, socialist society was one of the earliest and the most fully elaborated in the history of socialist ideas.

THE PATERNALISTIC SOCIALISM OF ROBERT OWEN

The most important of the early organizers of a socialist movement to transform capitalism was Robert Owen. Born in 1771, Owen served as a draper's apprentice from the age of 10. At 20 he was the manager of a large mill. Wise business decisions and good luck soon resulted in the acquisition of a considerable fortune. Owen was a perfect example of a benevolent autocrat. His factory at New Lanark became known throughout all England because he insisted on decent working conditions, livable wages, and education for working-class children. His workers received "affectionate tutelage" from him, and he thought of himself as their trustee and steward.

The paternalistic attitude did not interfere with Owen's very strict organizational discipline in his factory. Owen described one of his methods of maintaining discipline:

> that which I found to be the most efficient check upon inferior conduct was the contrivance of a silent monitor for each one employed in the establishment. This consisted of a four-sided piece of wood, about two inches long and one broad, each side colored—one side black, another blue, the third yellow, and the fourth white, tapered at the top, and finished with wire eyes, to hang upon a hook with either side to show front. One of these was suspended in a conspicuous place near to each of the persons employed, and the color at the front told the conduct of the individual during the preceding day, to four degrees of comparison. Bad, denoted by black and No. 4; indifferent by blue, and No. 3; good by yellow, and No. 2; and excellent by white, and No. 1. Then books of character were provided, for each department, in which the name of each one employed in it was inserted in the front of succeeding columns, which sufficed to mark by the number of daily conduct, day by day, for two months; and these books were changed

[22]Ibid., pp. 269–367.

six times a year, and were preserved; by which arrangement I had the conduct of each registered to four degrees of comparison during every day of the week, Sundays excepted, for every year they remained in my employment.[23]

So in his life and deeds, Owen, like other capitalists of his era, strove to maximize his profits. He believed his competitors' harsh treatment of their workers was stupid and shortsighted, and he based his life on the assumption that the Christian paternalist ethic was compatible with the capitalistic system, at least at the factory level. In his own words, "My time, from early to late, and my mind, were continually occupied in devising measures and directing their execution, to improve the condition of the people, and to advance at the same time the works and the machinery as a manufacturing establishment."[24]

Although Owen's life and actions did not differentiate him from many of the conservative Tory radicals of his time, some of his ideas did. He did not believe that any society in which one class was elevated to a position of power and used this power to exploit the lower classes could ultimately become a truly good society. Private ownership of the means of production (factories, machinery, tools) was the social institution by which one small class in the existing economic system gained immense power over the mass of farmers and workers. The profit motive was the force that drove this small class to use its power to exploit the workers and farmers in order to gain profits.

Owen believed that in an ideal society the people could most effectively control nature because they would reap the greatest collective benefit if they cooperated. This cooperation should take the form of self-governing industrial and agricultural communities. In such communities, private ownership of the means of production would be abolished and the selfish quest for profits eliminated. He maintained that only when such a society was established would it be true that

one portion of mankind will not, as now, be trained and placed to oppress, by force or fraud, another portion, to the great disadvantage of both; neither will one portion be trained in idleness, to live in luxury on the industry of those whom they oppress, while the latter are made to labor daily and to live in poverty. Nor yet will some be trained to force falsehood into the human mind and be paid extravagantly for so doing while other parties are prevented from teaching the truth, or severely punished if they make the attempt.[25]

There was something in these writings that differed very radically from his description of the way in which he ran his own factory at New Lanark.

[23]M. Beer, ed., *Life of Robert Owen* (New York: Knopf, 1920), p. 111.
[24]Ibid., p. 112.
[25]Robert Owen, "The Book of the New Moral World," reprinted in part in Carl Cohen, ed., *Communism, Fascism, and Democracy* (New York: Random House, 1962), pp. 47–48.

In the ideal society, for Owen, the paternalism of the traditional Christian ethic would be expressed as a brotherhood of equals, a considerable shift from the parent-child type of subordination expressed in the medieval and Tory radical versions of the Christian paternalist ethic.

The feudal version of that ethic had accepted a hierarchical society. In this version those at the top lived lavishly (by the standard of the day, at least), and they did so by exploiting those at the bottom. Chaucer's parson's description of the medieval view is apt: "God has ordained that some folk should be more high in estate and degree and some folk more low, and that everyone should be served in his estate and his degree."[26] This traditional feudal ethic seemed to most capitalists to be incompatible with the capitalist order, and it was gradually replaced by the new individualist philosophy of classical liberalism.

Classical liberalism, however, was a two-edged sword. Although this ideology was used to justify the new capitalist order (see Chapter 4), its individualistic assumptions were very radical. If the old feudal aristocracy had no inherent superiority over the middle class and if any member of the middle class was to be freed of the old restraints, and if individuals should be the best judge of their own affairs, then how could one stop short of asserting the same rights and advantages for the lowest classes? The ideal that each individual ought, in some abstract way, to be considered as important as any other individual was radical indeed.

If individualism seemed to imply equality in theory, it certainly did not lead to it in practice. The rugged battle for more profits led not only to the social misery described earlier but also to a new class division of society that was sharply defined and as exploitative in nature as the medieval class structure. Membership in the higher class of the new system depended not on genealogy but on ownership. Capitalists derived their income and their power from ownership of the means of production.

Socialism, then, was a protest against the inequality of capitalism and the social evils resulting from that inequality. The inequality itself, in the opinion of socialists from the earliest times to the present, resulted inevitably from the institution of private property in the means of production. Hence, socialism asserted as its most cardinal tenet the idea that social justice demanded the abolition of private ownership of capital.

Intellectually, socialism was a wedding of the liberal notion of the equality of all human beings to the notion inherent in the traditional Christian paternalist ethic that every man should be his brother's keeper. Incorporating the egalitarian elements of classical liberalism into the traditional Christian ethic made this a utopian ethic, in comparison with which existing society was criticized. Without this egalitarian element the Christian ethic served well as an ideological justification of the hierarchical class system of the Middle Ages

---

[26]Quoted in J. L. Hammond and Barbara Hammond, *The Rise of Modern Industry* (New York: Harper & Row, Torchbooks, 1969), p. 215.

and was sometimes used to defend the capitalist system, particularly in the late nineteenth and twentieth centuries.

OTHER IMPORTANT PRE-MARXIST SOCIALISTS

When Owen asserted that in the ideal society private property and acquisitive profit seeking would be eliminated, he became part of a socialist tradition that was already firmly established. One of the first voices of socialist protest against capitalist property relations was that of Gerrard Winstanley (1609–1652), a cloth merchant who had been bankrupted in the depression of 1643. He blamed his own misfortune as well as that of others on the "cheating art of buying and selling."[27] In 1649 he led a strange band of followers from London to Saint George's Hill, Surrey. There they occupied unused crown lands, which they cultivated in common and, in general, shared in a communal existence.

In the same year Winstanley published *The True Levellers Standard Advanced,* in which he rebuked "the powers of England" and "the powers of the world" for their failure to realize that "the great creator . . . made the Earth a common treasury for beasts and man."[28] He asserted that all who derived their incomes in part or in full from property ownership were violating God's commandment "Thou shalt not steal." "You pharaohs, you have rich clothing and full bellies, you have your honors and your ease; but know the day of judgment is begun and that it will reach you ere long. The poor people you oppress shall be the saviours of the land."[29]

Babeuf

Throughout the eighteenth and nineteenth centuries, a large number of writers argued that private property was the source of the inequities and exploitation that existed in the capitalist economy. In this chapter we can mention only a few of the better known among them. One of the most interesting was the Frenchman Gracchus Babeuf (1760–1797). Babeuf argued that nature had made all persons equal in rights and needs. Therefore the inequalities of wealth and power that had developed should be redressed by society. Unfortunately, most societies did the opposite: They set up a coercive mechanism to protect the interests of the property holders and the wealthy. For Babeuf the presence of inequality meant, of necessity, the presence of injustice. Capitalist commerce existed, he said, "for the purpose of pumping the sweat and blood of more or less everybody, in order to form lakes of gold for the benefit of the few."[30] The workers who created the wealth of society received the least in return; and unless private property were eliminated the inequalities in society could never be redressed.

[27]Quoted in Lee Cameron McDonald, *Western Political Theory: The Modern Age* (New York: Harcourt Brace Jovanovich, 1962), p. 63.
[28]Ibid.
[29]Ibid.
[30]Alexander Gray, *The Socialist Tradition* (London: Longmans, 1963), p. 105.

Babeuf led the extreme left wing of the French revolutionary movement. After the fall of Robespierre he masterminded a conspiracy to destroy the French government and replace it with one dedicated to equality and brotherhood. The plot was betrayed and its leaders were arrested. Babeuf and his lieutenant, Darthe, were executed on February 24, 1797.

Babeuf is important in the socialist tradition because he was the first to advance the notion that if an egalitarian socialist state is to be achieved, the existing government must be toppled by force. The issue of whether socialism can be achieved peacefully has divided socialists since Babeuf's time. Babeuf also believed that if his revolt were successful, a period of dictatorship would be necessary during the transition from capitalism to a communist democracy to extirpate the surviving remnants of the capitalist system. Thus in several important ways Babeuf was a precursor of the twentieth-century Russian Bolsheviks.

Godwin

Other important ideas in the socialist critique of capitalism can be seen in the writings of the Englishman William Godwin (1756–1836). While the classical liberals were bemoaning the natural laziness and depravity of the lower classes, Godwin argued that the defects of the working class were attributable to corrupt and unjust social institutions. The capitalist society, in Godwin's opinion, made fraud and robbery inevitable: "If every man could with perfect facility obtain the necessities of life . . . temptation would lose it power."[31] Men could not always obtain the necessities because the laws of private property created such great inequality in society. Justice demanded that capitalist property relations be abolished and that property belonged to that person whom it would benefit most:

> To whom does any article of property, suppose a loaf of bread, justly belong? To him who most wants it, or to whom the possession of it will be most beneficial. Here are six men famished with hunger, and the loaf is, absolutely considered, capable of satisfying the cravings of them all. Who is it that has a reasonable claim to benefit by the qualities with which the loaf is endowed? They are all brothers perhaps, and the law of primogeniture bestows it exclusively to the eldest. But does justice confirm this reward? The laws of different countries dispose of property in a thousand different ways; but there can be but one way which is most conformable to reason.[32]

That one way, of course, must be based on equality of all human beings. To whom could the poor turn to correct the injustices of the system? In Godwin's opinion it most certainly would not be the government. With economic power went political power. The rich were "directly or indirectly the

---

[31]William Godwin, *An Inquiry Concerning Political Justice,* pp. 33–34. Quoted in Gray, *The Socialist Tradition,* p. 119.
[32]Ibid., p. 131.

legislators of the state; and of consequence are perpetually reducing oppression into a system."[33] The law, then, is the means by which the rich oppress the poor, for "legislation is in almost every country grossly the favorer of the rich against the poor."[34]

These two ideas of Godwin's were to be voiced again and again by nineteenth-century socialists: (1) Capitalist social and economic institutions, particularly private property relations, were the causes of the evils and suffering within the system; and (2) government in a capitalist system would never redress these evils because it was controlled by the capitalist class. Godwin, however, had an answer to this seemingly impossible situation. He believed human reason would save society. Once people become educated about the evils of the situation, they would reason together and arrive at the only rational solution. As Godwin saw it, this solution entailed the abolition of government, the abolition of laws, and the abolition of private property. For this radical social transformation Godwin believed socialists could rely primarily on education and reason. Most subsequent socialists argued that education and reason alone were insufficient. Education, they believed, should be only a part of the larger objective of creating a mass socialist movement. The importance of education and intellectual persuasion in attaining socialist ends has remained a much-debated issue to this day.

Saint-Simon

Other important socialist ideas were advanced by Henri de Saint-Simon (1760–1825), who was actually closer to the Tory radicals than the socialists in many ways. He came from an impoverished family of nobility, and his writings show an aristocrat's disdain for the antisocial egoism of the rich capitalists.

He also condemned the idle rich who lived off the labor of the poor but contributed nothing to society's well-being:

> Suppose that France preserves all the men of genius that she possesses in the sciences, fine arts and professions, but has the misfortune to lose in the same day Monsieur the King's brother [and all of the other members of the royal household] . . . Suppose that France loses at the same time all of the great officers of the royal household, all the ministers . . . all the councillors of state, all the chief magistrates, marshals, cardinals, archbishops, bishops, vicars-general and cannons, all the prefects and subprefects, all the civil servants, and judges, and, in addition, ten thousand of the richest proprietors who live in the style of nobles. This mischance would certainly distress the French, because they are kind-hearted, and could not see with indifference the sudden disappearance of such a large number of their compatriots. But this loss of thirty thousand individuals . . . would result in no political evil for the state.[35]

[33]Ibid., p. 119.
[34]Ibid.
[35]F. M. H. Markham, ed., *Henri Comte de Saint-Simon, Selected Writings* (Oxford: Blackwell, 1952), pp. 72–73.

Saint-Simon was the first to emphasize the efficiency of huge industrial undertakings and argued that the government should actively intervene in production, distribution, and commerce in the interest of promoting the welfare of the masses. He sanctioned both private property and its privileges as long as they were used to promote the welfare of the masses.

Many of his followers were more radical. They wrote endless pamphlets and books exposing abuses of capitalism, attacking private property and inheritance, denouncing exploitation, and advocating government ownership and control of economic production in the interest of the general welfare. It was from Saint-Simon and his followers that socialism inherited the idea of the necessity of government administration of production and distribution in a socialist economy.

Fourier

There were many other important socialists in the first half of the nineteenth century. The Frenchman Charles Fourier popularized the idea of cooperatives (or *phalanxes,* as he called them) He attempted to change society by encouraging the formation of phalanxes. His failure proved to many socialists that capitalism could not be reformed by the mere setting of examples. He was also one of the first socialists to predict that competition among capitalists would lead inevitably to monopoly:

> Among the influences tending to restrict man's industrial rights, I will mention a formation of privileged corporations which, monopolizing a given branch of industry, arbitrarily close the doors of labour against whomsoever they please. . . . Extremes meet, and the greater the extent to which anarchical competition is carried, the nearer the approach to *universal monopoly,* which is the opposite excess . . . Monopolies . . . operating in conjunction with the great landed interest, will reduce the middle and labouring classes to a state of commercial vassalage . . . The small operators will be reduced to the position of mere agents, working for the mercantile coalition.[36]

Fourier believed that in a capitalist economy only one-third of the people really did socially useful work. The other two-thirds were directed by the corruption and distortion caused by the market system into useless occupations or were useless, wealthy parasites. He divided these wastes into four categories:

> First Waste: Useless or destructive labour. (1) the army (2) the idle rich (3) ne'er-do-wells (4) sharpers (5) prostitutes (6) magistrates (7) police (8) lawyers (9) philosophical cranks (10) bureaucrats (11) spies (12) priests and clergymen.
> Second Waste: Misdirected work, since society makes it repellent, and not a vehicle of man's personality, attractive to him. (a) Deflection of the

[36]Quoted in Sydney H. Coontz, *Productive Labor and Effective Demand* (Clifton, N.J.: Augustus M. Kelley, 1966), p. 54.

passions into greed and morbidity, instead of being utilized as society's motors. (b) Scale of production too small to utilize labour properly. (c) No co-operation. (d) No control of production. (e) No adjustment of supply to demand, except by the mechanism of the "blind" market. (f) The family: this economic and educational unit is absurdly small.

Third Waste: Commerce dominated by middlemen. It takes a hundred men to do what society, with warehouses, distributed according to need, could do with one. A hundred men sit at counters, wasting hours waiting for someone to enter, a hundred people write inventories, etc., competitively. These hundred wasted merchants eat without producing.

Fourth Waste: Wage labour in indirect servitude; cost of class antagonisms. Since class interests are opposed, the costs of keeping men divided are greater than the gains in making them co-operate.[37]

Most socialists agreed that capitalism was irrational and wasteful and led to extreme inequalities, and hence was unjust and immoral. They disagreed, however, on the tactics they should use to achieve socialism. Many famous socialists, such as Louis Blanc (1811–1882), believed that the government could be used as an instrument of reform and that socialism could be achieved through gradual, peaceful, piecemeal reform. Others, such as Auguste Blanchqui (1805–1881), a pupil of Babeuf, based his ideas on the assumption that capitalism involved a constant class war between capitalists and workers. He believed that as long as capitalists occupied the position of power that ownership of capital gave them, they would exploit the workers, and the government and laws would be weapons used in this exploitation. He therefore saw no hope of achieving socialism through gradual political reform. Revolution was, for him, the only answer.

Proudhon

Pierre Joseph Proudhon (1809–1865), in his well-known book *What Is Property?*, answered the question posed in the title with a slogan that made him famous: "Property is theft." He believed property was "the mother of tyranny." The primary purpose of the state was the enforcement of property rights. Because property rights were simply sets of special privileges for the few and general restrictions and prohibitions for the masses, they involved coercion, of necessity, in their establishment and continued enforcement. Hence the primary function of the state was to coerce.

"Every state is a tyranny," declared Proudhon. The state was the coercive arm of the ruling class, and Proudhon advocated resistance rather than servitude: "Whoever lays a hand on me to govern me is a usurper and a tyrant. I declare him to be my enemy." There could be no justice until property relations were abolished and the state was made unnecessary:

To be governed is to be watched over, inspected, spied on, directed, legislated, regimented, closed in, indoctrinated, preached at, controlled, as-

[37]Ibid., p. 55.

sessed, evaluated, censored, commanded; all by creatures that have neither the right, nor wisdom, nor virtue . . . To be governed means that at every move, operation, or transaction one is noted, registered, entered in a census, taxed, stamped, priced, assessed, patented, licensed, authorized, recommended, admonished, prevented, reformed, set right, corrected. Government means to be subjected to tribute, trained, ransomed, exploited, monopolized, extorted, pressured, mystified, robbed; all in the name of public utility and the general good. Then, at the first sign of resistance or word of complaint, one is repressed, fined, despised, vexed, pursued, hustled, beaten up, garroted, imprisoned, shot, machine-gunned, judged, sentenced, deported, sacrificed, sold, betrayed, and to cap it all ridiculed, mocked, outraged, and dishonored. That is government, that is its justice and its morality! . . . O human personality! How can it be that you have cowered in such subjection for sixty centuries?[38]

Property rights were not only the source of tyranny and coercion, but also the source of economic inequality. Whereas the amount of labor expended determined how much was produced in a capitalist society, ownership of property determined how that produce was divided. It was divided in such a way that those who produced received almost nothing of what they produced, whereas those who owned property used the laws of private ownership to "legally steal" from the workers. Proudhon's ideal state rejected not only capitalist property relations but industrialization as well. Like Thomas Jefferson, Proudhon envisioned a golden age of small-scale agriculture and handicraft production, in which each farmer and worker owned his or her own capital and no one lived through property ownership alone. The list could be continued, but we have included most of the important pre-Marxist socialist ideas and have introduced some of the most famous socialist thinkers. Unquestionably the most influential socialist thinker was Karl Marx, and it is to a summary of his ideas that we turn in Chapter 6.

SUMMARY

The workers bore the cost of industrialization. The new factory system reduced most of them to poor, unhealthy, dehumanized wretches. Classical liberalism was generally not only impervious to their plight but even taught that the desire to improve the conditions of the poor was quixotic and doomed to failure.

There were, however, a few exceptions among the classical liberals, the most outstanding of whom was Thomas Hodgskin. Hodgskin argued that capital was unproductive and the profits represented an unfair, coercive extraction of a parasitic elite from the produce of the producers, the working people. He believed that the invisible hand of the competitive market system could function effectively only in a market socialist economy.

William Thompson argued that market competition—even under its

[38]Quoted in Daniel Guerin, *Anarchism* (New York: Monthly Review Press, 1970), pp. 15–16; the quotations in the preceding paragraph are from the same source.

very best form, market socialism—contained several inherent evils that could be eliminated only in a planned, cooperative, socialist economy. Robert Owen was a wealthy capitalist who espoused and helped build a movement for cooperative socialism. The ideas of several other socialists were briefly discussed in this chapter. All of them protested the inequities of capitalism. They believed that by eliminating the capitalists' method of robbing workers—private ownership of capital—they could create an industrial society in which every man and woman was treated with dignity and in which the fruits of production were reasonably and equitably divided.

CHAPTER 6

Marx's Conception of Capitalism

Karl Marx (1818–1883) has been the most influential of all socialists. His writings have had, and continue to have, a profound impact not only on socialist thought but also on policy decisions that affect a large percentage of the world's population. Although he worked in close collaboration with Friedrich Engels (1820–1895) and was unquestionably deeply influenced by Engels, Marx was the intellectual leader in most matters of political economy, so no attempt is made in this chapter to distinguish Engels's separate contributions.

HISTORICAL MATERIALISM

Marx believed that most of the late eighteenth- and early nineteenth-century socialists were humanitarians who were rightly indignant about the harsh exploitation that accompanied early capitalism. Despite his admiration for many of them, he gave to them the derisive label "utopian socialists." He believed most of them to be quixotic utopians who hoped to transform society by appealing to the rationality and moral sensibilities of the educated class. In Marx's view, educated men were usually members of the upper classes, and thus they owed their position, prosperity, and superior knowledge and education to the privileges inherent in the capitalist system. Therefore they would generally do everything within their power to preserve that system. The few heretics and humanitarians among them would certainly never constitute the power base from which a transition from capitalism to socialism could be effected. Yet Marx had an undying faith that such a social and economic transition would occur. This faith was not the result of his belief in the rationality and humanity of men but rather was based on an analysis of capitalism. He concluded that internal contradictions and antagonisms within the capitalist system would eventually destroy it.

Marx based his study of capitalist society on a historical approach that has been called *historical materialism*. When he looked at the mass of ideas, laws, religious beliefs, mores, moral codes, and economic and social institutions that were present in all social systems, he tried to simplify the complex cause-and-effect relationships among these many facets of social systems. Such a simplification, he believed, would enable him to focus his attention on the relationships that were most fundamental in determining a social system's overall direction of movement and change.

He believed that although all social institutions and intellectual traditions were reciprocally related in a complex web of cause-and-effect relationships (each affecting and, in turn, affected by the others), a society's economic base, or mode of production, exerted the most powerful influence in determining the other social institutions as well as social and religious thought. The mode of production consisted of two elements: (1) the forces of production and (2) the relations of production. The forces of production included tools, factories, equipment, production skills, the level of knowledge of the labor force, natural resources, and the general level of technology. The relations of production were the social relationships among humans, particularly the relationship of each class of humans to the means of production. These relations included the ownership of productive facilities and the division of the fruits of productive activity. The whole economic system, or mode of production, was referred to by Marx as the base, or substructure of society. The religions, ethics, laws, mores, and political institutions of society he called the superstructure.

Although the mode of production and the superstructure interacted reciprocally as both cause and effect, the mode of production was the base on which the superstructure was built. Therefore, the line of causation running from this economic base to the superstructure was much more powerful and important than the reverse line of causation. To argue that Marx believed the economic base determined, completely and rigidly, every aspect of the superstructure is grossly inaccurate (although it is often done). He did assert, however, that the mode of production was the most important single aspect in determining not only the present social superstructure but also the direction of social change.

When he referred to the relations of production, Marx meant the class structure of society, the most important single aspect of the mode of production. The antagonisms between social classes were, for Marx, the propelling force in history. "The history of all hitherto existing society is the history of class struggles,"[1] he proclaimed. The importance of the mode of production

---

[1] Karl Marx and Friedrich Engels, "The Communist Manifesto," in Arthur P. Mendel, ed., *Essential Works of Marxism* (New York: Bantam, 1965), p. 13.

and the class antagonisms it engendered have been summarized by Marx in
a famous passage:

> In the social production which men carry on they enter into definite relations
> that are indispensable and independent of their will; these relations of pro-
> duction correspond to a definite stage of development of their material
> powers of production. The sum total of these relations of production consti-
> tutes the economic structure of society—the real foundation, on which rise
> legal and political superstructures and to which correspond definite forms of
> social consciousness. The mode of production in material life determines the
> general character of the social, political, and spiritual process of life. It is not
> the consciousness of men that determines their existence, but, on the con-
> trary, their social existence determines their consciousness.
>
> At a certain stage of their development, the material forces of produc-
> tion in society come into conflict with the existing relations of production,
> or—what is but a legal expression for the same thing—with the property
> relations within which they had been at work before. From forms of develop-
> ment of the forces of production the relations turn into their fetters. Then
> comes the period of social revolution. With the change of economic founda-
> tion the entire immense superstructure is more or less rapidly transformed.
> In considering such transformation a distinction should always be made
> between the material transformation of the economic conditions of produc-
> tion which can be determined with the precision of natural science and the
> legal, political, religious, aesthetic, or philosophic—in short ideological forms
> in which men become conscious of this conflict and fight it out.[2]

Marx identified four separate economic systems, or modes of production,
through which the European civilization had evolved: (1) primitive communal,
(2) slave, (3) feudal, and (4) capitalist. In any one of these economic systems
there was a unique mode of production that included forces of production as
well as a particular class structure, or relations of production. Increasing
demands for more production inevitably led to changes in the forces of production; yet the relationships of production, or class positions, remained fixed and
were fiercely defended. Therefore there were conflicts, tensions, and contradictions between the changing forces of production and the fixed social relations
(and vested interests) of production. These conflicts and contradictions grew
in intensity and importance until a series of violent social eruptions destroyed
the old system and created a new system. The new system would have new
class relationships compatible (for a time at least) with the changed forces of
production.

In each mode of production the contradictions that developed between
the forces of production and the relations of production showed themselves in
the form of a class struggle. The struggle raged between the class that controlled the means of production and received most of the benefit and privilege
of the system (such as the Roman slaveholders) and the much larger class they

²Karl Marx, "Critique of Political Economy," reprinted in part in Howard Selsam and
Harry Martel, eds., *Reader in Marxist Philosophy* (New York: International Publishers, 1963),
pp. 186–187.

controlled and exploited (such as the Roman slaves). In all economic systems prior to capitalism, this class struggle had destroyed one system only to create a new system based on exploitation of the masses by a new ruling class, and hence the beginning of a new class struggle. Capitalism, however, was, in Marx's opinion, the last mode of production that would be based on the existence of antagonistic classes. The capitalist class, which ruled by virtue of ownership of the means of production, would be overthrown by the proletariat, or working class, which would establish a classless society in which the means of production were owned in common by all.

Before we can understand Marx's views on the ways in which capitalism tended to create the seeds of socialism, however, we must understand his conception of capitalism. Capitalism is an economic system in which resources are allocated by, and income distribution is determined within, the market. Marx called this a "commodity-producing society." In addition to this, capitalism is characterized by a particular class structure. In the next section we discuss the market, and in the following section the class structure of capitalism.

THE MARKET

The most conspicuous aspect of capitalism is the pervasive or ubiquitous functioning of the market. In any society, human beings are interdependent, each relying upon and requiring innumerable things, services, and activities from many others. In capitalism, nearly all human social and economic interdependencies are mediated by the market. This means that in capitalism, every thing, service, or activity that I need from another I must buy in the market. Similarly, if I perform or act for others, it is only in response to their buying things, services, or activities from me in the market.

When one stops to consider any one of the thousands of things necessary to sustain daily life, one becomes aware of how extensive and complex human social interdependence is. For example, we may begin our day by eating a bowl of cereal. For that cereal we depend upon farm workers who plant and harvest the grain, transportation workers who take it to mills, production workers in mills who transform it into the cereal we eat, transportation workers who transport it to grocery stores, and clerks who sell it to us. But that is only the beginning. The farm workers (as well as all of the other workers in the process) use machinery and tools that must be constantly produced by thousands of other workers. These latter workers, in turn, require materials, partly finished goods, tools, and machinery produced by still other workers.

From this example we see that even the simplest act of consumption or production involves interdependencies among tens or even hundreds of thousands of productive individuals. Thus, above all else, an act of consumption or an act of production is a *social* act. It is social because it requires the cooperation and social coordination of countless productive activities on the part of other people.

This merely reflects the fact that in all societies people must *socially* transform the natural environment in order to make it livable. This social transformation of the environment *is* production. For Marx, three facts about production were true in every society: First, production did, of course, require a natural environment to transform. Human beings could not exist in a vacuum.

Second, nature itelf contributed nothing toward its own transformation—it simply was the "stuff" being transformed in production. Only human labor transformed nature. Marx's views contrast sharply with the conservative ideology of capitalism, which claims that nature and tools both contribute to production and that landlords and capitalists are entitled to rewards commensurate with the contributions of nature and tools. For Marx, the fact that we exist in a natural environment that can be transformed in such a way that it fulfills our needs, however, had nothing whatsoever to do with the fact that landlords own the natural environment. Likewise, tools, which certainly must be used in production, were themselves in existence, he insisted, only because working people had produced them, and not because of the peculiarities of ownership. Thus, labor was the *only* human cause or source of production.

Third, any individual laborer or producer was, Marx argued, very nearly helpless alone. Production was a social activity where the production of one laborer depended upon the simultaneous or previous production of many other laborers. These three facts were true in every socioeconomic system, including capitalism.

What distinguished capitalism was that productive activity was not directly or immediately social. An individual producer had no direct social relation to (and generally had no knowledge of) either the workers upon whom his own production depended or those who depended upon his production. He bought what he needed in the market and produced for sale in the market. Therefore, the labor of the workers upon whom he depended confronted him *not* as the activity of particular people but as the market prices of the commodities they had produced. Likewise, the people who depended upon his labor did not know him as an individual. They knew nothing of the peculiar characteristics of him as a person or of his labor. His labor existed for them only as the selling price of the commodity he had produced.

In capitalism, then, labor was not directly social. It became social only when it appeared as the price of a commodity that was exchanged. The prices of commodities and the buying and selling of commodities at these prices constituted the *indirect* social relations of interdependent laborers. Thus, in capitalism the social interdependence of workers appeared, in the form of commodity prices, to be a set of relations among things (commodities) rather than a set of relations among workers. In capitalism, Marx wrote,

articles of utility become commodities only because they are products of the labour of private individuals or groups of individuals who carry on their work independently of each other. The sum total of the labour of all these private individuals forms the aggregate labour of society. Since the producers do not come into social contact with each other until they exchange their products, the specific social character of each producer's labour does not show itelf except in the act of exchange. In other words, the labour of the individual asserts itself as a part of the labour of society, only by means of the relations which the act of exchange establishes directly between the products, and indirectly, through them, between the producers. To the latter, therefore, the relations connecting the labour of one individual with that of the rest appear, not as direct social relations between individuals at work, but as . . . social relations between things.[3]

The common belief that the exchange of commodities is merely a set of relations among *things,* rather than social relations among *human individuals,* makes a fetish of things, so Marx called this belief the "fetishism of commodities." Marxist economics focuses on the human relations directly involved in market exchange, as well as other social and productive relations that form the necessary economic foundation for the kind of exchange that characterizes capitalism.

The prices of commodities, for Marx, had no inherent relation to the physical characteristics of the commodities. Wheat, for example, had certain physical characteristics when it was produced for the use of the producer and those directly associated with him or her in a precapitalist society with no markets and no prices. Wheat had exactly the same physical characteristics when it was produced, in capitalism, only for sale at some price in the market where its users had no direct social relation with its producers. Since prices had no inherent connection to the physical characteristic or useful qualities of things, prices could only be mental abstractions that were socially attached to things in order to coordinate the interdependence of producers. The social coordination or allocation of productive labor, in capitalism, depended entirely on prices and buying and selling. Therefore, prices were abstractions whereby capitalism rendered private labor into social labor through market exchange. As such, prices represented this social labor. But they appeared to be attributes of commodities rather than attributes of people. These views were the foundation of Marx's labor theory of value, which we discuss in the next chapter.

Whether social labor is allocated to the production of food, shelter, clothing, and other necessities or to yachts, mansions, pornography, hydrogen bombs, and nerve gas depends upon whether sellers of commodities (who are generally capitalists) can find buyers who are able and willing to pay the price that makes production of those various commodities profitable. Marx and his disciples have put considerable stress on the fact that the search for profits, and not inherent human or social needs, allocates and directs labor in capitalism. No matter how useful or beneficial some particular productive activity may be, it will generally not be undertaken if it does not yield profit to a capitalist. Likewise, the most useless, or even socially harmful, activities will be undertaken if they yield a profit for a capitalist.

Already in our discussion of the market, however, we have found it

---

[3]Karl Marx, *Capital,* 3 vols. (Moscow: Foreign Languages Publishing House, 1960), vol. I, pp. 72–73.

necessary to introduce the other defining feature in Marx's conception of capitalism, the distinction between workers who produce and capitalists who, through their search for profit, direct and control (and hence socially allocate) productive workers.

Marx's first defining feature of capitalism was that the market coordinated and allocated social labor by mediating all productive relationships among workers in such a way that *the social nature of labor appeared as the prices of commodities.* This allocation was effected through the search for profits. To understand Marx's views on the nature and role of profits we must understand his second defining feature of capitalism, its peculiar *class structure.*

THE CLASS STRUCTURE OF CAPITALISM

Marx believed that in every historical setting and within every cultural or national boundary in which capitalism had existed, it had been characterized by the existence of four classes of people: the class of capitalists, the class of small shopkeepers and independent craftsmen or professional people, the class of workers, and a poverty-stricken class that generally owned little or no property and whose members for a variety of reasons could not work. In some settings capitalism had had other classes as well. In the period of early capitalism, for example, by the side of these four classes were peasants and nobility, the remaining vestiges of the two main classes characteristic of feudalism. But the above-mentioned four classes were always characteristic of capitalism, and together they constituted its second defining feature. We shall briefly discuss Marx's view of each of these four classes.

Of the four, the working class and the capitalist class were by far the most important. In most capitalist settings, and always in well-developed capitalist economies, the working class constituted the absolute majority of the population and created or produced nearly all of the commodities. The capitalist class had the bulk of economic and political power in a capitalist society. We therefore discuss these two classes first.

A capitalist class could not exist without a class of wage laborers. Working for wages, or wage labor, characterized the working class in capitalism. Wage labor came into existence in the sixteenth to eighteenth centuries when large numbers of peasants were pushed off the land by landlords who took over the peasant's land and the formerly common lands. Peasants were thus forced to migrate to the cities, where they found a commercial market-oriented economy. The peasants could no longer sell the commodities they produced in order to acquire the commodities necessary to sustain their lives because they had no access to the land or to means of production.

But workers in the city had to buy commodities in order to live, and they could not buy commodities without selling something first so as to acquire money for purchases. Such workers had but one salable thing—a body or capacity to produce. A worker could not sell his or her body once and for all, or we would have had a slave economy and not a capitalist economy. In capitalism, workers recurringly sold control over their capacity to work, or labor power, for definite periods of time only. For example, they "hired out" by the hour, the day, or the week. The wage was the price workers received for selling control of themselves for this period of time. Therefore, the defining characteristic of the working class of capitalism was that it was comprised of wage laborers who had to sell their labor power as a commodity in order to survive.

The class that owned the means of production, of course, was the capitalist class. Exactly the same historical forces that created the wage laborer created the capitalist. The enclosure movements and the other forms of the primitive accumulation of capital that we discussed in Chapter 2 deprived the working class of any access to the means of production while simultaneously putting these means into the hands of the capitalist class. Therefore, the creation of the wage labor class was also necessarily the creation of the capitalist class.

Because of their ownership, capitalists needed to do nothing productive. They were free to do almost anything they chose. A few of them might simply choose to engage in productive endeavors. Yet such endeavor had absolutely nothing to do with their role as capitalists. They could cease such endeavor at will and still remain capitalists. Thus, for example, the Rockefeller family has produced governors, bank presidents, a vice-president of the United States, and so forth. Any one of them was also free at any time, without jeopardizing the family's status as capitalists, to become a functionless playboy.

The capitalist class owned the materials necessary for production. They then bought labor power as a commodity on the market. They directed the laborers, whose labor power they had purchased, to produce. The laborers produced commodities having some given magnitude of value. These commodities were owned by the capitalists, of course, who then sold the commodities. The value that the laborers had produced was generally sufficient for the capitalist to pay the laborers their wage, to pay for raw materials used, to pay for the wear and tear of the machines and tools used, or to acquire new machines and tools, and to leave a surplus for the capitalist. Capitalists received the surplus purely as a result of their ownership of property.

Not all of this surplus, however, was profit. The capitalist might have borrowed funds to augment his capital, or he might have rented the land on which his factory was constructed. For the capitalist, the interest he paid on his debt and the rent he paid on the land were both expenses which he deducted, along with his other expenses, from the value his laborers had created in order to arrive at his profit. The persons who received this interest and rent were also, in Marx's view, receiving income purely from ownership. Thus, the surplus value created by workers, in excess of the value of their own wages and the materials and tools used up in production, went to profit, interest, and rent. All three of these latter forms of income were derived from ownership. Therefore they were all capitalist income. Ownership of money, land, or tools and machinery could thus all become capital under the right circumstances, and the return from owning capital could take the form of interest, rent, or profit.

The capitalist class comprised those people whose ownership was so significant that it brought them sufficient income to live in luxury and to have great economic and political power without ever having to engage in any form of socially useful toil.

In every capitalist economy there was another social class that stood between the capitalists and the wage laborers. This was the class of small shopkeepers, independent craftsmen, and professionals or other independent proprietors. This class had features resembling both capitalists and workers. They owned their own means of production and did much (and sometimes all) of the work in creating or selling their commodities. Most frequently they themselves, like wage laborers, had to work, but they also, like capitalists, hired wage laborers to assist them. Included in this class would be most doctors, lawyers, independent accountants, barbers, and many owners of such small businesses as hamburger stands, dry cleaners, repair garages, small retail shops, and the like. This class has always been much smaller than the working class and much larger than the capitalist class. In some circumstances the interests of this class might be very close to those of the capitalist class, whereas in other circumstances their interests might be closer to those of the working class.

Finally, the last class in capitalism was the poorest class. It included people who received little or no income from either owning or working. Included in this class were two distinctly different groups. First, there were those who could not work for a variety of reasons, such as mental, physical, or emotional handicaps or problems; people who were too young or too old to work and had no one to support them; and people such as single parents of very small children whose necessary activities left no time for wage labor. The second group included people who were able and willing to work but for whom capitalism did not provide enough jobs. Throughout the history of capitalism there have always been millions of such involuntarily unemployed people. They have generally performed two very important economic functions. First, they have weakened the bargaining power of employed laborers in their wage negotiations, since if employed workers demanded too much, they could easily be replaced. Second, capitalism has always been an unstable economy. It has experienced alternative periods of prosperity and depression. The involuntarily unemployed have constituted a reserve of workers who could be used in times of prosperity when the economy was growing and needed more workers and could be discarded when recession or depression set in and fewer workers were needed. Thus, the size of this lowest or poorest class in capitalism has always varied in accordance with general business conditions.

After examining the sources of income among all four classes, Marx concluded that interest, rent, and profit were not the only forms taken by the surplus created by the working class. Taxes also came from this surplus. Whether the taxes were collected from wage earners or from the recipients of interest, rent, and profits, they represented a claim on the product of labor and were hence a part of the surplus value created by but not received by workers. Thus we see that two of the classes in capitalism—the highest and the lowest—did not contribute to the production of commodities but lived off the surplus created by wage laborers.

Within the context of Marx's theory, it is interesting to note that whenever workers become angry or frustrated by their support of unproductive consumers, it is, of course, much more conducive to the peace and stability of capitalism if all of their anger and frustration is turned against those living in dire poverty—the unemployed and unemployable—rather than against those living in extravagant luxury—the capitalists. It is not surprising that conservatives generally protest the parasitic nature of the very poor and the powerless, while critics who have been influenced by Marx protest the parasitic nature of the wealthy and the powerful. In Marx's view, however, both classes were integral parts of capitalism and would continue to exist as long as capitalism existed.

Thus the market allocation of productive labor and natural resources, together with the four-level class structure of capitalism, constituted the main defining features of capitalism for Marx. In discussing this class structure, however, we have used the concepts of private property and capital, concepts which Marx understood somewhat differently than do most of us. We shall therefore discuss them at somewhat greater length.

MARX'S VIEW OF PRIVATE PROPERTY

It is difficult to find a general definition that will cover all property rights, in all societies, in all times. One thing, however, is clear. A property right is *not* simply or even primarily a relation between an isolated individual and a material thing. An isolated individual could use any material object in any way he or she chose, subject only to the laws of physics, chemistry, and human anatomy. He or she would have absolutely no need for, and no conception of, property rights. Property rights are essential social relations between people. But not all social relations are property rights.

An adequate general definition of property rights is, of necessity, fairly vague and complex. The best definition, in our opinion, is as follows: *Within a particular social or cultural setting* (e.g., a modern nation-state) *property rights represent a set of social relations that defines privileges and corresponding sanctions. The privileges and sanctions are related to objects* (whether material or not). *The privileges and sanctions are coercively established and coercively maintained by an agency of coercion that is widely believed to "rightly" or "properly" use coercive force* (such as the police).

For most of us, private property simply means private ownership of our personal means of consumption. We have the exclusive privilege of using and disposing of our own food, clothing, and assorted personal effects (though generally *not* of the dwelling in which we reside). Others cannot have this privilege with our personal effects. They face coercive sanctions. If they try to use or dispose of our personal effects, their action constitutes theft and they face coercion from the police, one of our institutionalized agencies whose use of coercion (within defined limits) is generally deemed proper.

Private ownership of the means of consumption strikes most of us as a reasonable and useful social convention. It would seem difficult for a society to function if certain items, such as food and clothing, were not allocated in such a manner as to give particular individuals the right to use and dispose of particular means of consumption, at least where that consumption is primarily a private matter. Defenders of private property generally use the means of personal consumption to illustrate that private property is "natural," "inevitable," and "just." Marx's concern, however, was not so much with private ownership of the means of consumption as with private ownership of the means of production.

Marx insisted that all production was social. Yet there were two different ways in which it was social. First, in handicraft production, a single or at most a few producers working together created a finished product. Even in the case of a single producer, there was an economic or productive dependence on other producers who had to provide the individual producer with materials on which to work as well as equipment, machines, and tools with which to work. Defenders of private ownership of the means of production have generally used examples of handicraft production to construct their defense. In such production, the individual's social dependence was similar to that involved in private consumption; that is, others produced both the necessary means of consumption and production. Thus, when handicraft production alone was considered, the same rationale would defend private ownership of both productive and consumptive goods.

Marx felt that it was ironic that handicraft production was frequently used as the basis for defending capitalist private ownership of the means of production. He argued that it was such historical processes as the enclosure movement and increased indebtedness, among other things, that had made independent handicraft production *impossible for the vast majority of workers* and, in so doing, had simultaneously created a supply of unemployed wage workers. In other words, the necessary condition for capitalism's historical creation was that the form of production that was used to defend capitalist ownership had to become inaccessible to most producers and therefore had to become relatively unimportant to the whole capitalist economy.

There were, of course, still a few independent handicraft producers in most capitalist economies of Marx's time (as there are today). They constituted a small part of the class of independent small shopkeepers, producers, and professionals that stood somewhere between the capitalist class and the working class. Obviously, this first form of productive interdependence, characteristic of handicraft production, was neither the most important form nor the characteristic form in a capitalist economy.

The second form of productive interdependence, then, was the one most characteristic of capitalism. This interdependence reflected the form of social production that inevitably went with a capitalist economy and was, historically, the outcome of the Industrial Revolution, which we discussed in Chapter

4. This form of productive interdependence was characteristic of factory and industrial production. In industrial production, no single worker or small group of workers produced a finished commodity. There was an elaborate division of labor in which each individual repetitiously performed a single task or a few tasks and only the coordinated effort of hundreds (and even, in some cases, tens of thousands) of individuals resulted in the production of a particular commodity. Such industrial production generally involved massive factories or work places, as well as very expensive and elaborate machines and tools.

Thus, industrial production, which was the form social productive interdependencies generally took in a capitalist economy, made it utterly impossible for the vast majority of working people to own individually as private property the means necessary for them to produce. In capitalism most production was totally social. It was social in the same way that handicraft production was social; that is, workers in a factory depended upon other workers to produce the materials on which they worked and the tools with which they worked. But it was also social in a new way: Any production process now involved the coordinated endeavors of hundreds or even thousands of workers working with complex, expensive machinery.

In this situation what then constituted the nature of private ownership of the means of production? Marx was aware that in the case of private ownership of the means of individual consumption—or private ownership of the means of individual, independent handicraft production—such ownership meant the privilege or right to use and dispose of the things owned. In industrial corporations, however, the ownership of stock (which constituted ownership of shares of the means of production) conferred this right to only a few of the biggest and most powerful owners. Even then, this right generally consisted only in naming powerful managers to oversee, direct, and control the use of these means of production by working people who did not own them. The common privilege of all ownership of stocks for every owner, from the smallest to the largest, was the right or privilege to take a proportionate share (depending on the amount of stock owned) of the surplus value created by workers. Ownership of the industrial means of production, in capitalism, thus had only one inherent or common privilege for all owners: to reap where they had not sown, to receive a part of the value of commodities produced without having to take any part whatsoever in the production of these commodities.

Thus Marx argued that capitalism had resulted in a

transformation of the actually functioning capitalist into a mere manager, administrator of other people's capital, and of the owner of capital into a mere owner, a mere money-capitalist. Even if the dividends which they receive include the interest and the profit of enterprise, i.e. the total profit (for the salary of the manager is, or should be, simply the wage of a specific type of skilled labour, whose price is regulated in the labour-market like that of any other labour), this total profit is henceforth received only in the form of interest, i.e. as mere compensation for owning capital that now is entirely divorced from its function in the actual process of reproduction just as this function in the person of the manager is divorced from ownership of capital. Profit thus appears . . . as a mere appropriation of the surplus-labour of others.[4]

During Marx's time (and, indeed, right up to the present) the dominant economic ideology of capitalism justified colossal incomes from ownership as being the fruits of high moral character. In capitalism, the ideologists argued, workers earned wages because of, or in payment for, the strain of producing. On the other hand, because it has always been extraordinarily difficult (very nearly impossible) for a noncapitalist to save enough to become a capitalist, the ideologists argued that whenever anyone did become a capitalist they must have undergone strain and sacrifices that were much more severe than the mere strain of productively creating things that were socially needed. Therefore, their profit, rent, and interest were earned because of, or in payment for, the strains and sacrifices of their abstinence.

There were many arguments by which Marx refuted the ideologists' apologetic views on profit. Here we shall mention only three of them.

First, the abstinence and strain that were necessary for one to become a capitalist involved no contribution to society. For example, if a person saved all his life in order to buy a factory, he saved only for himself. He had not, in so doing, done any of the work necessary to construct the factory. All the work had been done by working people. Rather, the extent of his stress and strain merely reflected the fact that in any class-divided society there had to be significant barriers to entrance into the ruling class. If it had been relatively easy for anyone to become a capitalist, then everyone would have become a capitalist; there would have been no workers; nothing would have been produced and everyone would have starved. There had been in history, and were in Marx's time, numerous socioeconomic systems that operated effectively without the abstinence of capitalists, in fact, without capitalists at all. But there had never been, and there never would be, a society without working people creating needed products.

Second, if sacrifice and abstinence could justify capitalists' income, then they could similarly justify the wealth, power, and income of any ruling class in any society. For example, in the American South prior to the Civil War, the economic system was one of commercial slavery. Slaves were very expensive, and most southern whites did not own slaves. Slave owners, of course, enjoyed great wealth and lavish incomes from the surplus their slaves produced over the costs of their maintainence. For a non–slave owner to become a slave owner was very difficult. It required extreme strain and abstinence. It is therefore clear that according to this ideology the surplus that these owners extracted from the sweat and toil of their slaves was merely the just reward for the owners' strain and abstinence.

Third, the majority of capitalists inherited their ownership of capital. Not only did they not strain and abstain, most of them lived lives of indolent luxury. And for those who had not inherited their wealth, most had become capitalists not because they had produced and abstained, but through some combination of ruthlessness, shrewdness, chicanery, and luck. Marx detailed the piracy, slave trading, and colonial plundering in the early process of building capitalist fortunes.

When confronted with these criticisms, defenders of capitalist ideology had two responses. The first response was that regardless of how a capitalist acquired his fortune, he abstained when he did not fritter the whole thing away. He could have consumed so incredibly profligately and luxuriously that he would soon have had none of his inherited fortune left. In fact, a few capitalists actually did this, and every capitalist constantly had the choice of, on the one hand, abstaining from such extreme profligacy and luxury in order that he or all of his descendents might live in ordinary profligacy and luxury or, on the other hand, recklessly throwing his entire fortune away. In fact, in order for a capitalist family to remain in the ruling class, generation after generation, the members of the family had to "abstain" to that degree just as they had to abstain from committing suicide before they had had any offspring to inherit their wealth. Such abstinence, in the ideology of capitalism, remained a moral justification for the large incomes of capitalists.

The second response to critics was that abstinence alone did not morally justify ruling-class income, but only abstinence that led to or perpetuated the ownership of nonhuman objects as capital. Thus the defenders of capitalism argued that abstinence in the acquiring of slaves did not justify property income because slave owning was inherently immoral, whereas the owner of capital did society a great service because capital was productive. The capitalist used his capital productively and thereby contributed to everyone's well-being.

Before we can understand all of Marx's critique of the ideology of capitalism, however, we must understand his conception of the nature of capital.

MARX'S VIEW OF CAPITAL

The standard ideology of capitalism was based on the notion that capital was one of the three factors of production—land, labor, and capital—that were necessary for production in every society. These factors were said to account for all production. Above all, the ideology held that the three were complementary and not alternatives or competitors. All production required the cooperation of all three. Without labor, no production was possible; without land, no production was possible; and without capital, no production was possible. Ideologists concluded that all three factors had to cooperate peacefully and harmoniously.

But the ideology went on to insist that all three factors of production were merely collections of three different kinds of commodities. Land, labor, and capital were names for three different sorts of commodities that are bought and sold in the market. Since commodities did not cooperate peacefully and harmoniously, it was obvious that the ideologists meant that the owners of the commodities must cooperate peacefully and harmoniously.

Next, the ideologists argued that entrepreneurs went into the market and bought certain quantities of each of the three commodity factors of production. The entrepreneur then combined these factors in a production process that yielded output in the form of commodities having certain value. He sold these commodities on the market. If everything had functioned properly, then two very interesting "facts" could be observed to result from the process. First, one could precisely ascertain the productive contribution of each of the factors: land, labor, and capital. Second, the price that the entrepreneur paid for each of these commodities—wages being the price of labor, rent being the price of land, and profit (or interest) being the price of capital—turned out to be exactly equal to the value of the productive contribution of each factor; that is, each factor was returned just what it had contributed to production. Hence there could not possibly be any economic exploitation. It is clear why the ideologists of capitalism held that harmony and not conflict is the natural social state of capitalism. This conservative ideology can still be found in many conservative economics textbooks on microeconomic theory.

Capital, in this ideology, was merely a commodity like the other factors of production. It produced for society and received a reward based on its productivity. If one doubted the productivity of capital, argued the ideologist, then one could try making steel without a blast furnace, or digging a trench without a shovel, or tightening a screw without a screwdriver, or, in general, producing without tools. Capital was identified as commodities that were tools (or other means of producing). And because tools were indispensable, they argued that capital was indispensable.

Marx immediately saw several difficulties with this analysis. Human beings had always used tools. Yet capitalism, capital, and profit were social categories that did not even exist as such in some societies. In fact, capitalism, capital, and profit had actually existed for only a few hundred years.

Obviously, land did not yield rent and tools did not yield profit simply because they entered into the production process. They had been used in societies that did not even have rent or profit. Clearly tools were not, per se, capital. Moreover, since one could own both land and tools and yet receive no rent or profit, it was equally clear that ownership of land or tools does not necessarily or automatically mean capitalistically owned land that yields rent or capital that yields profit. The problem of identifying the nature of capital remained unsolved within the context of capitalist ideology.

In Marx's opinion, the key to resolving these inconsistencies was to realize that land, labor, and capital were not, in the same sense, factors of production. Moreover, tools and land, simply purchased as commodities, required other social conditions before they could become profit-yielding capital and rent-yielding land.

The production process, Marx insisted, presupposed that human beings lived in an environment they could transform. Production was this transformation of nature by human beings. Although land, as this environment, was certainly necessary, to say that nature "produced" something was to engage in a kind of confusion (Marx called it fetishism) where human qualities were attributed to nonhuman things. It was the equivalent of saying that nature transformed itself expressly for human use.

Just as saying that land, as an inanimate object, could produce anything by itself was a confusion (or a form of fetishism), so was the notion that tools produced anything by themselves. A tool undertook no activity. It was an object produced by human labor. The producer of the tool had in mind, of course, that the tool would be used in further production. But the tool, as such, did not produce anything. Only people produced things—usually by using tools.

The statement that tools were absolutely necessary for modern production was true. It did not mean that tools engaged in production, however. It meant, rather, that production was social and that producers were interdependent. The carpenter, for example, depended upon the working people who produced hammers, nails, saws, and lumber. After the carpenter had built a house, the procapitalist ideologist would insist that a hammer, some nails, a saw, and some lumber—together with a carpenter—built the house. Contrary to this ideology, Marx argued that human beings had socially built the house by dividing the work in such a manner that some had produced the hammers, others nails, others saws, others lumber, and still others had brought all of these human exertions together by performing the last step (carpentering) in this social production process.

In fact, capital was not simply a commodity that produced. Capital was a word that was attached to tools only when a very specific set of social relations existed. Capital, then, did not refer to tools per se, or to tools sold as commodities per se, but to tools sold as commodities and used in a specific way within the context of a specific set of social relations.

Capital existed, then, only when three conditions were met: (1) Tools were produced as commodities. (2) These commodities were owned by a social class other than the class that productively used them. (3) The class that used the tools to produce received the permission to do so only on the condition that they did not receive ownership of the product that they produced; instead, these producers had to accept a wage having less value than the value of the commodities they produced. The difference, or extra value, went to owners in the form of interest, rent, or profit.

Capital, then, was the capacity of capitalists to place themselves between every human productive interdependency and to extract a return for allowing this interdependent production process to proceed. Between the carpenter who had to use a hammer, a saw, nails, and lumber and the producers of these items he required stood several capitalists. The worker-producer of nails produced nails for a capitalist, not for a carpenter. The same held true for the hammer, saw, and lumber worker-producers. But the carpenter did not receive these items directly from the capitalists involved. A capitalist owning the construction company bought them from the other capitalists.

In all human productive interdependencies one laborer required the labor of others and others required his labor. In capitalism, however, laborers never dealt with each other. Every interdependency of labor found actual expression in, or actually took effect through, financial dealings among capitalists. The interdependence of labor became, in capitalism, an absolute dependence of any particular laborer on a capitalist. At every point where one worker needed another worker stood a capitalist who demanded his share, in the form of profit, interest, or rent, before he would permit he process to go on.

Thus capitalism was a society in which labor became social by taking the form of the price of a commodity and in which every social interdependency of labor took the form of commodities owned by nonlaborers who extracted a concession for allowing producers to produce. In such a society and *only* in such a society did tools become capital that yielded profit.

Thus, for Marx, the historically specific social relations whereby the owners of the means of production exploited workers within a capitalist system were totally obscured when the procapitalist ideologists argued that rent and profit simply resulted from the physical nature of land and tools, which rendered them indispensable to production. Marx argued that this was a "complete mystification of the capitalist mode of production." The capitalism of the ideologists was "an enchanted, perverted, topsy-turvy world in which Monsieur le Capital and Madame La Terre do their ghost-walking as social characters and at the same time directly as mere things."[5]

By contrast, Marx's definition of capital stressed its historical specificity:

One thing . . . is clear—Nature does not produce on the one side owners of money or commodities [means of production], and on the other men possessing nothing but their own labour-power. This relation has no natural basis, neither is its social basis one that is common to all historical periods. It is clearly the result of a past historical development, the product of many economic revolutions, of the extinction of a whole series of older forms of social production.[6]

Capital is not a thing, but rather a definite social production relation, belonging to a definite historical formation of society, which is manifested in a thing and lends this thing a specific social character. . . . It is the means of production monopolized by a certain section of society, confronting living labour-power as products and working conditions rendered independent of this very labour-power.[7]

Capital was the social relation that defined the two most important classes of the capitalist mode of production. It did not exist on a significant scale prior to capitalism and it would not exist after capitalism had been overthrown.

[5]Ibid., vol. III, p. 809.
[6]Ibid., vol. I, p. 169.
[7]Ibid., vol. III, pp. 794–795.

SUMMARY

In Marx's historical materialism, the mode of production was the most significant aspect of any social system. The capitalist mode of production was one in which the market allocated labor and resources. It was made up of four classes: capitalists, small and independent shopkeepers and professionals, workers, and poor people with few if any sources of income. The most important classes were the capitalists and the workers. The capitalists' power was based upon private ownership of capital. Property ownership was a social relation involving privileges and sanctions coercively created and coercively maintained. Capital could not be identified as simply tools and machinery. Rather, capital involved ownership of tools and machines within the context of the social and economic relations between capitalists and laborers, whereby laborers received as wages only a part of the value they produced and capitalists demanded the remaining surplus as a necessary condition for permitting laborers to produce.

CHAPTER 7

Marx's Social and Economic Theory

Marx's conception of the nature of capitalism, which was described in the preceding chapter, furnished the intellectual foundation for his theories of how capitalism functioned. Many of Marx's economic arguments cannot be fully comprehended unless one first understands this overview of the nature of capitalism as a socioeconomic system. Likewise, many of Marx's economic theories are difficult to separate entirely from his moral critique of capitalism. We therefore begin this chapter with a discussion of that critique as it was spelled out in Marx's theory of alienation. After that we consider various aspects of his economic theory of how capitalism functions.

ALIENATION

Capitalism, in Marx's view, simultaneously increased society's capacity to produce while systematically rendering this increased productive capacity less serviceable in fulfilling some of the most basic of human needs. More production certainly made possible a more adequate fulfillment of the basic needs for food, shelter, and clothing. Because of the extreme inequalities in the distribution of wealth and income, however, millions of workers in the capitalist system of Marx's time suffered from extreme material poverty and deprivation.

Most of the socialists whose ideas we discussed in Chapter 5 based their moral critique of capitalism on a condemnation of the misery caused by this widespread poverty and inequality. Many interpreters of Marx's ideas have erroneously asserted that this was also the primary basis of Marx's moral critique. When Marx argued that the continued development of capitalism would only sharpen and increase the misery of workers, these interpreters have imagined him to have been arguing that the poverty and material deprivation of workers would grow worse. The fact that the purchasing power of workers' wages has generally risen during the century since Marx's death is therefore widely cited as a refutation of Marx's economic theory.

These interpreters have, however, misunderstood the primary basis of Marx's moral critique of capitalism. Although Marx was appalled by the inequities of capitalism and the material deprivation and suffering of the working class, he was well aware that with the increasing productivity of the capitalist system it would become possible for workers to win higher wages in their struggles with capitalists. If they did win such increases, Marx wrote, then

> a larger part of their own surplus . . . comes back to . . . [workers] in the shape of means of payment, so that they can extend the circle of their enjoyments; can make some additions to their consumption-fund of clothes, furniture, etc., and can lay by small reserve-funds of money. But just as little as better clothing, food, and treatment, and a larger peculium, do away with the exploitation of the slave, so little do they set aside that of the wage-workers.[1]

The most fundamental evil of capitalism was not, Marx insisted, the material deprivation of workers. Rather, it was to be found in the fact that capitalism systematically prevented individuals from achieving their potential as human beings. It diminished their capacity to give and receive love and it thwarted the development of their biological, emotional, aesthetic, and intellectual potential. In other words, capitalism severely crippled human beings by preventing their development.

This crippling effect could not, moreover, be overcome within a capitalist system. The forces that increased social productivity could only be utilized in capitalism through the very methods that degraded workers. This was because the technological improvements were always introduced for one purpose and only one purpose: to increase profit. Profit was the source of capitalists' wealth; profit could only be increased by extending and solidifying the control of the capitalists over the work process. Yet it was the control of capital over nearly all processes of human creativity that was the source of the degradation of workers in capitalism. Marx concluded that the "accumulation of wealth at one pole is, therefore, at the same time accumulation of misery, agony of toil, slavery, ignorance, brutality, [and] mental degradation at the opposite pole."[2]

The social nature of the work process was, for Marx, extremely important. It was through social cooperation in transforming nature into useful things that human beings achieved their sociality and developed their potential as individual human beings. If that production were a cooperative venture

---

[1]Karl Marx, *Capital,* vol. 1 (Moscow: Foreign Language Publishing House, 1961), p. 618.
[2]Ibid., p. 645.

among social equals, it would develop bonds of affection, love, and mutual affirmation among people. Moreover, such creative endeavor was the source of human aesthetic development. It is significant that when ancient people spoke of the "arts" they were referring to various productive skills. Moreover, the creation and use of tools have always been involved in the advancement of human knowledge and scientific understanding.

The production process, however, had exactly the opposite set of effects on workers in a capitalist system. In feudalism the exploitative class structure had severely limited human development. Yet because these exploitative social relations were also personal and paternalistic, not all of the human developmental potential of the work process was stunted or thwarted. Work in feudalism was more than merely a means of making a livable wage for the worker while he created wealth for his overlord. This changed with capitalism, when, in Marx's opinion:

> the bourgeoisie, wherever it has got the upper hand, has put an end to all feudal patriarchal, idyllic relations. It has pitilessly torn asunder the motley feudal ties that bound man to his "natural superiors," and has left remaining no other nexus between man and man than naked self-interest, than callous "cash payment." It has drowned the most heavenly ecstasies of religious fervor, of chivalrous enthusiasm, of philistine sentimentalism, in the icy water of egotistical calculation. It has resolved personal worth into exchange value.[3]

In a capitalist society the market separated and isolated "exchange value," or money price, from the qualities that shaped a person's relations with things as well as with other human beings. This was especially true in the work process. To the capitalist, wages were merely another expense of production to be added to the costs of raw materials and machinery in the profit calculation. Labor became a mere commodity to be bought if a profit could be made on the purchase. Whether the laborer could sell his or her labor power was completely beyond his or her control. It depended on the cold and totally impersonal conditions of the market. The product of this labor was likewise totally outside of the laborer's life, being the property of the capitalist.

Marx used the term *alienation* to describe the condition of individuals in this situation. They felt alienated or divorced from their work, from their institutional and cultural environment, and from their fellow humans. The conditions of work, the object produced, and indeed the very possibility of working were determined by the numerically small class of capitalists and their profit calculations, not by human need or aspirations. The effects of this alienation can best be summarized in Marx's own words:

> What, then, constitutes the alienation of labour? First, the fact that labour is external to the worker, i.e., it does not belong to his essential being; that in

[3]Karl Marx and Friedrich Engels, "The Communist Manifesto," in Arthur P. Mendel, ed., *Essential Works of Marxism* (New York: Bantam, 1965), p. 15.

his work, therefore, he does not affirm himself but denies himself, does not feel content but unhappy, does not develop freely his physical and mental energy but mortifies his body and ruins his mind. The worker therefore only feels himself outside his work, and in his work feels outside himself. He is at home when he is not working, and when he is working he is not at home. His labour is therefore not voluntary but coerced; it is *forced labour*. It is therefore not the satisfaction of a need; it is merely a *means* to satisfy needs external to it. Its alien character emerges clearly in the fact that as soon as no physical or other compulsion exists, labour is shunned like the plague. External labour, labour in which man alienates himself, is a labour of self-sacrifice, or mortification. Lastly, the external character of labour for the worker appears in the fact that it is not his own, but someone else's, that it does not belong to him, that in it he belongs, not to himself, but to another . . . As a result, therefore, man (the worker) no longer feels himself to be freely active in any but his animal functions—eating, drinking, procreating, or at most in his dwelling and in dressing up, etc.; and in his human functions he no longer feels himself to be anything but an animal. What is animal becomes human and what is human becomes animal.[4]

It was this degradation and total dehumanization of the working class, thwarting man's personal development and making an alien market commodity of man's life-sustaining activities, that Marx most thoroughly condemned in the capitalist system. His moral critique thus went far beyond those of most of his socialist precursors.

His faith in the possibility of a better future for the working class, however, was not based on the hope that ever-increasing numbers of people would share his moral indignation and therefore attempt to reform the system. Rather, he believed the capitalist mode of production and the class conflict inherent in it would lead to the destruction of capitalism. Capitalism, like all previous modes of production in which class conflicts were present, would destroy itself. In order to understand the basis for his faith, it is necessary to examine his economic theory, in which he attempted to analyze the "laws of motion" of capitalism.

THE LABOR THEORY OF VALUE AND SURPLUS VALUE

Because for Marx the capitalist mode of production—was based on the opposition of labor and capital, he began by analyzing the capital-labor relationship. This relationship was essentially one of exchange. The worker sold his or her labor power to the capitalist for money, with which the worker bought the necessities of life. Thus this exchange relation was obviously merely a special case of the general problem of exchange values within a capitalist market economy. Marx therefore began volume I of *Capital* with a section entitled "Commodities," in which he defined *commodities* as objects that are usually

⁴Karl Marx, *Economic and Philosophic Manuscripts of 1844* (Moscow: Progress Publishers, 1959), p. 69.

intended for exchange rather than for the direct personal use of the producer. He then attempted to analyze the basic determinant of the exchange value of commodities. In other words, he analyzed the ratio in which commodities could be exchanged for other commodities, as opposed to use value, which was a measure of the usefulness of commodities to their possessor.

Like Adam Smith, David Ricardo, and most of the pre-Marxist classical economists, Marx believed the exchange value of a commodity was determined by the amount of labor time necessary for its production. His theory is therefore usually called the *labor theory of value.* He recognized that laborers differed in abilities, training, and motivation, but he believed skilled labor could be calculated as a multiple of unskilled labor. Thus all labor time could be reduced to a common denominator.

He also realized that labor time expended in the production of a useless commodity (one for which there was no demand) would not create a commodity with an exchange value equal to the labor time embodied in it. The desire of capitalists to maximize their profits would, however, prevent the production of objects for which there was no demand. Capitalists would produce only commodities for which market demand would permit the realization of at least their costs of production. Market demand would determine not only what commodities were produced but also the relative quantities in which they were produced.

Marx began by describing how the capitalist buys the means of production and the labor power. Then when the laborers complete the production process, the capitalist sells the commodities for more money. Thus the amount of money at the end of the production process is greater than that at the start. This difference is what Marx called *surplus value.* He considered it the source of capitalist profits.

Surplus value originated in the fact that capitalists bought one commodity—labor power—and sold a different commodity—that which labor produced in the production process. Profits were made because the value of labor power was less than the value of the commodities produced with the labor power. The value of labor power was "determined, as in the case of every other commodity, by the labor time necessary" for its maintenance and reproduction, which meant that "the value of labor power . . . [was] the value of the means of subsistence necessary for the maintenance of the laborer at a socially defined standard of living."[5] The fact was that the average length of the working day exceeded the time necessary for a laborer to produce the value equivalent of his or her subsistence wage, which enabled the capitalist to appropriate the surplus produced over and above this subsistence. Marx called this process the *exploitation* of workers by capitalists. If the worker works for 8 hours but uses only 6 hours to produce the value of his or her wage goods, then that worker is exploited because he or she works 2 surplus hours for the capitalist.

[5]Marx, *Capital,* vol. I, pp. 170–171.

THE ACCUMULATION OF CAPITAL

Ownership of capital enabled the capitalist to gain profit. Most of these profits were reinvested in order to increase capital and hence increase future profits, which could then be plowed back into more capital, and so forth. This was the process of capital accumulation: Capital led to profits, which led to more capital. When and how did the process originate? Many classical economists and liberals, particularly the English economist Nassau Senior (1790–1864), had answered this question in a way favorable to the capitalist, arguing that through hard, diligent work and abstemious behavior a modest saving program was begun, which enabled the capitalist to accumulate slowly the fortunes many nineteenth-century capitalists owned. Laborers, on the contrary, rather than devoting themselves to working and living abstemiously, had profligately squandered their earnings.

Marx accused these defenders of the capitalist system of being totally ignorant of history. In a famous passage, which gives the flavor of some of his most colorful writing, Marx described the process of "primitive accumulation" by which the fortunes were originally made:

> This primitive accumulation plays in Political Economy about the same part as original sin in theology. Adam bit the apple, and thereupon sin fell on the human race. Its origin is supposed to be explained when it is told as an anecdote of the past. In times long gone by there were two sorts of people; one the diligent, intelligent, and above all, frugal elite; the other, lazy rascals, spending their substance, and more, in riotous living. . . . Thus it came to pass that the former sort accumulated wealth, and the latter sort had nothing to sell except their own skins. And from this original sin dates the poverty of the great majority that, despite all its labour, has up to now nothing to sell but itself, and the wealth of the few that increases constantly although they have long ceased to work. Such insipid childishness is every day preached to us in the defence of property. . . . As soon as the question of property crops up, it becomes a sacred duty to proclaim the intellectual food of the infant as the one thing fit for all ages and for all stages of development. In actual history it is notorious that conquest, enslavement, robbery, murder, briefly force, play the great part. . . . The methods of primitive accumulation are anything but idyllic.[6]

Marx listed the important forms of primitive accumulation as the enclosure movement and the dislocation of the feudal agrarian population, the great price inflation, monopolies of trade, colonies, "the extirpation, enslavement and entombment in mines of the aboriginal population, the beginning of the conquest and looting of the East Indies, [and] the turning of Africa into a warren for the commercial hunting of black skins."[7]

Once this initial accumulation of capital had taken place, the drive to acquire more capital became the moving force of the capitalist system. The

[6]Ibid., pp. 713–714.
[7]Ibid., p. 751.

capitalist's social standing and prestige as well as his economic and political power depended on the size of capital he controlled. He could not stand still; he was beset on every side by fierce competition. The system demanded that he accumulate and grow more powerful in order to outdo his competitors, or else his competitors would force him to the wall and take over his capital. Competitors were constantly developing new and better methods of production. Only by accumulating new and better capital equipment could this challenge be met. Thus Marx believed the capitalist

> shares with the miser the passion for wealth as wealth. But that which in the miser is a mere idiosyncrasy, is in the capitalist the effect of the social mechanism of which he is but one of the wheels. Moreover, the development of capitalist production makes it constantly necessary to keep increasing the amount of capital laid out in a given industrial undertaking, and competition makes the imminent laws of capitalist production to be felt by each individual capitalist as external coercive laws. It compels him to keep constantly extending his capital, in order to preserve it, but extend it he cannot except by means of progressive accumulation.[8]

SECTORAL IMBALANCES AND ECONOMIC CRISES

It was this ceaseless drive to accumulate more capital that created many of the contradictions to capitalist development. The capitalist would begin with the acquisition of more machines and tools of the types that were currently being used. This would require a proportional increase in the number of workers employed in order to operate the new equipment. But the capitalist had been able to keep the wage rate at the subsistence level only because there existed what Marx called an "industrial reserve army" of unemployed labor, which was living below the subsistence level and striving to take jobs that would pay a mere subsistence wage. Therefore, capitalists usually had no problem in keeping wage rates down. As the industrial expansion took place, however, the increasing demand for labor soon depleted the ranks of the reserve. When this happened, the capitalist began to find that he had to pay higher wages to get enough labor.

The individual capitalist took the wage level as given and beyond his power to change, so he attempted to make the best of the situation. The most profitable course of action seemed to be changing the techniques of production by introducing new labor-saving machinery so that each laborer would then be working with more capital, and output per laborer would be increased. This labor-saving investment would enable the capitalist to expand output with the same or an even smaller work force. When all or most of the capitalists, acting individually, did this, the problem of high wages was temporarily alleviated as the reserve army was replenished by workers who had been displaced by the new productive techniques, introducing new problems and contradictions.

Labor-saving expansion permitted increases in total production without

[8]Ibid., p. 592.

increasing the wages paid to workers. Therefore, while new goods were flooding the market, workers' wages were being restricted, with the result that consumer demand was limited. As Marx put it, the workers were still producing more profits in the form of goods, but the capitalists could not "realize" the profits by selling these goods in the market because of lack of consumer demand.

In order to clarify this process further, Marx divided the capitalist economy into two sectors, one producing consumer goods and the other producing capital goods. Lack of consumer demand meant that capitalists in the consumption goods sector would find that they could not sell their entire output and thus would lower their expectations of profits and would certainly *not* want to add to their productive facilities. They would therefore cancel any plans to add to their already excessively large capital stock. These decisions would, of course, significantly reduce the demand for capital goods, which would result in a decrease in production in the capital goods sector. Unlike the naïve underconsumptionist theories of the earlier socialists, Marx's view held that the first obvious sign of a depression might thus appear in the capital goods sector.

The actual decrease in capital goods production would mean that some workers in that sector would be fired, which would lower total wages, decrease national income, and reduce consumer demand. Thus there would be a cutback in consumer goods production, and layoffs of workers would spread to those industries. Wages and incomes would then be further reduced, causing a glut, or surfeit, of consumer goods. The entire process of successive repercussions in both sectors would then be one of economic collapse.

The resulting depression would more than restore the reserve army of unemployed and push labor's standard of living back to or below the subsistence level. Marx, however, was not a "stagnationist"—that is, he did not believe capitalism would suffer one long depression or that mass unemployment at high levels would last forever. During the depression, workers' wages would fall, but not as rapidly as the output of goods. Thus eventually supply would be lower than consumer demand, and therefore recovery would occur. Marx believed that capitalism does grow, but jerkily, in cycles of boom and bust, with periodic high levels of unemployment for the workers.

ECONOMIC CONCENTRATION

Concentration of wealth and economic power in the hands of fewer and fewer capitalists was another important consequence of capital accumulation. This concentration was the result of two forces. First, competition among capitalists tended to create a situation in which the strong either crushed or absorbed the weak. "Here competition rages in direct proportion to the number, and in inverse proportion to the magnitudes, of the antagonistic capitals. It always ends in the ruin of many small capitalists, whose capitals partly pass into the hands of their conquerors, partly vanish."[9]

[9]Ibid., p. 626.

Second, as technology improved there was "an increase in the minimum amount of . . . capital necessary to carry on a business under its normal conditions." In order to remain competitive, a firm would constantly have to increase the productivity of its laborers. The "productiveness of labor . . . depended] on the scale of production."[10] Thus changing technology as well as competition among capitalists created an inexorable movement of the capitalist system toward larger and larger firms owned by fewer and fewer capitalists. In this way the gulf between the small class of wealthy capitalists and the great majority of society, the proletariat, would continually widen.

THE IMMISERIZATION OF THE PROLETARIAT

At the same time that this increasing concentration of capital was taking place, the misery of the proletariat grew constantly worse. In his famous "doctrine of increasing misery" (immiserization), Marx argued that the conditions of labor would worsen relative to the affluence of the capitalists until the laborers could stand no more—and revolution became inevitable. Because Marx's doctrine of immiserization is very often misrepresented, we quote his own writings on this point:

> Within the capitalist system all methods for raising the social productiveness of labour are brought about at the cost of the individual labourer; all means for the development of production transform themselves into means of domination over, and exploitation of, the producers; they mutilate the labourer into a fragment of a man, degrade him to the level of an appendage of a machine, destroy every remnant of charm in his work and turn it into hated toil; they estrange from him the intellectual potentialities of the labour-process in the same proportion as science is incorporated in it as an independent power; they distort the conditions under which he works, subject him during the labour-process to a despotism the more hateful for its meanness; they transform his life time into working time, and drag his wife and children beneath the wheels of the Juggernaut of capital. But all methods for the production of surplus-value are at the same time methods of accumulation; and every extension of accumulation becomes again a means for the development of those methods. It follows therefore that in proportion as capital accumulates, the lot of the labourer, be his payment high or low, must grow worse. The law . . . establishes an accumulation of misery, corresponding with accumulation of capital. Accumulation of wealth at one pole is, therefore, at the same time accumulation of misery, agony of toil, slavery, ignorance, brutality [and] mental degradation at the opposite pole.[11]

It should be noted that Marx asserted that the laborer would become worse off even if his or her wages increased. There were two reasons for this. First, Marx believed that even if workers' wages increased, they would not increase by as much as capitalists' profits increased. The worker would therefore become continuously worse off relative to the capitalist. Second, Marx

[10]Ibid.
[11]Ibid., p. 645.

correctly foresaw that as the capitalist system progressed, there was to be an increasingly minute division of labor.

A finer division of labor makes the worker's activities less varied, and the job becomes more repetitious and tedious. Marx agreed with Adam Smith, who had stated that "the man whose whole life is spent in performing a few simple operations . . . generally becomes as stupid and ignorant as it is possible for a human creature to become."[12] Forced into a condition of stupor and increasingly severely alienated, "the lot of the labourer, *be his payment high or low,* must grow worse."[13]

THE CAPITALIST STATE

Marx rejected the notion that socialism could be created through gradual, piecemeal reforms undertaken by the state. By *the state* Marx meant something more than simply any government: "We may speak of a state where a special public power of coercion exists which, in the form of an armed organization, stands over and above the population."[14]

Many socialists believed the state was (or could be) an impartial arbiter in the affairs of society, and they had faith in moral and intellectual appeals to the state. Marx rejected this idea. "Political power," he declared in the *Communist Manifesto,* "is merely the organized power of one class for oppressing another." During each period of history, or for each mode of production, the state is the coercive instrument of the ruling class.

Friedrich Engels has summarized the Marxist argument:

> Former society, moving in class antagonisms, had need of the state, that is, an organization of the exploiting class at each period for the maintenance of external conditions of production; that is, therefore, for the forcible holding down of the exploited class in the conditions of oppression (slavery, villein-age or serfdom, wage labor) determined by the existing mode of production. The state was the official representative of society as a whole, its embodiment in a visible corporation; but it was this only in so far as it was the state of that class which itself, in its epoch, represented society as a whole; in ancient times, the state of the slave-owning citizens; in the Middle Ages, of the feudal nobility; in our epoch, of the bourgeosie.[15]

Thus the state is simply a dictatorship of the ruling class over the remainder of society.

In the capitalist system a dictatorship has two functions. First, it has the traditional function of enforcing the dictatorship of the capitalists over the rest of society. The state achieves this primarily by enforcing property rights, the

---

[12]Adam Smith, *The Wealth of Nations,* ed. Andrew Skinner (London: Penguin Books, 1970), p. 80.
[13]Marx, *Capital,* p. 645.
[14]Sidney Hook, *Towards the Understanding of Karl Marx* (New York: Day, 1933), p. 256.
[15]Friedrich Engels, "Anti-Duhring," in *Handbook of Marxism* (New York: Random House, 1935), p. 295.

source of the capitalists' economic power. It also serves in innumerable other ways—for example, jailing or harassing critics of capitalism, fighting wars to extend capitalists' markets, and providing roads, railroads, canals, postal service, and hundreds of other prerequisites for profitable commerce. Second, the government acts as the arbiter of rivalries among capitalists. Each capitalist is interested only in his own profits, and therefore it is inevitable that the interests of capitalists will clash. If not resolved, many of these clashes would threaten the very existence of the system. Thus the government intervenes, and in doing so it protects the viability of the capitalist system. This is why it is sometimes possible to observe the government acting in a way that is contrary to the interests of some of the capitalists. But the government never acts in a way that is contrary to the interests of *all* capitalists taken as a class.

For these reasons Marx rejected the notion that socialists could rely on the government for help in bringing about the transition from capitalism to socialism. The establishment of socialism, in Marx's opinion, would require a revolution.

THE SOCIALIST REVOLUTION

In his overall view of capitalism Marx saw the process of capital accumulation as inevitably involving several steps. Business cycles or crises would occur regularly and with increasing severity as the capitalist economy developed. There would be a long-run tendency for the rate of profit to fall, and this would exacerbate the other problems of capitalism. Industrial power would become increasingly concentrated in fewer and fewer giant monopolistic and oligopolistic firms, and wealth would become concentrated in the hands of fewer and fewer capitalists. The plight of the laborer would steadily deteriorate.

Given these increasingly bad conditions, the system could not be perpetuated. Eventually life under capitalism would become so intolerable that workers would revolt, overthrow the whole system, and create a more rational socialist economy:

> Along with the constantly diminishing number of magnates of capital, who usurp and monopolize all advantages of this process of transformation, grows the mass of misery, oppression, slavery, degradation, exploitation; but with this too grows the revolt of the working-class, a class always increasing in numbers, and disciplined, united, organized by the very mechanism of the process of capitalist production itself. The monopoly of capital becomes a fetter upon the mode of production, which has sprung up and flourished along with, and under it. Centralization of the means of production and socialization of labour at last reach a point where they become incompatible with their capitalist integument. This integument is burst asunder. The knell of capitalist private property sounds. The expropriators are expropriated.[16]

[16]Marx, *Capital,* vol. I, p. 763.

In subsequent chapters we shall examine the defenses of capitalism offered in opposition to Marx, as well as the further development of socialist thought after Marx.

SUMMARY

Karl Marx, the most influential of all socialists, based his economic analysis on a theory of history called historical materialism. Most social and political institutions, he believed, were significantly shaped by the economic base of society: the mode of production. Over time, conflicts developed between the forces of production and the relations of production. The working out of these conflicts was the most important element in the historical evolution of society.

Marx's economic writings were aimed at understanding the conflicts between the class system (or private property system) of capitalism and the methods of production and commodity exchange under capitalism and its replacement by a classless, socialist society.

CHAPTER *8*

The Rise of Corporate Capitalism and Its Ideological Defenses

The period from the mid-1840s to 1873 (the year that marked the beginning of the Long Depression in Europe) has been called the golden age of competitive capitalism.[1] These were years of rapid economic expansion throughout most of Europe. Industrialization was getting under way in the United States and continental Europe. The new capital goods necessary for industrialization were, to a large extent, imported from England. Between 1840 and 1860 England experienced an expansion of exports that was more rapid than ever before or since. Capital goods increased from 11 percent of English exports to 22 percent, and exports of coal, iron, and steel also rose sharply.

Between 1830 and 1850, England experienced a railroad-building boom in which some 6000 miles of railroads were constructed. This railroad building created a strong demand for iron, and iron production doubled between the mid-1830s and the mid-1840s. During the next 30 years the increases in industrial production were also very impressive. Between 1850 and 1880 the production of pig iron increased from 2,250,000 to 7,750,000 tons per year; steel production went from 49,000 to 1,440,000 tons; and coal increased by 300 percent, to 147,000,000 tons. The Bessemer converter (in the 1850s), the open-hearth furnace (in the 1860s), and the basic process (in the 1870s) completely revolutionized the steel industry, making large-scale production of

---

[1]Dudley Dillard, *Economic Development of the North Atlantic Community* (Englewood Cliffs, N.J.: Prentice-Hall, 1967), p. 363.

high-quality steel possible at much lower costs. The capital goods industries also prospered in the second half of the nineteenth century. Production of machines, ships, chemicals, and other important capital goods employed twice as many workers in 1881 as in 1851.

THE CONCENTRATION OF CORPORATE POWER

Just as competitive capitalism seemed to be achieving its greatest successes, the forces Marx had predicted would lead to the concentration of capital began to show themselves. Improvements in technology were such that larger-sized plants were necessary to take advantage of more efficient methods of production. Competition became so aggressive and destructive that small competitors were eliminated. Large competitors, facing mutual destruction, often combined in cartels, trusts, or mergers in order to ensure their mutual survival. In the United States this competition was particularly intense. (It is described in greater detail in Chapter 9.)

A factor that Marx had nearly overlooked, the revolutionary changes in transportation and communication, led to ever-widening markets that could be efficiently supplied by single companies or corporations. The joint stock company, or corporation, became an effective means by which a single business organization could gain control over vast amounts of capital. A large, well-organized money market evolved in Europe and North America that successfully channeled the smaller capital holdings of many thousands of individuals and small businesses into the hands of large corporations.

In the late nineteenth-century world of giant corporations, in which articles were mass produced for nationwide or worldwide markets, price competition (and indeed sometimes any kind of competition) proved so destructive that it was abandoned almost completely in the large and important industries. There was an inexorable trend toward monopoly power accruing to a few corporations. Many business giants entered into voluntary combinations in which each firm remained somewhat autonomous (e.g., cartels and pools). Other combinations used a financial enterprise such as a trust or holding company to control the voting stock of the corporations involved. Still others used direct mergers and amalgamations from which a single unified corporation emerged.

The English Case

England, where the classical liberal laissez-faire philosophy had taken root most firmly, was perhaps least affected by this movement to corporate monopolies. Advances in technology led to a steel industry made of very large producers. Nevertheless, the fact that England had very few restrictions on imports prevented the industry from combining into an effectively coordinated group until after the trade restrictions of 1932. However, producers of some heavy steel products, such as ship and boiler plate, were able to create effective monopolies much earlier.

In other industries, amalgamations led to heavy concentrations. English railroads were combined very early into four main companies. Banking was consolidated until five large commercial banks dominated the industry by the time of World War I. In 1896 the five rivals in the cotton sewing-thread industry had merged into a single monopoly (J. & P. Coats), which came to dominate the world market for that commodity and regularly made profits of 20 percent or more. The firm of Lever Brothers, through amalgamations, gained dominance over the soap business in England as well as in several other countries. Monopolies or closely coordinated oligopolies came to control the wallpaper, salt, petroleum, and rubber industries. Many other industries were either dominated or strongly influenced by a few large firms.

The German Case

In Germany the classical liberal ideology had never really taken root. During Germany's rapid rise to industrial power during the second half of the nineteenth century, there were neither philosophical nor ideological nor legal barriers to large-scale monopolistic industries. It is therefore not surprising that monopolies and combinations were more widespread in Germany than in any other country in Europe. The cartel was the main type of monopolistic business combination in Germany. There were approximately 16 cartels in 1879; the figure rose to 35 by 1885, to 300 by 1900, to 1000 by 1922, and to 2100 by 1930.

Thus by the early twentieth century monopolistic cartels completely dominated almost all the important sectors of the German capitalist economy. (The legal and philosophical justifications of these monopolistic German cartels are discussed in Chapter 9.)

The American Case

In the United States the Civil War gave a great stimulus to industrialization. The war not only increased the demand for industrially produced commodities but also led to the passage of laws that were beneficial to the newly emerging corporations that were soon to dominate American industry.

In an effort to provide civil and political rights for all Americans, Congress had passed the first Civil Rights Act in 1866. By 1868 the Fourteenth Amendment to the U.S. Constitution had been ratified by the states. The ostensible aim of these laws was to confer citizenship and equal rights on American blacks. The Civil Rights Act declared that citizens "of every race and color" were to have equal rights to make contracts, to sue, and enjoy "full and equal benefit of all laws and proceedings for the security of person and property."[2]

Most of the Civil Rights Act was incorporated into the Fourteenth

[2]Quoted in Kenneth M. Stampp, *The Era of Reconstruction, 1865–1877* (New York: Random House, Vintage Books, 1967), p. 136.

Amendment. The Amendment also included the famous due process clause, which prohibited any state government from depriving "any person of life, liberty, or *property,* without due process of law."[3]

For decades after its ratification the Fourteenth Amendment had no effect at all on the civil rights of American blacks; many of them were thrust into situations worse than slavery. Rather, most court decisions based on the Fourteenth Amendment involved corporations. The courts ruled that corporations were persons and, as such, were protected under the due process clause.

Each time a state government attempted to curb the extravagant excesses of corporations by passing regulatory legislation, the federal courts would invalidate the legislation because it violated the due process clause of the amendment. State governments became powerless before the growing strength of large corporations.

Representative John A. Bingham, who had written the due process clause, later admitted that he had phrased it "word for word and syllable for syllable" to protect the rights of private property and corporations. Representative Roscoe Conkling, who had also helped frame the Amendment, later declared: "At the time the Fourteenth Amendment was ratified, individuals and *joint stock companies* were appealing for congressional and administrative protection against invidious and discriminating state and local taxes. . . . [The Fourteenth Amendment embodies] the Golden Rule, so entrenched as to curb the many who would do to the few as they would not have the few do to them."[4]

With the knowledge that they could go to almost any length in their pursuit of profits without fear of state government controls, the corporations thrived. They grew through internal expansion and, more important, by absorbing their competitors. As the giant corporations flourished, the entire American economy thrived and grew.

By the turn of the century, the United States had become the leading industrial power in the world. By 1913, when the American economy produced over one-third of the world's industrial output—more than double that of its closest competitor, Germany—most of the strategic industries (railroads, meatpacking, banking in the large cities, steel, copper, and aluminum) and important areas of manufacturing were dominated by a relatively small number of immensely powerful corporations.

With the exception of the railroads, most industries in the immediate post–Civil War years had been relatively atomistic by present-day standards. Although accurate statistics are not available for this early period, it has been estimated that the 200 largest nonfinancial enterprises would have controlled a very minor and inconsequential percentage of all business assets. By the end of the 1920s this had grown to 33 percent of all assets.[5]

The primary cause of this concentration was the wave of combinations and mergers that took place at an unprecedented rate during the last quarter

---

[3]Ibid.; italics added.
[4]Ibid., p. 136.
[5]Joe S. Bain, *Industrial Organization* (New York: Wiley, 1959), pp. 191–192.

of the nineteenth century. This merger movement was the outgrowth of the particularly severe competition that had ravaged and destroyed scores of businesses. During this period many people began to question seriously the liberal notion of the invisible hand. It seemed to them that unrestrained individualism had led to unrestrained warfare.

As growing giant businesses locked horns, railroad against railroad, steel mill against steel mill, each sought to assure the coverage of its fixed expenses by gaining for itself as much of the market as it could. The outcome was the steady growth of cutthroat competition among massive producers. . . . On the Railroads for example, constant rate-wars were fought in the 1870s. In the oil fields, the coal fields, among the steel and copper producers, similar price-wars repeatedly broke out as producers sought to capture the markets.[6]

The outcome of such competition was the destruction or absorption of small competitors. Eventually only giants remained, and at this point further competition was immensely destructive to all competitors. The merger movement represented the means whereby the surviving firms could escape this competition.

The scope of the merger movement was so great that by 1904 it had basically altered the structure of American industry. By the beginning of that year there were over three hundred large industrial combinations with a combined capitalization in excess of $7,000,000,000. They controlled more than two-fifths of the manufacturing capital of the country and had affected about four-fifths of important American industries.[7]

THE CONCENTRATION OF INCOME

Accompanying this concentration of industry was an equally striking concentration of income in the hands of a small percentage of the population. Although no accurate statistics for the early part of the period exist, it seems reasonably certain that the degree of concentration increased substantially between 1870 and 1929. By 1929 just 5 percent of the population received 34 percent of personal disposable income in the United States.[8] The degree of concentration had probably reached this extreme as early as 1913. By the end of the 1920s, the highest one-fifth of "families and unattached individuals" were receiving more than 50 percent of all personal income.[9]

[6]Robert L. Heilbroner, *The Making of Economic Society* (Englewood Cliffs, N.J.: Prentice-Hall, 1962), p. 120.

[7]Joe S. Bain, "Industrial Concentration and Anti-Trust Policy," in Harold F. Williamson, ed., *Growth of the American Economy,* 2d ed. (Englewood Cliffs, N.J.: Prentice-Hall, 1951), p. 619.

[8]U.S. Department of Commerce, *Historical Statistics of the United States* (Washington, D.C.: GPO, 1961), p. 167.

[9]Ibid.; the data for 1913 do not give a figure for the income going to the top 5 percent. The amount going to the top 1 percent, however, was 14.98 percent in 1913 and 14.94 percent in 1928.

REEMERGENCE OF THE CLASSICAL LIBERAL IDEOLOGY

With this immense concentration of economic power in the hands of a small number of giant firms and a small percentage of the population, it would seem that the classical liberal ideology of capitalism would have been abandoned. The economic creed of classical liberalism, as developed by Adam Smith and refined by such well-known classical economists as David Ricardo, Nassau Senior, and J. B. Say, was based on an analysis of an economy composed of many small enterprises. In such an economy no individual enterprise could exercise a significant influence on the market price or on the total amount sold in the market. The actions of any firm were dictated to it by consumer tastes, as registered in the marketplace, and by the competition of innumerable other small firms, each vying for the consumer's dollars.

As wide as the gulf between classical economic theory and late nineteenth-century economic reality seems to have been, the economic creed of classical liberalism did not fall by the wayside in this later period. Rather, it was combined with Benthamite utilitarianism (which was already implicit in Adam Smith's normative model of the invisible hand) and refurbished within an elaborate and esoteric framework of algebra and calculus. This resurgence of the classical liberal economic creed was accomplished by a new school of economic thinkers known as *neoclassical* economists.

THE NEOCLASSICAL THEORY
OF UTILITY AND CONSUMPTION

During the early 1870s, at precisely the time when the drive toward the economic concentration of corporate capitalism was taking place, three very famous economics texts were published. William Stanley Jevons's *The Theory of Political Economy*[10] and Karl Menger's *Grundsätze der Volkswirtschafts-lehre*[11] both appeared in 1871, and three years later Léon Walras's *Eléments d'économie politique pure* was published.[12] Although there were many differences among the analyses of these men, the similarities in both approach and content of these books were striking.

Their theories pictured an economy composed of large numbers of small producers and consumers, each having insufficient power to influence the market significantly. The business firms hired or bought factors of production; they utilized the factors in the production process in such a way that their profits were maximized. Prices of the final products and factors of production were taken as given and beyond their control. The firms could control only the productive process chosen and the amount produced.

Households likewise sold their land and capital, as well as their labor,

---

[10]William Stanley Jevons, *The Theory of Political Economy,* 1st ed. (London: Macmillan, 1871).

[11]Karl Menger, *Grundsätze der Volkswirtschaftslehre* (Vienna: Braumuller, 1871), translated as *Principles of Economics* (New York: Free Press, 1950).

[12]Léon Walras, *Eléments d'économie politique pure* (Lausanne: Corbaz et Cie, 1874), translated as *Elements of Pure Economics* (Homewood, Ill.: Irwin, 1957).

at prices determined in the market and used the receipts (their incomes) to buy goods and services. Consumers apportioned their income among the various commodities they wished to purchase in a way that maximized the utility they received from these commodities.

Commodities were the ultimate source of pleasure or utility, and the utility they yielded was assumed to be quantifiable. Jevons wrote, "A unit of pleasure or pain is difficult even to conceive; but it is the amount of these feelings which is continually prompting us to buying and selling, borrowing and lending, laboring and resting, producing and consuming; *and it is from the quantitative effects of the feelings that we must estimate their comparative amounts.*"[13]

Walras was less ambiguous in arguing that utility was quantifiable: "I shall, therefore, assume the existence of a standard measure of intensity of wants or intensive utility, which is applicable not only to similar units of the same kind of wealth but also to different units of various kinds of wealth."[14]

These economists, having presumably quantifiable magnitudes with which to work, next set up general mathematical formulas purporting to show a functional relationship between the utility a consumer received and the amounts of the various commodities he or she consumed. The problem then was to show how the consumer could get the maximum utility, given his or her income and the commodity prices prevailing in the market.

Consumers maximized utility when the increase in utility derived from the last unit consumed, expressed as a ratio over the price of that commodity, was an equal proportion for all commodities. In other words, the last dollar spent on a commodity should yield the same increase in the utility derived by the consumer as the last dollar spent on any other commodity. Jevons explained the same thing in a different way, stating that the consumer maximized utility because he or she "procures such quantities of commodities that the final degrees of utility of any pair of commodities are inversely as the ratios of exchange [prices] of the commodities."[15]

Suppose there were a free market in which consumers could freely exchange their incomes for commodities. They would be led by their self-interest to maximize utility. Therefore it was concluded that consumers distributed their income among purchases of commodities in such a way that the welfare of all would be maximized, given the existing distribution of wealth and income.

THE NEOCLASSICAL THEORY OF PRODUCTION

In neoclassical production theory the analysis of the business firm was perfectly symmetrical with the analysis of consumer behavior. In order to maximize profits, the firm would operate at its highest efficiency and hence produce

[13]Jevons, *Theory of Political Economy,* p. 11.
[14]Walras, *Principles of Economics,* p. 117.
[15]Jevons, *Theory of Political Economy,* p. 139.

at the lowest possible cost. It purchased factors of production (such as labor) until the amount added to production by the last unit of each factor of production, expressed as a ratio over the price of the factor, was an equal proportion for all factors. The last dollar spent on each factor should yield the same increase in production from all factors. In a free market, firms would always attempt to maximize efficiency in order to maximize profits. Therefore this condition would always hold. Thus the factors of production would all be used in such a way that no possible reorganization of production (given the existing technology) could result in a more efficient use of the factors of production.

Neoclassical economists also believed that if an economy were characterized by a free market with many small competitive firms, then each commodity would be produced in such quantities and with such methods that it would be impossible to shift resources from the production of one commodity to the production of a different one without diminishing that total value of what was produced in the market economy.

LAISSEZ-FAIRE

Thus the neoclassical economists gave a very elaborate and esoteric analytic defense of Adam Smith's notion of the invisible hand of market competition and the economic policy of laissez-faire. They showed that, in a competitive market economy made up of innumerable small producers and consumers, the market would guide the consumers in such a way that they would end up with an optimal mix of commodities, *given their original income and wealth.* Factors of production would be used in the most efficient way possible. Moreover, commodities would be produced in amounts that would maximize the value of society's production. This optimal result depended, however, on a minimum of interference by government in the processes of the free market.

They recognized that this result was optimal if one accepted the existing distribution of income. Some (particularly the American economist John Bates Clark) tried to defend the distribution of income that obtained in a free-market economy. They argued that the principles of profit maximization would lead to a situation in which each category of productive factors would be paid an amount equal to the value of its marginal contribution to the productive process. This seemed to them a model of distributive justice, with each unit of the productive factors being paid an amount equal to what it produced. Critics were quick to point out, however, that units of productive factors were not people (at least as far as land, natural resources, and capital were concerned). In order for such a system to be fair, these critics insisted, an equitable distribution of ownership of the factors of production would be necessary.

Nevertheless, the neoclassical economists did succeed in erecting an impressive intellectual defense of the classical liberal policy of laissez-faire. They did it by creating a giant chasm between economic theory and economic reality, however. From the 1870s until today, many economists in the neoclassical tradition have abandoned any real concern with existing economic institutions and problems. Instead, many of them have retired to the rarefied stratosphere of mathematical model building, constructing endless variations on esoteric trivia.

SUBSEQUENT MODIFICATIONS OF NEOCLASSICAL THEORY

Some economists in the second and third generations of neoclassical analysis recognized the need to make the theory more realistic. The economic system was *not* characterized by "perfect competition"; it had flaws. The principal admitted weaknesses were as follows: (1) Some buyers and sellers *were* large enough to affect prices; moreover, the economics of large-scale production seemed to render this inevitable. (2) Some commodities should be "consumed socially," and their production and sale might never be profitable in a laissez-faire capitalist economy, even though they might be deemed highly desirable by most citizens (e.g., roads, schools, or armies). (3) The costs to the producer of a commodity (such as automobiles) might differ significantly from the social costs (such as smog) of producing that commodity. In such a case it was possible that for society as a whole the costs of production might exceed the benefits of production for the commodity, even though the producer still profited from making and selling it. For example, consider the poisoning of the water and air by producers making profits but doing little or nothing about the evil, even though its side effects could endanger human life itself. (4) An unrestrained free-market capitalist system appeared to be quite unstable, being subject to recurring depressions that incurred enormous social waste.

It was generally agreed that such flaws did exist and did disrupt the otherwise beneficial workings of the capitalist system, but they could be corrected only by some amount of government intervention in the market system. Government antitrust actions, it was argued, could force giant firms to act as if they were competitive, and something called "workable competition" could be achieved. Roads, schools, armies, and other socially consumed commodities could be provided by the government. Extensive systems of special taxes and subsidies could be used to equate private and social costs in cases where they differed. Finally (especially after the 1930s), it was believed that through wise use of fiscal and monetary policy the government could eliminate the instability of the system. (This last point is discussed in more detail in Chapter 12.)

The flaws in the system were thus seen as minor and ephemeral. An enlightened government could correct them and free the invisible hand once again to create the best of all possible worlds. There did develop, however, an inability to agree on the extent and significance of the flaws. Those who believe them to be fairly widespread and quite significant have, during the course of the twentieth century, become known as *liberals*. They have sometimes advocated fairly extensive government intervention in the economic system, but most have continued to use neoclassical economic theory as an ideology to defend the private-ownership, capitalist market economic system.

Economists who see the flaws as minor and unimportant continue to advocate a minimum of government intervention in the market economy. Despite the fact that the laissez-faire policies advocated by these economists have been much closer to those advocated by the nineteenth-century classical liberals, they have become known in the twentieth century as *conservatives.* Both liberals and conservatives, as we have described them here, have used neoclassical economic theory to justify the capitalist system.

LAISSEZ-FAIRE AND THE SOCIAL DARWINISTS

Before we leave the topic of late nineteenth- and early twentieth-century advocates of laissez-faire capitalism, a brief discussion of social Darwinism is necessary. *Social Darwinists* believed the government should allow capitalists to compete freely in the marketplace with a minimum of government restrictions and, in general, favored as little government intervention as possible in all spheres of life. Therefore many people have imagined their defense of laissez-faire capitalism to be similar to that of the neoclassical economists. This is not so. Their policy recommendations were based on a substantially different theoretical framework.

The social Darwinists took Darwin's theory of evolution and extended it to a theory of social evolution (in a manner that Darwin himself strongly disapproved of, it may be added). Competition, they believed, was a teleological process in which each succeeding generation was superior to the preceding one. This upward progress was made possible because those least fit to survive did not succeed in maintaining themselves and procreating. Greater ability to survive was equated with a biological as well as a moral superiority.

Herbert Spencer (1820–1903), the father of social Darwinism, based his evolutionary as well as his moral theory on what he called the *law of conduct and consequence.* He believed survival of the human species could be ensured only if society distributed its benefits in proportion to a person's merit, measured by his or her power to be self-sustaining. One ought to reap the benefits or suffer the evil results of one's own actions. Thus the people most adapted to their environment would prosper, and those least adapted would be weeded out—provided that the laws of conduct and consequence were observed. If the government, wishing to mitigate inequalities of wealth and income in society, took "from him who . . . [had] prospered to give to him who . . . [had] not, it [violated] its duty towards the one to do more than its duty towards the other."[16] This type of action slowed social progress and could, if carried to excess, destroy the human species. Survival and progress could be ensured only if the weak were weeded out and destroyed by the impersonal forces of social evolution.

In Spencer's opinion, "the poverty of the incapable, the distresses that come upon the imprudent, the starvation of the idle and those shoulderings aside of the weak by the strong . . . are the decrees of a large, far-seeing

---

[16]Quoted in Sidney Fine, *Laissez Faire and the General Welfare State* (Ann Arbor: University of Michigan Press, 1964), p. 38.

benevolence."[17] Spencer categorically opposed any action by the government that interfered with trade, commerce, production, or the distribution of wealth or income. He rejected welfare payments of any kind, attempts to decrease the economic insecurity of workers, and government provision of schools, parks, or libraries as detrimental to human progress. His laissez-faire was thus much more extreme than that of the classical economists or most of the conservative neoclassical economists.

Social Darwinists accepted the large monopolistic and oligopolistic industries as the beneficial result of evolution. Neoclassical economists, if they did not simply define away or ignore the concentrations of economic power, believed government should attempt to create a more competitive and atomistic market situation. In this very important respect the two theories were thus quite antagonistic.

LAISSEZ-FAIRE AND THE IDEOLOGY OF BUSINESSMEN

Most businessmen, however, were not very concerned with intellectual inconsistency. They feared radical and socialist reformers who wanted to use the government as a means of achieving greater equality, and they welcomed any theory that concluded that the government should not intervene in the economic process. Even though they themselves used the government to promote their own interests (through special tariffs, tax concessions, land grants, and a host of other special privileges), they relied on laissez-faire arguments when threatened with any social reform that might erode their status, wealth, or income. Thus in the ordinary businessman's ideology of the late nineteenth and early twentieth centuries there was a general attempt to combine neoclassical economics and social Darwinism.

In this ideology the accumulation of wealth was considered de facto proof of evolutionary superiority, whereas poverty was believed to be evidence of evolutionary inferiority. Success, asserted writer Benjamin Woods, was "nothing more or less than doing thoroughly what others did indifferently." Andrew Carnegie equated success with "honest work, ability and concentration"; another businessman argued that "wealth has always been the natural sequence to industry, temperance, and perseverance, and it will always so continue." At the same time, S. C. T. Dodd, solicitor for Standard Oil, maintained that poverty existed "because nature or the devil has made some men weak and imbecile and others lazy and worthless, and neither man nor God can do much for one who will do nothing for himself."[18]

The beneficial results of competition in neoclassical economic theory seemed to reinforce reliance on the "survival of the fittest" in the "struggle for survival." "Competition in economics," asserted Richard R. Bowker, "is the same as the law of . . . 'natural selection' in nature."[19]

[17]Ibid.
[18]All quotations in this paragraph are cited in ibid., p. 98.
[19]Ibid., p. 100.

Although some businessmen and their spokesmen were trying to perpetuate the laissez-faire conclusions of the classical liberal ideology of capitalism, many defenders of the capitalist system believed that in the new age of
mass production (with gigantic concentrations of wealth and power in the
hands of so few corporations and capitalists) the older, individualistic, laissez-
faire ideology was no longer appropriate. The late nineteenth century witnessed a rebirth of the older paternalistic ethic. In the next section we examine
a new ideology of capitalism that was based, in many essential respects, on a
new version of the Christian paternalist ethic.

A NEW CHRISTIAN PATERNALIST ETHIC

The distance separating the neoclassical liberal ideology of capitalism and
economic reality impressed itself on the minds of many academicians and
businessmen. The result was a new ideology for the new age of corporate
capitalism. Just as the new industrial and financial entrepreneurs came to
resemble the feudal robber barons, so the new ideology resembled the feudal
version of the Christian paternalist ethic. It emphasized the natural superiority
of a small elite, the new industrial and financial magnates, and the paternalistic
functions of that elite in caring for the masses.

The new ideology reflected the fact that many of the wealthy capitalists
of the era were becoming something of folk heroes among the general public.
The last two decades of the nineteenth century and the first three of the
twentieth were an age during which the businessman became the most admired
social type. The success of businessmen was viewed as de facto proof that they
possessed virtues superior to those of the ordinary person. This version of
success was the theme of the biographies of William Makepeace Thackeray
and the novels of Horatio Alger. These men and other writers created a cult
of success that viewed the increase of industrial concentration as proof of
Darwinian superiority on the part of the industrialists, glorified the self-made
individual, and kept the Horatio Alger rags-to-riches myth constantly in the
public mind.

The veneration of businessmen, added to the strong rejection of destructive competition by both businessmen and the general public, led to a new
conservative version of the Christian paternalist ethic, which resembled the
philosophy of the Tory radicals of the late eighteenth and early nineteenth
centuries. The unfortunate plight of the poor received prominent mention in
the new writings. This problem, as well as that of economic instability, could
best be solved, according to the new ideology, by encouraging cooperation
among the leaders of the giant corporations. Competition was viewed as antisocial. Through cooperation business cycles could be eliminated and the plight
of the poor improved.

This new version of the Christian paternalist ethic received the support
of Pope Leo XIII (1810–1903). Between 1878 and 1901 the pope sought to
analyze the problems of corporate capitalism and to suggest remedies in a
series of encyclicals. In *Rerum novarum* (1891) he argued that "a remedy must

be found . . . for the misery and wretchedness which press so heavily at this moment on the large majority of the very poor." He continued with a condemnation of unrestrained laissez-faire competition:

> Working men have been given over, isolated and defenseless, to the callousness of employers and the greed of unrestrained competition. The evil has been increased by rapacious usury . . . still practiced by avaricious and grasping men. And to this must be added the custom of working by contract, and the concentration of so many branches of trade in the hands of a few individuals, so that a small number of very rich men have been able to lay upon the masses of the poor a yoke little better than slavery itself.[20]

This passage, which sounds so socialist in tone and content, was followed by a strong condemnation of socialism and a defense of private property. The pope hoped the problems could be corrected by rejection of competition and a return to the Christian virtues of love and brotherhood, with the leaders of business and industry leading the way to a new Christian paternalism within the context of a private property capitalist system.

The German Version

The new paternalistic ideology was probably strongest in Germany, where classical liberalism had never gained a good hold and industrial concentration was most pronounced. A famous German economist expressed the very widely held view that

> the proper kind of cartelization creates more or less a system of justice and equity. . . . The directors of the cartels are educators who wish to bring about the triumph of wide interests of a branch of industry over the egoistic interests of the individual. . . . The cartel system is like a co-operative or merchant's association, an important element in the education of commercial and technical officials who want to make money but who have also learned to put themselves in the service of general interests and to administer the property of others in a loyal and honorable fashion.[21]

Cartels were also widely justified as means of eliminating economic crises. A German court decision, one of several that formed the legal justification of the cartel system in that country, stated, "Indeed the formation of syndicates and cartels . . . has repeatedly been considered a device especially useful for the economy as a whole, since they can prevent uneconomic overproduction and ensuing catastrophe."[22]

[20]Quoted in Daniel R. Fusfeld, *The Age of the Economist* (Glenview, Ill.: Scott, Foresman, 1966), p. 86.
[21]Gustave Schmoller, quoted in Koppel S. Pinson, *Modern Germany: Its History and Civilization* (New York: Macmillan, 1954), p. 236.
[22]Quoted in Dillard, *Economic Development*, p. 396.

The American Version

In the United States, as mentioned earlier, the new ideology thrived in an atmosphere that venerated the successful businessman and was extremely weary of destructive competition. The view of many American industrial and financial magnates was expressed by Andrew Carnegie, one of the most successful of the magnates:

> Not evil, but good, has come to the race from the accumulation of wealth by those who have the ability and energy that produce it. . . . We have the true antidote for the temporary unequal distribution of wealth, the reconciliation of the rich and the poor—a reign of harmony—another ideal, differing, indeed, from that of the Communist in requiring only further evolution of existing conditions, not the total overthrow of our civilization. . . . Under its sway we shall have an ideal state, in which the surplus wealth of the few will become in the best sense, the property of the many, because administered for the common good, this wealth passing through the hands of the few can be made a more potent force for the elevation of our race than if it were distributed in sums to the people themselves.[23]

Carnegie argued, and many businessmen and their spokesmen agreed, that the millionaire would be "a trustee for the poor, entrusted for a season with a great part of the increased wealth of the community, but administering it for the community far better than it could or would have done for itself.[24]

The Right Reverend William Lawrence gave the new elitist view the sanction of religion. "In the long run, it is only to the man of morality that wealth comes. . . . Godliness is in league with riches."[25] Railroad president George F. Baer had the same idea in mind when he tried to assure railroad workers that "the rights and the interests of the laboring man will be protected and cared for, not by the labor agitators, but by the Christian men to whom God, in his infinite wisdom, has given control of the property interests of the country."[26]

SIMON PATTEN'S ECONOMIC BASIS FOR THE NEW ETHIC

Perhaps the most influential academic spokesman for the new corporate ideology was Dr. Simon N. Patten, professor of economics at the University of Pennsylvania from 1888 to 1917 and one of the founders of the American Economic Association.[27] In keeping with the paternalistic element of the new ideology, Patten denounced the poverty and economic exploitation of his era. The following passage could almost have been written by a Marxist of that era:

[23]Andrew Carnegie, "Wealth," in Gail Kennedy, ed., *Democracy and the Gospel of Wealth* (Lexington, Mass.: Raytheon/Heath, 1949), pp. 3, 5, 6.
[24]Cited in Kennedy, *Democracy and the Gospel of Wealth,* p. xii.
[25]Ibid.
[26]Ibid.
[27]For a more complete account of Patten's ideas, see E. K. Hunt, "Simon N. Patten's Contribution to Economics," *Journal of Economic Issues,* December 1970, pp. 38–55.

There have flowed then, side by side, two streams of life, one bearing the working poor, who perpetuate themselves through qualities generated by the stress and mutual dependence of the primitive world, and the other bearing aristocracies, who dominate by means of the laws and traditions giving them control of the social surplus.[28]

In the same vein, 15 years later, he wrote:

The glow of Fifth Avenue is but the reflection of a distant hell into which unwilling victims are cast. Some resource is misused, some town degraded, to create the flow of funds on which our magnates thrive. From Pennsylvania, rich in resources, trains go loaded and come back empty. For the better half no return is made except in literary tomes designed to convince the recipients that exploitation is not robbery. . . . But Nature revolts! Never does the rising sun see children yanked from bed to increase the great Strauss dividends, nor the veteran cripples of the steel mill tramping in their beggar garb, but that it shrivels, reddens, and would strike but for the sight of happier regions beyond.[29]

This poverty and exploitation were, in Patten's opinion, the last vestiges of an earlier age characterized by scarcity. In the economy of scarcity capitalists competed aggressively with each other, with the result that laborers as well as the general public suffered. The fierce competition of the robber barons, however, had marked a watershed in history. The merger movement that followed this competition was the beginning of a new era, an era of plenty rather than scarcity. Capitalists were becoming socialized. They were putting the public welfare ahead of their pursuit of profits, and in doing this they eschewed competition, recognizing that the public welfare could best be promoted by cooperation. (Of course we have seen that capitalists cooperated with each other mostly to squeeze more profit from the public.)

Evidence that the conditions of economic prosperity at the turn of the century were socializing capitalists could be seen in the fact that "hospitals . . . [were] established, schools . . . [were] made free, colleges . . . [were] endowed, museums, libraries, and art galleries . . . [received] liberal support, church funds . . . [grew] and missions . . . [were] formed at home and abroad."[30] On almost every policy issue of his day, Patten took a strongly proindustrial capitalist position. He viewed the late nineteenth-century captains of industry as a paternally beneficent elite:

The growth of large-scale capitalism has resulted in the elimination of the unsocial capitalist and the increasing control of each industry by the socialized groups. . . . At bottom altruistic sentiment is the feeling of a capitalist expressing itself in sympathy for the laborer. This desire of upper class men to improve the conditions of lower classes is a radically different phenome-

[28]Simon Nelson Patten, *The New Basis of Civilization* (New York: Macmillan, 1907), p. 39.
[29]Simon Nelson Patten, *Mud Hollow* (Philadelphia: Dorrance, 1922), p. 226.
[30]Simon Nelson Patten, *The Theory of Prosperity* (New York: Macmillan, 1902), p. 170.

non from the pressure exerted by the lower classes for their own betterment. The lower class movement stands for the control of the state by themselves in their own interests. The upper class movement directs itself against the bad environmental conditions preventing the expression of character.[31]

He believed competition should be discouraged by taxing competitive firms and exempting trusts and monopolies from these taxes. This would benefit all society by eliminating the extensive waste created by competition. In *The Stability of Prices* he argued that competition was largely responsible for the economic instability of the late nineteenth century. When the movement toward trusts and monopolies had been completed, production would be controlled and planned in such a way that this instability would be eliminated.

Patten's paternalistic ideology was, like the liberal ideology of capitalism, ultimately a plea for a minimum of government interference with the actions of businessmen. The government was to interfere in the economy only by encouraging trusts and monopolies and discouraging competition. In Patten's scheme all important social and economic reforms were to be carried out voluntarily by the socialized capitalists in a system of cooperative corporate collectivism.

THE NEW PATERNALISM AND THE NEW DEAL[32]

Patten's version of the new ideology of corporate capitalism was to be very important historically. When the Great Depression of the 1930s struck, two of Patten's students and devotees, Rexford Guy Tugwell and Frances Perkins, had influential positions as members of Roosevelt's original cabinet. Tugwell had asserted that Patten's views "were the greatest single influence on my thought. Neither Veblen nor Dewey found their orientation to the future as completely and instinctively as did Patten. The magnificence of his conceptions and the basic rightness of his vision become clearer as time passes. I am eternally grateful to him."[33] Perkins believed her former teacher to be "one of the greatest men America has ever produced."[34]

Through these two former students Patten exerted a considerable influence on the economic policies of the early phase of the New Deal. His ideas helped create the intellectual basis of the National Industrial Recovery Act of 1933 (NIRA).[35] Patten was not, of course, the only source of these ideas. During World War I, the War Industries Board had generated enthusiasm for corporate collectivism. Throughout the 1920s, trade associations prospered

---

[31]Simon Nelson Patten, "The Reconstruction of Economic Theory," reprinted in Rexford Guy Tugwell, ed., *Simon Nelson Patten, Essays in Economic Theory* (New York: Knopf, 1924), p. 292.

[32]For a more complete discussion of the material covered in this section, see E. K. Hunt, "A Neglected Aspect of the Economic Ideology of the Early New Deal," *Review of Social Economy,* September 1971, pp. 180–192.

[33]Quoted in Allan G. Gruchy, *Modern Economic Thought: The American Contribution* (Clifton, N.J.: Augustus M. Kelley, 1967), p. 408.

[34]Quoted in Arthur M. Schlesinger, Jr., *The Coming of the New Deal* (Boston: Houghton Mifflin, 1965), p. 229.

[35]Ibid., p. 98.

and the doctrine of business self-government gained many adherents in the business world. In 1922, Franklin Roosevelt was president of one such association: the American Construction Council. However, Patten's teachings were unquestionably influential. His protégés, Tugwell and Perkins, were both instrumental in the actual framing of the NIRA.

The National Industrial Recovery Act proclaimed the intent of Congress "to promote the organization of industry for the purpose of cooperative action among trade groups."[36] The bill contained sections providing for codes of fair competition that permitted and even encouraged cooperative price fixing and market sharing and for virtually complete exemption from antitrust laws. Section 7A was designed to promote labor organization but was so diluted that very often it promoted the formation of company unions. "If it [the NIRA] worked, Tugwell thought, each industry would end with a government of its own under which it could promote its fundamental purpose ('production rather than competition'). NIRA could have been administered, Tugwell later wrote, so that a 'great collectivism' would have channeled American energy into a disciplined national effort to establish a secure basis for well-being."[37]

In explaining the bill to the National Association of Manufacturers, General Hugh S. Johnson, the first head of the National Recovery Administration (NRA), declared that "NRA is exactly what industry organized in trade associations makes it." He further asserted that before the NRA the trade associations had about as much effectiveness as an "Old Ladies' Knitting Society; now I am talking to a cluster of formerly emasculated trade associations about a law which proposes for the first time to give them power."[38]

Most of the economics literature that appeared in 1934 recognized that the early New Deal reforms had not significantly extended government control over business. On the contrary, it had given voluntary trade associations the support of the government in forcing the controls of trade associations on all industry.[39]

This experiment in business self-government proved disastrous. The distinguished historian Arthur M. Schlesinger, Jr., has assessed the success of this phase of the early New Deal. With Schlesinger we concur:

> And the result of business self-government? Restriction on production, chiseling of labor and of 7A, squeezing out of small business, savage personal criticism of the President, and the general tendency to trample down everyone in the rush for profits. Experience was teaching Roosevelt what instinct and doctrine had taught Jefferson and Jackson; that to reform capitalism you must fight the capitalists tooth and nail.[40]

[36]Quoted in ibid., pp. 98–99.
[37]Ibid., p. 108.
[38]Quoted in ibid., p. 110.
[39]See Leo Rogin, "The New Deal: A Survey of Literature," *Quarterly Journal of Economics,* May 1935, pp. 338, 346, 349–355. Typical of the comments of supporters of the early New Deal is this quotation from Tilly: "Here *industry* is setting up a legal and enforceable Golden Rule." Ibid., p. 351.
[40]Arthur M. Schlesinger, Jr., "The Broad Accomplishments of the New Deal," in Edwin C. Rozwenc, ed., *The New Deal: Revolution* (Lexington, Mass.: Raytheon/Heath, 1959), pp. 30–31.

The early New Deal philosophy underlying the NIRA was very quickly abandoned. The NIRA was declared unconstitutional by the Supreme Court. The new paternalistic ideology of capitalism, however, was to receive more elaborate statements after World War II.

SUMMARY

In the late nineteenth century capitalism was characterized by the growth of giant corporations. Control of most of the important industries became more and more concentrated. Accompanying this concentration of industry was an equally striking concentration of income in the hands of a small percentage of the population.

In view of these facts it would seem that the classical liberal ideology (which depended on an analysis of an economy based on many small, relatively powerless enterprises) would have had to be abandoned. The gulf that separated the theory from reality had widened into a giant chasm. But the idea that the market economy channeled acquisitive profit seeking into socially benevolent practices was simply too elegant an apologia for unrestrained profit-making activity. The classical liberal ideology of capitalism was thus even more assiduously disseminated in a new school of neoclassical economics.

An elaborate deductive theory permitted the neoclassical economists to defend the classical policy prescription of laissez-faire. Conservative neoclassical economists assigned to the government only the tasks that would directly or indirectly promote business profits. Liberal neoclassical economists also believed the government should enter a limited number of other areas in which the operation of the free market did not maximize the social welfare. Whether in the hands of the conservative or the liberal faction, neoclassical economics remained essentially an ideological defense for the status quo.

Social Darwinist ideology and the ideology of most businessmen defended many of the neoclassical economists' conclusions. They did so, however, on entirely different grounds. They accepted the fact that corporate power, personal wealth, and personal income were highly concentrated. This, they believed, was evidence of the evolutionary superiority of the wealthy and, as such, was socially beneficial.

During this period, however, many ideologists of capitalism rejected classical liberalism because of its unrealistic assumptions. These thinkers created a new version of the Christian paternalist ethic that pictured capitalists as beneficent, fatherly protectors of the public welfare. This new ethic was to become particularly influential in the social and economic legislation of the early New Deal in the 1930s.

CHAPTER 9

The Consolidation of Monopoly Power and the Writings of Veblen

The process of industrialization in the United States after the Civil War involved, in its initial stages, a competition among industrial and financial capitalists that was unique in its ferocity. From 1860 until the early 1880s the strongest and shrewdest businessmen built great empires with the fruits of economic conquest. The great improvements in transportation that occurred during this period, the rise of standardization in parts and finished products, and the increased efficiency in large-scale mass production created the possibility of nationwide markets. The stakes in the economic struggle were very large, and the participants neither asked for quarter nor received any.

COMPETITION AS INDUSTRIAL WARFARE

Examples of the industrial warfare of the time have filled many books.[1] In the oil industry, for example, John D. Rockefeller and Henry M. Flagler shipped so much oil that they were able to demand large concessions from the railroads. With this cost advantage they could undersell competitors. Their company, which was incorporated in 1870 under the name of Standard Oil Company of Ohio, was able to force many competitors to the wall and

---

[1]See, for example, Matthew Josephson, *The Robber Barons* (New York: Harcourt Brace Jovanovich, Harvest Books, 1962), for a fascinating account of the exploits of the capitalists of this era.

thus achieve regional monopolies, at which point the price could be substantially increased without fear of competition. After securing large rebates on transport costs, Standard Oil's share in the petroleum industry quickly increased from 10 to 20 percent. But the company did not stop there. Next it succeeded in forcing the railroads to give it rebates on its *competitors'* shipments as well as "all data relating to shipper, buyer, product, price and terms of payment," a scheme that "provided Rockefeller and his associates with rebates on all their own shipments, rebates on all shipments by their competitors, and in addition a complete spy system on their competitors."[2] With his power Rockefeller was able to smash most of his competitors. By 1879, only 9 years after incorporation, Standard Oil controlled between 90 and 5 percent of the nation's output of refined petroleum. A sympathetic biographer of Rockefeller has written, "Of all the devices for the extinction of competition, this was the cruelest and most deadly yet conceived by any group of American industrialists."[3]

Competition among the railroad magnates was particularly intense. Rate wars were common, forcing weaker competitors out of business and giving stronger competitors monopoly power over large regions. The battles sometimes got so brutal that locomotives were crashed into each other and track was destroyed. The railroads also extorted money from towns along proposed railroad lines. A member of the California Constitutional Convention of 1878 described the technique:

> They start out their railroad track and survey their line near a thriving village. They go to the most prominent citizens of that village and say, "If you will give us so many thousand dollars we will run through here; if you do not we will run by." And in every instance where the subsidy was not granted this course was taken and the effect was just as they said, to kill off the little town.[4]

According to the same report, the railroad "blackmailed Los Angeles County for $230,000 as a condition of doing that which the law compelled them to do." The railroads also manipulated connections with politicians to get government handouts of public lands. It is estimated that these giveaways amounted to 158,293,000 acres—a greater land area that that of some whole countries.[5] The railroads were certainly not in favor of a laissez-faire policy in practice.

The great entrepreneurs of that age were definitely not men of estimable social conscience. Many founded their fortunes on the Civil War. When shortages of supplies became desperate, they received high prices for selling to the army "shoddy blankets, so many doctored horses, and useless rifles, [and] . . .

[2] Dudley Dillard, *Economic Development of the North Atlantic Community* (Englewood Cliffs, N.J.: Prentice-Hall, 1967), p. 410.
[3] Allan Nevins, *John D. Rockefeller, The Heroic Age of American Enterprise,* vol. 1 (New York: Scribner's, 1940), p. 325.
[4] Quoted in Josephson, *Robber Barons,* pp. 84–85.
[5] Ibid., p. 79.

stores of sickening beef."[6] In order to eliminate their competitors, they did not hesitate to use hired thugs, kidnapping, and dynamite. Likewise, they stopped at nothing as they milked the public of millions of dollars through stock frauds, schemes, and swindles. Some of these actions were legal and some were not, but the dominant mood of these capitalist entrepreneurs was expressed by Cornelius Vanderbilt, who, when cautioned about the questionable legality of a desired course of action, exclaimed, "What do I care about the law? Hain't I got the power?"[7] Much the same idea was expressed by William Vanderbilt during a public outcry against one of his policy decisions: "The public be damned. I am working for my stockholders."[8]

BUSINESS COLLUSION AND GOVERNMENT REGULATION

After a few years of this type of competition, however, most of the remaining business firms were battle-tested giants. Continuing such competition would have been ruinous for all. So, whereas competition was the road to large profits before 1880, after that date it became obvious that cooperative collusion would be more beneficial for the remaining firms. In that way they could exercise monopolistic power for their mutual benefit. Thus, pools, trusts, and mergers (described in Chapter 8) were the consequence of the earlier competition. Increasingly as the turn of the century neared, the neoclassical vision of many small competing firms diverged from the reality of massive corporations acting cooperatively to maximize their joint profits.

With the rise of big corporations there was a parallel growth of grass-roots popular opposition to these companies and their blatant disregard for the public welfare. This popular antagonism became so widespread and intense that in the presidential campaign of 1888 both the Democrats and the Republicans advocated federal laws to curb the abuses of big corporations.

After the 1888 election, both parties became extremely reluctant to take any such action. Many of the most important Republicans controlled the very corporations they had promised to curb, and the Democrats were only slightly less involved with big business. Only when public pressure reached incredible heights did Congress respond, in December 1889, by passing the Sherman Anti-Trust Act. The act, an obvious concession to aroused public opinion, passed both houses of Congress with only a single dissenting vote. But the wording of the law was so weak and vague that it appeared to be designed to ensure that it would be ineffective. Another proposal, which recommended meaningful punishment of firms that violated the law, was overwhelmingly defeated.

The law proscribed "every contract, combination in the form of a trust or otherwise, or conspiracy, in restraint of trade or commerce among the several states or with foreign nations." It also declared that any person who attempted

[6]Ibid., p. 67.
[7]Ibid., p. 72.
[8]Ibid.

"to monopolize, or combine or conspire with any other person . . . to monopolize any part of the trade or commerce among the several states, or with foreign nations" was guilty of a misdemeanor.

The primary effect of the Sherman Act over the next few decades was to weaken labor unions. What had begun as a concession to the public's hatred of abuses by big business became an antilabor law. This effect followed because the courts ruled that many union strikes constituted constraints of trade. On this basis the government arrested numerous union leaders and broke up many unions.

While President McKinley was in office there were only five cases initiated under the Sherman Act, despite the fact that 146 major industrial combinations were formed between 1899 and 1901 alone. One of these was the massive United States Steel Corporation. In 1901 U.S. Steel controlled or acquired 785 plants worth $1,370,000,000, which would be many times that amount in today's dollars.

Staggeringly high profits, graft, corruption, and discriminatory practices on the part of the nation's railroads led to the establishment of the first federal government regulatory agency. The Interstate Commerce Act of 1887 established the Interstate Commerce Commission (ICC), which was designed to regulate the railroads in order to protect the public interest.

Competition among the railroads had been so destructive that the railroads themselves were the leading advocates of extended federal regulation. A few years after the passage of the Interstate Commerce Act, U.S. Attorney General Olney wrote a letter to a railroad president that read, in part, "The [ICC] . . . is, or can be made, of great use to the railroads. It satisfies the popular clamor for a government supervision of railroads, at the same time that supervision is almost entirely nominal. Further, the older such a commission gets to be, the more inclined it will be found to take the business and railroad view of things."[9]

The attorney general's prediction has certainly been borne out by the facts. In the years since the establishment of the ICC, many other federal regulatory agencies have been established. The Federal Communications Commission (FCC), the Civil Aeronautics Board (CAB), and the Securities and Exchange Commission (SEC) were among the federal agencies that joined the ICC as "protectors" of the public interest. Most serious students of government regulation would agree that "the outstanding political fact about the . . . regulatory commissions is that they have in general become promoters and protectors of the industries they have been established to regulate."[10] The agencies help the industries make extraordinary profits at the expense of the public.

Many oligopolistic industries seemed unable to cooperate and act collectively as a monopoly. There is a considerable body of evidence indicating that

---

[9] Quoted in Grant McConnell, "Self-Regulation, the Politics of Business," in D. Mermelstein, ed., *Economics: Mainstream Readings and Radical Critiques* (New York: Random House, 1970), p. 197.

[10] Ibid., p. 199.

these industries turned to the government and to federal regulatory agencies as a means of achieving this monopolistic coordination.[11] Regulatory agencies have generally performed this function very effectively.

The collusive behavior of the oligopolistic businesses seemed to go unnoticed by neoclassical economists. They continued to frame their analyses in terms of innumerable small, competing business firms. In their advocacy of laissez-faire policies, they failed to see that it was primarily big business that supported active government intervention.

Neoclassical economists also continued to accept the classical economists' view that as long as free competition prevails, the economy will tend toward full utilization of its productive capacity, and full employment will be more or less continuous. During the second half of the nineteenth century, however, economic depressions became more frequent and more severe. During the first half of the nineteenth century, the United States had had two economic crises (in 1819 and 1837), and England had had four (in 1815, 1825, 1836, and 1847). During the second half of the century, the number increased to five in the United States (1854, 1857, 1873, 1884, and 1893), and six in England (in 1857, 1866, 1873, 1882, 1890, and 1900). Thus, the neoclassical economic ideology was as poor a reflection of economic performances as it was of industrial concentration.

CHANGES IN THE STRUCTURE OF CAPITALISM

During the late nineteenth and early twentieth centuries, capitalism underwent an important and fundamental transformation. Although the foundations of the system the laws of private property, the basic class structure, and the processes of commodity production and allocation through the market—remained unchanged, the process of capital accumulation became institutionalized in the large corporation. In the earlier stages of capitalist development, individual capitalists had played a central role in the accumulation process. The process from their standpoint had depended on organizational skills, cunning, business acumen, ruthlessness, and no small amount of luck. From the standpoint of society, however, the fortune of any particular capitalist was irrelevant—accumulation was an inexorable, ceaseless, spiraling process that had momentum and patterns of development that were quite independent of the actions of any particular capitalist.

The late nineteenth century saw the accumulation process rationalized, regularized, and institutionalized in the form of the large corporation. "Taylorism" and scientific management replaced the older, more individualistic mode of capital accumulation. A new managerial class became increasingly important. Ownership of the means of production remained the principal source of economic, social, and political power in capitalism. The new managerial class was primarily composed, at least in its highest echelons, of important and

---

[11]The most thoroughly documented defense of this assertion can be found in Gabriel Kolko, *The Triumph of Conservatism* (New York: Free Press, 1963).

powerful owners of capital. The managerial class was clearly and decisively subordinated to the entire capitalist class.

Among the consequences of this institutional transformation were two changes of particular importance. The first was the internationalization of capital. We discuss this in Chapter 11. The second was a change in the structure of the capitalist class. Although the social, political, and economic dominance of the capitalist class remained unchanged, the institutionalization of the accumulation process permitted the majority of capitalists to perpetuate their status merely through passive absentee ownership. The majority of capitalists became a pure rentier class, while a minority engaged in managerial functions (in both the economy and the polity) and acted as a kind of executive committee to protect the interests of the entire capitalist class. This committee performed its function by "managing the managers" of the new corporate structure; meanwhile, the remaining capitalists simply enjoyed lavish incomes derived from ownership alone.

These changes in economic organization and activities were reflected in diverse ways in the realm of economic theory. But the economic writings that most completely reflected and described the institutional and cultural transformation of this period were those of Thorstein Veblen (1857–1929). Veblen was probably the most significant, original, and profound social theorist in American history.

Veblen taught at the University of Chicago and at Stanford University, and was mistreated at both institutions, particularly the latter. He wrote prolifically, publishing ten important books and innumerable articles and reviews in journals and periodicals. His great genius and unusual writing style make all of his works enormously enjoyable and intellectually valuable.

THE ANTAGONISTIC DICHOTOMY OF CAPITALISM

Veblen believed that there were two generally antagonistic clusters of behavioral traits, which were manifested in different historical eras through the social institutions and modes of behavior peculiar to those eras. Central to one of the clusters was Veblen's notion of the "instinct of workmanship." Central to the other cluster was his notion of the instinct to "exploit," or the "predatory instinct." Associated with workmanship were traits that Veblen referred to as the "parental instinct" and the "instinct of idle curiosity." These traits were responsible for the advances that had been made in productivity and in the expansion of human mastery over nature. They were also responsible for the degree to which the human needs for affection, cooperation, and creativity were fulfilled. Associated with exploit, or the predatory instinct, were human conflict, subjugation, and sexual, racial, and class exploitation. Social institutions and habitual behavior often tended to hide the true nature of exploitation and predatory behavior behind facades that Veblen referred to as "sportsmanship" and "ceremonialism."

The antithesis between these two sets of behavioral traits, and the social institutions through which they were manifested, was the central focal point of Veblen's social theory. Veblen was primarily interested in analyzing the capitalist system of his era within the context of this social theory. Just as Marx in the mid-nineteenth century had taken England as the prototype of capitalist society, Veblen, writing during the last decade of the nineteenth and first quarter of the twentieth centuries, took the United States as the prototype. The central question for him was how these two antagonistic clusters of behavioral traits were manifested in and through the institutions of capitalism.

The question could be approached from several vantage points; Veblen used at least three. From a social psychological point of view, he distinguished individuals and classes whose behavior was dominated by the propensity to exploit, or the predatory instinct, from those whose behavior was dominated by the instinct of workmanship, the parental bent, and the development of idle curiosity. From the standpoint of economics, Veblen saw the same dichotomy between the forces that he referred to as "business"—which he defined as grubbing for profit—and the forces that he referred to as "industry"—which he defined as production of socially useful commodities. From the standpoint of sociology, the dichotomy was manifested in the differences between the "ceremonialism" and "sportsmanship" characteristic of the "leisure class" and the more creative and cooperative behavior characteristic of the "common man."

Each of these three levels of analysis tended to merge with the other two, for Veblen was in fact analyzing a society that was mainly constituted of two major classes. One class was the capitalists, whom he variously referred to as the "vested interest," the "absentee owners," the "leisure class," or the "captains of industry." The other class was the productive or working class, whom he variously referred to as the "engineers," the "workmen," and the "common man."

PRIVATE PROPERTY, CLASS-DIVIDED SOCIETY, AND CAPITALISM

At the foundation of this class structure was the institution of private property. In the earliest stages of human society, low productivity made a predominance of the instinct of workmanship a social prerequisite for survival. During this period, "the habits of life of the race were still perforce of a peaceful and industrial character, rather than contentious and destructive."[12] During this early period, "before a predacious life became possible" and while society was still dominated by the instinct of workmanship, "efficiency [or] serviceability commends itself, and inefficiency or futility is odious."[13] In this type of society, property was social and not private.

[12]Thorstein Veblen, "The Instinct of Workmanship and the Irksomeness of Labor," in *Essays in Our Changing Order* (New York: Augustus M. Kelley, 1964), p. 86.

[13]Ibid., pp. 87, 89.

Only after production became substantially more efficient and technical knowledge and tools were socially accumulated did predatory exploitation become possible. Invidious distinctions among different members of society became possible only at that point. With greater productivity, it became possible to live by brute seizure and predatory exploitation. "But seizure and forcible retention very shortly gain the legitimation of usage, and the resultant tenure becomes inviolable through habitation."[14] In other words, private property came into existence.

Private property had its origins in brute coercive force and was perpetuated both by force and by institutional and ideological legitimization. Class-divided societies inevitably came with the development of private property: "Where this tenure by prowess prevails, the population falls into two economic classes: those engaged in industrial employments, and those engaged in such nonindustrial pursuits as war, government, sports, and religious observances."[15]

Private property and the predatory instinct led to the predatory, class-divided societies of the slave and feudal eras. Capitalism was the outgrowth of feudalism in western Europe. Whereas the predatory instinct totally dominated society in slavery and feudalism, in capitalism there had occurred an important, profound growth of the instinct of workmanship. Capitalism—or as Veblen sometimes referred to capitalism, "the régime of absentee ownership and hired labor"[16]—had begun as a "quasi-peaceable" society in which the forces of workmanship had originally developed very rapidly. With the passage of time, however, the forces of workmanship and the predatory forces of exploitation had become locked in a struggle. This antagonism was expressed by Veblen as a conflict between "business" and "industry," or between "salesmanship" and "workmanship."

These two social forces were embodied in entirely different classes of people in capitalism. "The interest and attention of the two typical . . . classes . . . part company and enter on a course of progressive differentiation along two divergent lines."[17] The first class embodied the instinct of workmanship or industry:

The workman, laborers, operatives, technologists—whatever term may best designate that general category of human material through which the community's technological proficiency functions directly to an industrial effect—those who have to work, whereby they get their livelihood and their interest as well as the discipline of their workday life converges, in effect, on a technological apprehension of material facts.[18]

[14]Thorstein Veblen, "The Beginnings of Ownership," in ibid., p. 43.
[15]Ibid.
[16]Veblen, *Absentee Ownership and Business Enterprise in Recent Times* (New York: Augustus M. Kelley, 1964), p. 291.
[17]Thorstein Veblen, *The Instinct of Workmanship* (New York: Augustus M. Kelley, 1964), pp. 187–188.
[18]Ibid., p. 188.

The second class embodied the predatory instinct, the business viewpoint, and salesmanship:

> These owners, investors, masters, employers, undertakers, businessmen, have to do with the negotiating of advantageous bargains. . . . The training afforded by these occupations and requisite to their effectual pursuit runs in terms of pecuniary management and insight, pecuniary gain, price, price-cost, price-profit, and price-loss; . . . that is to say in terms of the self-regarding propensities and sentiments.[19]

While the essence of success for laborers involved workmanship or productive creativity, the essence of success for owners and businessmen involved exploitative advantage over others. Profit making, or business, created behavior that was totally removed from industry or workmanship. Increasingly, owners had less and less to do in the direction of production, which became entrusted to a "professional class of 'efficiency engineers.' "[20] But the concern of this new managerial class of efficiency engineers was never with productivity itself or with serviceability to the community at large. "The work of the efficiency engineers . . . [is] always done in the service of business . . . in terms of price and profits."[21]

The nature of the control of business over industry was described by Veblen in one term: "sabotage." Business sabotaged industry for the sake of profit. Sabotage was defined as "a conscientious withdrawal of efficiency."[22] For business owners, "a reasonable profit always means, in effect, the largest obtainable profit."[23] The problem in capitalism was that large-scale industry and the forces of workmanship were always increasing the quantity of output that could be produced with a given quantity of resources and workers. But given the existing, extremely unequal distribution of income, this added output could only be sold if prices were reduced substantially. Generally, the necessary price reductions were so great that selling a larger quantity at lower prices was less profitable than selling a lesser quantity at higher prices. Therefore, in modern capitalism

> [there] is an ever increasing withdrawal of efficiency. The industrial plant is increasingly running idle or half idle, running increasingly short of its productive capacity. Workmen are being laid off. . . . And all the while these people are in great need of all sorts of goods and services which these idle plants and idle workmen are fit to produce. But for reasons of business expediency it is impossible to let these idle plants and idle workmen go to work—that is to say for reasons of insufficient profit to the business men interested, or

[19]Ibid., pp. 189–190.
[20]Ibid., p. 22.
[21]Ibid., p. 224.
[22]Thorstein Veblen, *The Engineers and the Price System* (New York: Augustus M. Kelley, 1965), p. 1.
[23]Ibid., p. 13.

in other words, for the reasons of insufficient income to the vested interests.[24]

The normal state of modern capitalism, Veblen believed, was one of recurring depressions: "It may, therefore, be said, on the basis of this view, that chronic depression, more or less pronounced, is normal to business under the fully developed regimen of the machine industry."[25] Moreover, throughout the business cycle and at all times, capitalism necessarily involved a continuous class struggle between owners and workers:

> In the negotiations between owners and workmen there is little use for the ordinary blandishments of salesmanship. . . . And the bargaining between them therefore settles down without much circumlocution into a competitive use of unemployment, privation, restriction of work and output, strikes, shutdowns and lockouts, espionage, maneuvers, pickets, and similar maneuvers of mutual derangement, with a large recourse to menacing language and threats of mutual sabotage. The colloquial word for it is "labor troubles." The business relations between the two parties are of the nature of hostilities, suspended or active, conducted in terms of mutual sabotage; which will on occasion shift from the footing of such obstruction and disallowance as is wholly within the law and custom of business, from the footing of legitimate sabotage in the way of passive resistance and withholding of efficiency, to that illegitimate phase of sabotage that runs into violent offenses against person and property. The negotiations . . . have come to be spoken of habitually in terms of conflict, armed forces, and warlike strategy. It is a conflict of hostile forces which is conducted on the avowed strategic principle that either party stands to gain at the cost of the other.[26]

GOVERNMENT AND THE CLASS STRUGGLE

The ultimate power in the capitalist system was in the hands of the owners because they controlled the government, which was the institutionally legitimized means of physical coercion in any society. As such, the government existed to protect the existing social order and class structure. This meant that in capitalist society the primary duty of government was the enforcement of private property laws and the protection of the privileges associated with ownership. Veblen repeatedly insisted that

> modern politics is business politics. . . . This is true both of foreign and domestic policy. Legislation, police surveillance, the administration of justice, the military and diplomatic service, all are chiefly concerned with business relations, pecuniary interests, and they have little more than an incidental bearing on other human interests.[27]

[24]Ibid., p. 12.
[25]Thorstein Veblen, *The Theory of Business Enterprise* (New York: Augustus M. Kelley, 1965), p. 234.
[26]Veblen, *Absentee Ownership*, pp. 406–407.
[27]Veblen, *Theory of Business Enterprise*, p. 269.

The first principle of a capitalist government was that the "natural freedom of the individual must not traverse the prescriptive rights of property. Property rights . . . have the indefeasibility which attaches to natural rights."[28] The principal freedom of capitalism was the freedom to buy and sell. The laissezfaire philosophy dictated that "so long as there is no overt attempt on life . . . or the liberty to buy and sell, the law cannot intervene, unless it be in a precautionary way to prevent prospective violation of . . . property rights."[29] Above all else, therefore, a "constitutional government is a business government."[30]

Thus, in the ceaseless class struggle between workers and absentee owners, the owners have nearly always prevailed. Government, as the institutionally legitimized means of physical coercion, was firmly in their hands. Since workers greatly outnumbered owners, the maintenance of the owners' supremacy—that is, the maintenance of the existing class structure of capitalism—depended on the absentee owner being in control of the government. At any point in the class struggle when the workers of a particular industry appeared to be getting the upper hand, the government was called in.

Whenever the prerogatives of private property were threatened in any way, the property-owning class responded by force of arms. Property rights were the basis of this class's power and of its "free income," and it would protect them at any cost: "And it is well known, and also it is right and good by law and custom, that when recourse is had to arms the common man pays the cost. He pays it in lost labor, anxiety, privation, blood, and wounds."[31]

CAPITALIST IMPERIALISM

During the last quarter of the nineteenth century and the early twentieth century, aggressive, imperialist expansion was one of the dominant features of industrial capitalism. In Chapter 11 we discuss some economic theories of imperialism. Veblen also wrote extensively on this topic. He believed that the quest for profits knew no national boundaries. The absentee owners of business saw rich possibilities for profits in different areas of the world if those areas could be brought under the domination of capitalist countries or domestic governments that approved of foreigners extracting profits from their countries. The absentee owners' success in getting the population to believe that everyone's interest was identical to the corporations' interest extended into the realm of patriotism. Patriotism was a nationalist sentiment that could be used to gain support for the government's aggressive, imperialist policies on behalf of business interests. "Imperialism is dynastic politics under a new name," Veblen wrote, "carried on for the benefit of absentee owners."[32] He was con-

[28]Ibid., p. 272.
[29]Ibid., p. 278.
[30]Ibid., p. 285.
[31]Veblen, *Essays in Our Changing Order,* p. 413.
[32]Veblen, *Absentee Ownership,* p. 35.

vinced that there was "a growing need for such national aids to business."[33] Continuous economic expansion was necessary to maintain high profits.

But the profits that imperialism brought to the absentee owners were not, in Veblen's opinion, its most important feature. Imperialism was a conservative social force of the utmost social importance. With the development of the techniques of machine production, human productivity had expanded rapidly during the capitalist era. The natural concomitant of the growth of productivity was the growth of the instinct of workmanship and its related social traits. As workmanship and its attendant traits became dominant in the culture, the social basis of absentee ownership and predatory business practices became endangered. The ethos of workmanship stressed cooperation rather than competition, individual equality and independence rather than pervasive relations of subordination and superordination, logical social interrelationships rather than ceremonial role playing, and peaceable rather than predatory dispositions generally. Thus the traits associated with workmanship were subversive to the very foundation of the existing class structure. The absentee owners had to find some means to counteract the subversive effects of workmanship, cooperation, individual independence, and the quest for a peaceable brotherhood.

For this important task the absentee owners turned to imperialism. This social role of imperialism was so central to Veblen's view of the functioning of capitalism that we quote him at length:

> The largest and most promising factor of cultural discipline—most promising as a corrective of iconoclastic vagaries—over which business principles rule is national politics. . . . Business interests urge an aggressive national policy and business men direct it. Such a policy is warlike as well as patriotic. The direct cultural value of a warlike business policy is unequivocal. It makes for a conservative animus on the part of the populace. During war time, . . . under martial law, civil rights are in abeyance; and the more warfare and armament the more abeyance. Military training is a training in ceremonial precedence, arbitrary command, and unquestioning obedience. A military organization is essentially a servile organization. Insubordination is the deadly sin. The more consistent and the more comprehensive this military training, the more effectually will the members of the community be trained into habits of subordination and away from the growing propensity to make light of personal authority that is the chief infirmity of democracy. This applies first and most decidedly, of course, to the soldiery, but it applies only in a less degree to the rest of the population. They learn to think in warlike terms of rank, authority, and subordination, and so grow progressively more patient of encroachments upon their civil rights. . . . The disciplinary effects of warlike pursuits . . . direct the popular interest to other noble, institutionally less hazardous matters than the unequal distribution of wealth or creature comforts. Warlike and patriotic preoccupations fortify the barbarian virtues of subordination and prescriptive authority. Habituation to a warlike, predatory scheme of life is the strongest disciplinary factor that can be brought to counteract the vulgarization of modern life wrought by peaceful industry and the machine process,

---

[33]Ibid.

and to rehabilitate the decaying sense of status and differential dignity. Warfare, with the stress on a military organization, has always proved an effective school in barbarian methods of thought.

In this direction, evidently, lies the hope of a corrective for "social unrest" and similar disorders of civilized life. There can, indeed, be no serious question but that a consistent return to the ancient virtues of allegiance, piety, servility, graded dignity, class prerogative, and prescriptive authority would greatly conduce to popular content and to the facile management of affairs. Such is the promise held out by a strenous national policy.[34]

THE SOCIAL MORES OF PECUNIARY CULTURE

Where the instinct of workmanship held sway, the social tendency was toward the advancement of knowledge, cooperation, equality, and mutual aid. But the class division of capitalism depended on the continued social prominence of the traits associated with predatory exploit—the admiration of predatory skills, acquiescence in the hierarchy of subordination, and the widespread substitution of myth and ceremony for knowledge. The free and unearned income of the absentee owners ultimately depended on the cultural and social domination of the mores of the predatory or (what in capitalism amounted to the same thing) the pecuniary or business aspects of the culture.

When the predatory instinct dominated society, the prevailing mores were those of the leisure class, which constituted the ruling element of society. Veblen believed that "the emergence of a leisure class coincides with the beginning of ownership. . . . They are but different aspects of the same general facts of social structure."[35] In all class-divided societies there had always been a fundamentally significant differentiation between the occupations of the leisure class and those of the common people. "Under this ancient distinction," he wrote, "the worthy employments are those which may be classed as exploit; unworthy are those necessary everyday employments into which no appreciable element of exploit enters."[36]

Under capitalism there came to be a hierarchy of occupations ranging from the most honorific—absentee ownership—to the most vulgar and repulsive—creative labor.

Employments fall into a hierarchical gradation of reputability. Those which have to do immediately with ownership on a large scale are the most reputable. . . . Next to these in good repute come those employments that are immediately subservient to ownership and financering, such as banking and law. Banking employments also carry a suggestion of large ownership, and this fact is doubtless accountable for a share of the prestige that attaches to the business. The profession of law does not imply large ownership; but since no taint of usefulness, for other than competitive purpose, attaches to

[34]Veblen, *Theory of Business Enterprise,* pp. 391–393.
[35]Thorstein Veblen, *The Theory of the Leisure Class* (New York: Augustus M. Kelley, 1965), p. 22.
[36]Ibid., p. 8.

the lawyer's trade, it grades high in the conventional scheme. The lawyer is exclusively occupied with the details of predatory fraud either in achieving or in checkmating chicane, and success in the profession is therefore accepted as marking a large endowment of that barbarian astuteness which has always commanded men's respect and fear. . . . Manual labour, or even the work of directing mechanical processes, is of course on a precarious footing as regards respectability.[37]

But wealthy absentee owners usually lived in large cities and spent most of their time with lawyers, accountants, stockbrokers, and other advisers, buying and selling stocks and bonds, manipulating financial deals, and generally engineering schemes of sabotage and fraud. Therefore, whereas the predatory virtues in more barbarian cultures were so obvious and immediate as to easily incite the admiration of the populace, the predatory virtues in a capitalist society were largely hidden from view and could not so readily incite admiration. Therefore, capitalists had to conspicuously display their prowess.

Most of *The Theory of the Leisure Class* was devoted to a detailed description of how the leisure class displayed its predatory prowess through conspicuous consumption and the conspicuous use of leisure. For Veblen, conspicuous consumption often coincided with conspicuous waste. The housing of the rich, for example, "is more ornate, more conspicuously wasteful in its architecture and decoration, than the dwelling houses of the congregation."[38] It was always necessary for the rich to have expensive, ornate, and largely useless—but above all, expensive—paraphernalia prominently displayed. For the wealthy, the more useless and expensive a thing was, the more it was prized as an article of conspicuous consumption. Anything that was useful and affordable to common people was thought to be vulgar and tasteless.

The beauty and elaborate dressing and display of one's wife were essential for a substantial citizen of good taste. Innumerable servants were indicators that a wife had to do none of the vulgar work of an ordinary housewife and that she was herself primarily an ostentatious trophy of beauty and uselessness that added to the esteem of her husband. Villas on the sea, yachts, and elaborate mountain chateaus, all of which were rarely used but prominently visible, were essential for respectability.

Veblen had much more in mind in describing the conspicuous consumption of the rich than merely giving an amusing anecdotal account. Pecuniary culture was above all else a culture of invidious distinction. When an individual's personal worth was measured primarily in a pecuniary system of invidious distinction, one of the most powerful forces in society was emulation, which was the most important guarantor of social, economic, and political conservatism.

If the majority of working people came to realize that capitalists contributed nothing to the production process, that the capitalists' business and pecuniary activities were the cause of depressions and other malfunctions in

[37]Ibid., pp. 231–232.
[38]Ibid., p. 120.

the industrial system, that the disproportionately large share of wealth and income going to the capitalists caused the impoverishment of the majority of society, that the degradation of the work process was the result of the prevailing predatory ethos of capitalists—if the workers came to realize these facts, then they would surely free the industrial system from the oppressive and archaic fetters of the laws, governments, and institutions of the pecuniary business culture. There would be a revolutionary overthrow of capitalism.

The capitalists relied on two principal means of cultural discipline and social control. The first, as we have seen, was patriotism, nationalism, militarism, and imperialism. The second means of emotionally and ideologically controlling the population was through emulative consumption (or "consumerism," as this phenomenon later came to be called). The importance of this phenomenon in Veblen's total theory was so great that we quote him at length:

> A certain standard of wealth . . . and of prowess . . . is a necessary condition of reputability, and anything in excess of this normal amount is meritorious.
>
> Those members of the community who fall short of this somewhat indefinite, normal degree of prowess or property suffer in the esteem of their fellow-men; and consequently they suffer also in their own esteem, since the usual basis of self-respect is the respect accorded by one's neighbours. Only individuals with an aberrant temperament can in the long run retain their self-esteem in the face of the disesteem of their fellows. . . .
>
> So soon as the possession of property becomes the basis of popular esteem, therefore, it becomes also a requisite to that complacency which we call self-respect. In any community . . . it is necessary, in order to have his own peace of mind, that an individual should possess as large a portion of goods as others with whom he is accustomed to class himself; and it is extremely gratifying to possess something more than others. But as fast as a person makes new acquisitions, and becomes accustomed to the resulting new standard of wealth, the new standard forthwith ceases to afford appreciably greater satisfaction than the earlier standard did. The tendency in any case is constantly to make the present pecuniary standard the point of departure for a fresh increase of wealth; and this in turn gives rise to a new standard of sufficiency and a new pecuniary classification of one's self as compared with one's neighbours. So far as concerns the present question, the end sought by accumulation is to rank high in comparison with the rest of the community in point of pecuniary strength. So long as the comparison is distinctly unfavourable to himself, the normal average individual will live in chronic dissatisfaction with his present lot; and when he has reached what may be called the normal pecuniary standard of the community, or of his class in the community, this chronic dissatisfaction will give place to a restless straining to place a wider and ever-widening pecuniary interval between himself and this average standard. The invidious comparison can never become so favourable to the individual making it that he would not gladly rate himself still higher relative to his competitors in the struggle for pecuniary reputability.[39]

[39]Ibid., pp. 30–32.

When people were caught on this treadmill of emulative consumption, or consumerism, they led a life of "chronic dissatisfaction," regardless of the amount of income they received. The misery of workers, in Veblen's view, arose predominantly from material deprivation only in that part of the working class that lived in abject poverty. For the remainder of the working class, the misery was caused by both the social degradation of labor and the "chronic dissatisfaction" associated with emulative consumption. The misery of the materially advantaged workers was spiritual. But Veblen insisted that this misery "is . . . none the less real and cogent for its being of a spiritual kind. Indeed it is all the more substantial and irremediable on that account."[40]

It seemed irremediable because the workers' response to the misery furthered and perpetuated the misery, the reaction being to believe that they would be happy if they acquired more and consumed more. So the workers went into debt, depended more and more heavily on moving up in their jobs and securing more income, and ultimately were convinced that their only possibility for transcending their chronic dissatisfaction was to please their employers and never do or say anything disruptive or radical.

But such a treadmill was endless. The harder one tried to overcome one's chronic dissatisfaction and misery, the more dissatisfied and miserable one became. In a system of invidious social ranking and conspicuous consumption, workers rarely blamed the "system," the "vested interest," or the "absentee owners" for their plight. They generally blamed themselves, resulting in a further decline in self-esteem and self-confidence and a tighter clinging to the values of pecuniary culture.

Veblen hoped that the more secure elements of the working class, in whom the instinct of workmanship was most highly developed, might someday transform capitalism. He envisioned a better society in which absentee ownership would be a thing of the past, in which there would no longer be a business class to subvert industry, and in which production would reflect the needs of all people rather than being controlled solely by the profits, and greed, of a tiny minority. But his social theory showed that capitalism systematically created an overwhelming conservative prejudice in most people and that, therefore, this transformation of capitalism would certainly be a profoundly difficult task.

SUMMARY

In the late nineteenth century the potential profits made possible by mass production and nationwide markets led to intense industrial warfare. Through the crushing of competitors and not infrequently the swindling of the general public, a handful of giant corporations came to dominate the American economy.

The passage of the Sherman Act and the establishment of various government regulatory agencies were ostensibly aimed at controlling these giant corporations. In practice, however, government tended to aid these giants in consolidating and stabilizing their massive empires.

[40]Veblen, *Instinct of Workmanship,* p. 95.

Thorstein Veblen's writings best reflect and describe the effects of this collusion of government and big business on the welfare of the general public. Veblen stressed the distinction between industry (which produces needed articles for human well-being) and business (which produces profits for the wealthy absentee owners by sabotaging industry). He analyzed imperialism, militarism, and the general "chronic misery" caused by emulative consumption in an acquisitive, competitive, capitalist society. The profundity of many of Veblen's insights is unmatched in American intellectual history.

CHAPTER *10*

Economic Prosperity and Evolutionary Socialism

In the late nineteenth and early twentieth centuries, the socialist analysis of capitalism was profoundly affected by two developments: (1) the economic and political gains made by the working class and (2) the imperialistic carving up of the economically less developed areas of the world by the major capitalist powers. These developments split the socialist movement into two camps. Some became convinced that governmental power could be peacefully acquired by socialists and used to promote economic and social reforms that would result in gradual evolution to socialism. The more militant socialists, however, continued to accept the Marxist view of the class nature of capitalist governments and to insist on the necessity of revolution. This chapter considers the economic and political gains of the working class and the resultant conservative reformist tendency in the socialist movement. Imperialism and revolutionary socialism are discussed in Chapter 11.

THE ECONOMIC AND POLITICAL GAINS OF THE WORKING CLASS

During the second half of the nineteenth century, the real income of workers rose throughout the capitalist world. In England the average real wage increased rapidly throughout the 1860s and early 1870s. By 1875 it was 40 percent higher than it had been in 1862. After 10 years in which wages sagged, they again rose sharply between 1885 and 1900. By 1900, the average real wage was 33 percent higher than in 1875 and 84 percent higher than in 1850. Most of the gains in real wages can be attributed to the advent of mass production techniques that permitted the prices of many commodities consumed by laborers to be lowered. As a result of new methods of producing and labor's greater purchasing power, there was a fundamental change in patterns of consumption. Workers began to eat more meats, fruits, and sweets. Mass-produced shoes and clothing, furniture, newspapers, bicycles, and other new products came within the reach of many. Unquestionably, the average worker's lot improved substantially during the period.

It should be mentioned, however, that averages can be misleading. Two late nineteenth-century social surveys revealed that about 40 percent of the working class in London and York still lived in abject poverty. The fact that this could be so after a half-century of rapid increases in average real wages gives an indication of the truly pitiful conditions that must have existed in the early nineteenth century.

Similar gains were being made in western Europe and the United States during this period, and in most of these countries economic gains were accompanied by political gains. Most of the industrialized capitalist countries had nearly complete male suffrage by the early twentieth century. Political parties were created that were devoted to furthering the cause of workingmen. The most successful of these was the German Social Democratic party, formed at a meeting in Gotha in 1875 between the followers of Marx, led by Wilhelm Leibknecht and August Bebel, and the followers of Ferdinand Lassalle. The program adopted in this first party congress was known as the *Gotha Programme.* It represented a compromise that was bitterly attacked by Marx.

Marx believed his followers had made too many concessions to the Lassallian outlook, which conceived of the government as a neutral instrument to be used by workers to achieve socialism through peaceful reform. Excessive concern with reformism could, he believed, divert workers from their task of overthrowing capitalism. The conflict between the revolutionary socialists and the reformers was to remain important in the Social Democratic party for the next 40 years. Ultimately Marx's misgivings proved prophetic, however, and the reformists became dominant in the party.

In 1874 the two socialist groups had polled 340,000 votes. In the election of 1877 the newly formed party received more than 500,000 votes and had 12 representatives elected to the Reichstag. This show of strength frightened Bismarck, and in 1878 a series of infamous antisocialist laws was passed. Many of the more militant socialist leaders were exiled, and the Social Democratic party was prohibited from holding meetings or publishing newspapers.

In spite of this repression the party continued to grow. It received 549,000 votes in 1884 and 763,000 in 1887. By 1890 the Social Democratic party polled 1,427,000 votes and had become the largest single party in the Reich. The repression had not worked; the antisocialist laws were abandoned.

In both England and Germany, as well as several other western European countries, it appeared to many socialists that the capitalist system had provided the workers with an escalator on which they could steadily and peacefully advance in both economic well-being and political power.

THE FABIAN SOCIALISTS

In England, despite the brilliant achievements of individual Marxists like William Morris, the socialist movement was largely non-Marxist; the Fabian Society was the primary influence on English socialism, and it rejected Marx's analysis completely. In their economic analysis the Fabians used orthodox neoclassical utility theory. They believed labor received an amount equal to what it produced, and capitalists and landlords received the value of what was produced with their capital and land. The chief cause of the injustice was not that labor's surplus value was appropriated by capitalists but rather that all the income from ownership accrued to a tiny percentage of the population. The only way to achieve an equitable society would be to divide the income from ownership equally, and this could be done only through government ownership of the means of production.

On the issue of the nature and role of the government, the Fabians differed radically from Marx. For Marx, the government was an instrument of coercion controlled and used by the ruling class to perpetuate the privileges inherent in the capitalist system. The Fabians believed that in a parliamentary democracy based on universal suffrage the state was a neutral agency that could be freely used by the majority to reform the social and economic system. Because the working class was the majority in a capitalist economy, they were confident that, step by step, piecemeal reforms would strip away the privileges of the owning class and result in socialism achieved by peaceful evolution rather than violent revolution.

The most influential of the Fabians were George Bernard Shaw, Sidney and Beatrice Webb, and Graham Wallas. For many years Shaw was the principal draftsman of Fabian publications and was widely known as the society's most lucid and forceful spokesman. The worst evil of capitalism was, in Shaw's opinion, the enormous inequality of wealth and income that prevailed in every capitalist country. The cause of the most egregious inequality was the income that accrued from ownership of land and capital. Such unearned incomes, which Shaw combined under the label of "rents," created extremes of incredible wealth and power for a tiny minority while the majority of those who created the wealth lived in poverty. He also believed the capitalist system suffered from periods of chronic underproduction and incurred enormous wastes by devoting productive capacity to the creation of mountains of useless consumption goods for the rich. By expropriating these rents and eliminating the wastes and inefficiencies of capitalism, a socialist government could easily provide economic security and an ample livelihood for everyone.

The only ultimately just distribution of income was absolute equality. To achieve this, it would be necessary to sever any connection between productive services rendered and monetary remuneration. This, in turn, would require a reliance on noneconomic, or social, incentives to accomplish the necessary productive tasks. Shaw envisioned this equality not as an immediate possibility but only as a long-run goal.

Perhaps the least attractive aspect of Shaw's socialism was his extreme elitist bias. He had little faith in democracy. Rather, he believed an efficient and just organization of society required that policymaking and administrative tasks be handled by experts. According to one eminent historian of socialism, Shaw "was apt to admire dictators, if only they would give the experts a free hand."[1]

Shaw's elitism was shown most clearly in his defense of British imperialism. He believed that

> no group or nation had any right to stand in the way of the full development in the interest of the whole world of any productive resource of which it stood possessed, and that accordingly higher civilizations had a complete right to work their will upon backward peoples and to override national or sectional claims, provided only that by doing so they increased the total wealth of the human race.[2]

In view of these opinions, Shaw's leadership of the pro-imperialist faction of the Fabian Society is easily understandable.[3]

Among the general public Shaw was probably the most influential of the Fabians. Within the Fabian Society itself, however, the most influential theoreticians were Sidney and Beatrice Webb. The Webbs were probably the most serious scholars in the Fabian Society and undoubtedly among the most prolific writers in the history of socialism.

One of their first and most influential books, *Industrial Democracy,* rejected the notion that workers had neither the desire nor the capability to run their enterprises. Rather, industrial democracy under socialism was envisioned as a scheme in which industry was controlled by professional managers, who in turn were to be made accountable to the general population through supervision by a democratically elected parliament, local governments, and consumers' cooperatives.

They rejected the idea that socialism would involve ownership of all industry by the national government. Ownership should reside both in national government and in any of a variety of smaller local or regional administrative units. The scope of an enterprise's activities and the portion of the population affected by these activities should, they believed, determine the nature of social ownership of any particular business firm.

In *A Constitution for the Socialist Commonwealth of Great Britain* they proposed the creation of two separate, democratically elected parliaments. One was to handle political affairs and the other to preside over social and economic affairs. In addition, they advocated a system of local governments based on

---

[1]G. D. H. Cole, *A History of Socialist Thought,* vol. III, part 1 (London: Macmillan, 1956), p. 211.

[2]Ibid., p. 219.

[3]See Chapter 11.

local units with fixed geographic boundaries. These local governments, however, were to be combined in various ways to form administrative units to supervise and control different economic and social services. The particular size, shape, and location of these administrative units would depend on the nature of the service involved.

In general, it may be said that the Webbs wrote a great deal about the nature of the socialist society they would have liked to have seen created at some future time but very little about specific tactics for transforming existing society into that future socialist system. They believed labor unions should confine their activities to representing the economic interests of their members in the collective bargaining process and should not act as insurgents. In fact, they seemed to see little hope for political change coming from a broadly based movement of workers. Rather, they assumed that an intellectual appeal might ultimately change the general public's opinions in a manner that would lead to the election of members of Parliament who were sympathetic to socialist ideas.

The Fabian Society gradually succeeded in gaining influence in the parliamentary Labour party. By 1918 the Labour party had adopted a socialist program that reflected the Fabian Society's views and attitudes. By the 1920s the Labour party had formed a government, and the cause of socialism via the voting booth seemed to many to be on the road to triumph.

The Fabians had never wanted to be a mass membership society. They were a small, select group, and most of their efforts were devoted to educating the middle class to accept socialism. They published innumerable tracts exposing the poverty and injustice they found in early twentieth-century England. Remedies for these evils would be forthcoming through paternalistic government actions and programs, they believed, once the government was made truly democratic and the people were made aware of these conditions.

However debatable their certainty that socialism could be achieved through education, it is undeniable that the Fabians offered an impressive group of teachers. Some of the most brilliant of the English intellectual elite were members of the society, including, in addition to the Webbs and Shaw, H. G. Wells, Sydney Olivier, and Graham Wallas. With such sponsorship the Fabians' reformist, evolutionary socialism became eminently respectable. One could espouse socialism and still remain completely secure in a comfortable middle-class niche in English capitalistic society.

THE GERMAN REVISIONISTS

The German counterparts of the English Fabians were the Revisionists. At the turn of the century the Social Democratic party was nominally a Marxist party. A large portion of the membership argued, however, that the course of history had proved Marx wrong on many issues, and that a "revision" of Marx's ideas was necessary to make them relevant to German economic and social life. The most famous of the Revisionists was Eduard Bernstein, who presented a detailed critique of Marxist ideas in his best-known work, *Evolu-*

tionary Socialism, published in 1899. Bernstein maintained that capitalism was not approaching any kind of crisis or collapse and, indeed, had never been more viable. Marx was also wrong, Bernstein declared, in predicting the concentration of all industries in the hands of a few giant firms. He argued that enterprises of all sizes thrived and would continue to do so (despite the fact that corporate concentration and the cartel movement were more extreme in Germany than in any other capitalist country). Even if large trusts did dominate the economy, Bernstein insisted, there would be a "splitting up of shares," making petty capitalists of a very large percentage of the population, including many workers. He believed the economy had already gone far in this direction: "The number of members of the possessing classes is today not smaller but larger. The enormous increase of social wealth is not accompanied by a decreasing number of large capitalists, but by an increasing number of capitalists of all degrees."[4]

Furthermore, even workers who received no profits, rents, interest, or dividends were rapidly becoming much better off. Improvements in the general standard of living and the democratization of the government had made revolution not only highly unlikely but also morally undesirable. The hopes of the working class lay more "in a steady advance than in the possibilities offered by a catastrophic crash."[5]

Bernstein's book contained much more than the simple substitution of "peaceful evolution" for "revolution": It was, in fact, a direct attack on nearly all of the intellectual foundations of Marxism. Capitalism was not, he asserted, characterized by two polarized, conflicting classes. Class struggle could hardly be the moving force of history when class distinctions were rapidly breaking down and frequently nonexistent. Workers were far from being a homogeneous mass, he argued, and therefore "the feeling of solidarity between groups of workers . . . is only very moderate in amount."[6] Instead of two fundamentally antagonistic classes, Bernstein saw a multiplicity of interest groups that were often in conflict but even more often united in a collective "community."

From his rejection of the class nature of capitalist society, it follows that Bernstein had to reject Marx's theory of historical materialism. He argued that as society developed, economic forces were coming to be less and less important and ideological and ethical forces becoming increasingly significant:

Modern society is much richer than earlier societies in ideologies which are not determined by economics and by nature operating as an economic force. Science, the arts, a whole series of social relations are nowadays much less dependent on economics than formerly they were; or let us say, in order to leave no room for misunderstanding, the point of economic development that has now been reached leaves the ideological, and especially the ethical, factors greater scope for independent activity than used to be the case.

[4]Eduard Bernstein, *Evolutionary Socialism* (New York: Schocken Books, 1961 [first published in 1899]), p. xii.
[5]Ibid., p. xiv.
[6]Ibid., p. 120.

Consequently, the interdependence of cause and effect between technological, economic evolution and the evolution of other social tendencies is becoming continually more indirect; and accordingly the necessities of the former are losing much of their power to dictate the form of the latter.[7]

He similarly rejected Marx's theory of surplus value. Marx had asserted that surplus value was created in the process of production by living labor alone. Bernstein simply dismissed this theory by stating that surplus value "can only be grasped as a concrete fact by thinking of the whole economy of society."[8] This, he believed, was a most damning criticism of Marx because the theory of surplus value was seen as the scientific basis for Marx's socialism. Henceforth, Bernstein averred, socialism would have to be based on ethical and not scientific foundations.

Perhaps the most fundamental difference between Marx and Bernstein was their difference concerning the nature of government in a capitalist society. Marx had asserted (and Bernstein's contemporary Marxist adversaries continued to assert) that capitalist governments were primarily instruments of class rule. Capitalists maintained their economic status and privileges through capitalistic property relations. They used their wealth, in turn, to control the political process in order to ensure the continuation of governments that were, above all else, committed to the defense of these property relations.

Bernstein dismissed the Marxist view of capitalist government as "political atavism." The Marxist notion may have once been valid, but contemporary extensions of suffrage had, he believed, invalidated it. Universal suffrage could make all people equally powerful in selecting the government and could thereby destroy class conflict by making each individual an "equal partner" in the community. "The right to vote," he wrote, "in a democracy makes its members virtually partners in the community, and this virtual partnership must in the end lead to real partnership."[9]

Thus Bernstein, like the Fabians, rejected the notion that the government in a capitalist society had an inherent class bias. In a capitalist democracy each worker was seen as an equal partner with each capitalist, and they could all be induced, through moral appeals, to use peaceful political means to promote the general interests of the entire community.

THE FATE OF EVOLUTIONARY SOCIALISM

Throughout the period from the publication of *Evolutionary Socialism* until the outbreak of World War I, Bernstein's ideas evoked intense controversy in the Social Democratic party and also throughout the entire worldwide socialist movement. The issue at stake was of the utmost significance.

The Fabians and the Revisionists argued that persistence in legislating reforms would ultimately achieve socialism. No single reform would, by itself,

[7]Quoted in Cole, *History of Socialist Thought,* p. 280.
[8]Bernstein, *Evolutionary Socialism,* p. 38.
[9]Ibid., p. 144.

threaten the capitalist structure, but eventually the cumulative effect of many reforms would be the peaceful abdication of the capitalist class.

Marxists continued to believe, however, that as soon as any reforms seriously threatened the privileges and prerogatives of property rights, the capitalist class would resort to intimidation, repression, and ultimately abolition of the democratic rights of workers rather than seeing their economic power and social status eroded. When this happened, the working class would have to be prepared for revolution. If it were not, all of its hard-won concessions and advances would be lost.

By the beginning of World War I, it was obvious that the conservatives in the socialist movement had won at least a temporary victory over the revolutionaries. Capitalism in both England and Germany had passed through a period of prosperity in which the plight of workers had improved and a general feeling of optimism prevailed. In England the Fabian philosophy had come to dominate the Labour party, and in Germany the Revisionists had gained control of the Social Democratic party.

The subsequent history of those two parties was to illustrate the basic weakness of socialism that relied entirely on legislative reforms. Even though many party leaders continued to propound socialist ideas for some time, it was found that the pressure to attain an electoral majority continually forced party policies toward greater conservatism. In the 1950s both parties officially announced that they had given up the quest for social ownership of the means of production, distribution, and exchange. They asserted that ameliorative legislation to improve the living standards of the poor was all that remained to achieve a good and just society.

SUMMARY

In the late nineteenth and early twentieth centuries, improved working conditions, living standards, and political rights led to a split in the socialist movement. While the Marxist revolutionary socialists continued to affirm the necessity of a socialist revolution, a new school of reformist, evolutionary socialists argued that socialism could be achieved through gradual, peaceful legislative reforms.

In England, reformist socialism found its ablest leaders in George Bernard Shaw, Sidney and Beatrice Webb, and the other members of the Fabian Society. In Germany, it was Eduard Bernstein and the Revisionists who led the movement toward reformism. Both of these parties were ultimately pushed, by the pressures of achieving electoral majorities, to abandon the most fundamental tenet of socialism—socialization of the means of production.

CHAPTER 11

Imperialism and Revolutionary Socialism

The idea that a democratic government in a capitalist country could be used to effect a gradual and peaceful transition from capitalism to socialism led to a controversy that split the European socialist movement.[1] However, the issue of imperialism was of equal if not greater significance in precipitating this division among socialists. During the late nineteenth and early twentieth centuries, European economic imperialism was most intensive. The nature and importance of an appropriate socialist response to imperialism were issues that created profound divisions among socialists—divisions that persist to this day.

EUROPEAN IMPERIALISM

India was one of the earliest and most dramatic cases of European imperialism. The East India Company had traded extensively in India for 150 years before the conquest of Bengal in 1757. During this period India was relatively advanced economically. Its methods of production and its industrial and commercial organization could definitely be compared with those prevailing in western Europe. In fact, India had been manufacturing and exporting the finest muslins and luxurious fabrics since the time when most western Europeans were backward primitive peoples.

[1]See Chapter 10.

After the conquest of Bengal, however, the East India Company became the ruling power in much of India, and the trade of the previous 150 years turned to harsh exploitation. It has been estimated that between 1757 and 1815 the British took between £500 million and £1000 million of wealth out of India.[2] The incredible magnitude of this sum can be appreciated when compared with the £36 million that represented the total capital investment of all the joint stock companies operating in India.[3]

The policy of the East India Company in the last decades of the eighteenth century and in the early nineteenth century reflected two objectives. First, in the short run the myriad of greedy officials sought personal fortunes overnight: "These officials were absolute, irresponsible and rapacious, and they emptied the private hoards. Their only thought was to wring some hundreds of thousands of pounds out of the natives as quickly as possible, and hurry home to display their wealth. Enormous fortunes were thus rapidly accumulated at Calcutta, while thirty millions of human beings were reduced to the extremity of wretchedness."[4]

A British observer described this ruthless quest for wealth in similar terms: "No Mahratta raid ever devastated a countryside with the thoroughness with which both the Company [East India Company] and, above all, the Company's servants in their individual capacities, sucked dry the plain of Bengal. In fact, in their blind rage for enrichment they took more from the Bengali peasants than those peasants could furnish and live. And the peasants duly died."[5]

The second was a long-run goal: to discourage or eliminate Indian manufacturers and make India dependent on British industries by forcing the Indians to concentrate on raw materials and export them to supply the textile looms and other British manufacturers. The policy was brutally, methodically—and successfully—executed.

The total effect of this was that the British administration of India systematically destroyed all the fibres and foundations of Indian economy and substituted for it the parasitic landowner and moneylender. Its commercial policy destroyed the Indian artisan and created the infamous slums of the Indian cities filled with millions of starving and diseased paupers. Its economic policy broke down whatever beginnings there were of an indigenous industrial development and promoted the proliferations of speculators, petty businessmen, agents, and sharks of all descriptions eking out a sterile and precarious livelihood in the meshes of a decaying society.[6]

[2]Paul A. Baran, *The Political Economy of Growth* (New York: Monthly Review Press, 1962), p. 145.
[3]Ibid.
[4]Brooks Adams, *The Law of Civilization and Decay, An Essay on History* (New York: Macmillan, 1896); quoted in ibid., p. 146.
[5]John Strachey, "Famine in Bengal," in Robert Lekachman, ed., *The Varieties of Economics,* vol. 1 (New York: Meridian, 1962), p. 296.
[6]Baran, *Political Economy of Growth,* p. 149.

It was only later, however, after the period of extensive railroad construction beginning in 1857, that the British thoroughly penetrated the interior of India. British investors who sank money into these railroads were guaranteed a 5 percent return by the government, which enforced a provision that if profits fell below 5 percent the Indian people would be taxed to make up the difference. Thus Indians were taxed to ensure that British investors would have adequate transport for further economic exploitation of the Indian interior.

Despite such harsh measures, the age of European imperialism really did not get under way on a broad, pervasive front until the last quarter of the nineteenth century. Between 1775 and 1875 the European countries had lost about as much colonial territory as they had won. The opinion was widely held that colonies were expensive luxuries.

All this changed suddenly and drastically after 1875. By 1900 Great Britain had grabbed 4,500,000 square miles, which she added to her empire; France had gobbled up 3,500,000; Germany, 1,000,000; Belgium, 900,000; Russia, 500,000; Italy, 185,000; and the United States, 125,000. Imperialism ran rampant as one-fourth of the world's population was subjugated and put under European and American domination.

Imperialism in Africa

By 1800 the Europeans had hardly penetrated beyond the coastal areas of Africa. By the early twentieth century, after a 100-year orgy of land grabbing and empire building, they controlled over 10 million square miles, or about 93 percent of the continent. In that gigantic plunder, various European powers sought to acquire the abundant minerals and agricultural commodities of the "dark continent."

The brutality of the European exploitation of Africa was perhaps most severe in the Belgian Congo. Belgian King Leopold II had sent H. M. Stanley into central Africa in 1879. Serving a private, profit-seeking company headed by Leopold and some of his associates, Stanley had a network of trading posts constructed and also duped native chiefs into signing "treaties" that established a commercial empire stretching over 900,000 square miles. Leopold set himself up as sovereign ruler of the Congo Free State and proceeded to exploit the natural and human resources of the area for the profits of his company.

The exploitation was ruthless. Natives were forced through outright physical coercion to gather rubber from the wild rubber trees and ivory from the elephants. Leopold confiscated all land that was not directly cultivated by the natives and placed it under "government ownership." Atrocities of the worst sort were committed to force the natives to submit to a very burdensome tax system that included taxes payable in rubber and ivory as well as in labor obligations.

By the twentieth century the Congo had also become a rich source of diamonds, uranium, copper, palm oil, palm kernels, and coconuts. In general, it can be said that the Congo was one of the most profitable of European imperialistic exploits as well as one of the most scandalous.

The British grabbed the most populous and also the richest holdings in Africa. In 1870 Cecil Rhodes went to South Africa for his health. Within two years his genius for organizing and controlling joint stock companies and his ability to corner the market on diamonds had made him a millionaire. In later years, the British South Africa Company, which Rhodes headed, came to control South Africa completely. Although it was a private, profit-seeking company, it had all the power of government, including the authority (given in its charter of 1889) to "make treaties, promulgate laws, preserve the peace, maintain a police force, and acquire new concessions."

The expansionist policies of the British South Africa Company led to the Boer War (1899–1902), which crushed the Dutch republics (the Orange Free State and the Transvaal republic) and gave Britain complete control over all South Africa. South Africa proved to be a rich mining region. But the legacy of British and Dutch imperialism is most vividly seen today in the suppression of the blacks, who constitute the vast majority of the population.

The other instances of imperialism in Africa are no less deserving of study. It must suffice in this short account, however, to mention that on the eve of World War I France held about 40 percent of Africa (much of it within the Sahara desert), England controlled 30 percent, and roughly 23 percent was divided among Germany, Belgium, Portugal, and Spain.

Imperialism in Asia

The results of the British takeover of India were evident by the turn of the twentieth century. In 1901 the per capita income was less than $10 per year, over two-thirds of the population were badly undernourished, and most native Indian manufacturing had been either ruined or taken over by the British. Nearly 90 percent of the population struggled to subsist in villages where the average holding was only 5 acres and farming techniques were primitive. Much of the meager produce was paid out in taxes, rents, and profits that accrued to the British. Famine, disease, and misery were rife. In 1891 the average Indian lived less than 26 years and usually died in misery.

Much of the rest of Asia was also subjugated during this period. In 1878 the British overran Afghanistan and placed it under the Indian government, and in 1907 Persia was divided between Russia and Britain.

In 1858 the French had used the murder of a Spanish missionary as the rationalization for invading Annam, a tributary state of China. They soon established a French colony in what is now Vietnam. With this toehold the French succeeded, through war and intrigue, in bringing all the territory of Indochina under their domination by 1887.

The Malay Peninsula and the Malay Archipelago (which stretches for nearly 3000 miles) were also carved up. The British grabbed Singapore and the Malay States, the northern part of Borneo, and south New Guinea. Another part of New Guinea was taken by the Germans, and most of the remaining islands (an area comprising about 735,000 square miles) went to the Dutch.

AMERICAN IMPERIALISM

Throughout much of the nineteenth century American imperialism channeled all its energies into conquering the continent and exterminating the native American Indian population. The Samoa Islands were America's first overseas imperialist acquisition. In 1878 the natives of Pago Pago granted the Americans the right to use their harbor. Eleven years later, the islands had been conquered and divided between the United States and Germany.

Similarly, Pearl Harbor became a U.S. naval station in 1887. In a very short time American capitalists controlled most of Hawaii's sugar production. The tiny minority of white Americans soon revolted against Queen Lili-uokalani's rule and, with the help of U.S. Marines, subjugated the native population. In 1898 Hawaii was officially annexed by the United States.

It was also in 1898 that the United States used the convenient sinking of the battleship *Maine* as an excuse to declare war on Spain and "liberate" the Cubans from Spanish oppression. Recognizing that it was no match for the United States, the Spanish government accepted every American demand, but the United States declared war anyway as a "measure of atonement" for the *Maine.* The American victory gave it Puerto Rico, Guam, and the Philippine Islands outright, and the newly "independent" Cubans soon found American capitalists taking over most of their agriculture and commerce. Cuban independence had been restricted by a provision that the United States could intervene at its own discretion into Cuba's internal affairs "for the protection of life, property and individual liberty," a slogan that has been used to justify imperialism more than a few times. American troops invaded Cuba in 1906, 1911, and 1917 before secure control was finally established.

The Filipinos, who had been fighting for their independence from Spain, discovered the American brand to be no better than Spanish domination. President McKinley had decided that Americans were obligated "to educate the Filipinos and uplift and Christianize them," but the Filipinos, who had been Roman Catholics for centuries, resisted American "Christianization." It took 60,000 American troops, as well as endless atrocities and concentration camps, before the Filipinos were finally "uplifted" and "educated."

In 1901, when the republic of Colombia refused to sell a strip of land (on which the Panama Canal was to be constructed) to the United States, President Roosevelt took action. A Panamanian insurrection was organized with American approval and help. United States warships were strategically placed to prevent Colombian troops from moving in to suppress the rebellion. The revolt started on November 3, 1903; on November 6, the United States extended diplomatic recognition to the "new nation"; on November 18, the United States had the Canal Zone on much more favorable terms than it had originally offered.

In 1904 President Roosevelt announced that the United States believed in the principle of self-determination for nations that acted "with reasonable efficiency and decency in social and political matters." He added, however, that "chronic wrongdoing, or any impotence which results in a general loosening of the ties of civilized society, may in America, as elsewhere, ultimately require intervention by some civilized nation."[7]

In 1909 U.S. Marines invaded Nicaragua to overthrow José Santos Zelaya, who threatened American economic concessions there. American troops were back in Nicaragua in 1912. In 1915 American Marines invaded Haiti, and in 1916 American troops overwhelmed the Dominican Republic and established a military government there.

By World War I the United States had seized or otherwise controlled Samoa, Midway Island, Hawaii, Puerto Rico, Guam, the Philippines, the island of Tutuila, Cuba, Santo Domingo, Haiti, Nicaragua, and the Panama Canal Zone.

IMPERIALISM AND EVOLUTIONARY SOCIALISM

The Boer War jolted British public opinion and resulted in strong conflicts among many radicals and socialists. On the one hand, it produced an abundance of jingoist sentiment and imperialist ideology that influenced some socialists; on the other hand, J. A. Hobson's *Imperialism: A Study* caustically ridiculed this sentiment and ideology and advanced a theory of imperialism that was to have a profound influence on Marxists and many non-Marxist socialists.

Imperialism, according to Hobson, was a struggle for political and economic domination of areas of the world occupied by "lower races." Its "economic taproot" was the necessity for advanced capitalist countries to find markets for goods and capital produced domestically but for which there was inadequate domestic demand. Evoking traditions of nationalism and militarism, it could "appeal to the lust of quantitative acquisitiveness and of forceful domination surviving in a nation from early centuries of animal struggle for existence."[8]

The basic cause of the deficiency in domestic demand was, Hobson believed, a severely inequitable distribution of income that resulted in a distorted allocation of resources, which led, in turn, to the quest for foreign markets. Hobson argued that the imperialist tendencies of the late nineteenth and early twentieth centuries could be reversed only by reform radical enough to effect a more equitable distribution of income. He summarized his position succinctly in the following passage:

> There is no necessity to open up new foreign markets; the home markets are capable of indefinite expansion. Whatever is produced in England can be consumed in England, provided that the "income," or power to demand commodities, is properly distributed. This only appears untrue because of the unnatural and unwholesome specialization to which this country has been subjected, based upon a bad distribution of economic resources, which

[7]Quoted in G. C. Fite and J. D. Reese, *An Economic History of the United States*, 2d ed. (Boston: Houghton Mifflin, 1965), p. 472.

[8]Quotations in this paragraph are from J. A. Hobson, *Imperialism: A Study* (London: Allen & Unwin, 1938 [first published in 1902]), p. 368.

has induced an overgrowth of certain manufacturing trades for the express purpose of effecting foreign sales. If the industrial revolution had taken place in an England founded upon equal access by all classes to land, education, and legislation, specialization in manufactures would not have gone so far . . . ; foreign trade would have been less important though more steady; the standard of life for all portions of the population would have been high, and the present rate of national consumption would probably have given full, constant, remunerative employment to a far larger quantity of private and public capital than is now being employed.[9]

The issue of whether publicly to denounce English imperialism bitterly divided the Fabians. Sydney Olivier's insistence that the society's executive committee issue a pronouncement condemning the Boer War in particular and imperialism in general was rejected by one vote, but the committee agreed to the demand that the issue be put to a general vote.

Led by George Bernard Shaw, the pro-imperialist faction argued that small, backward nations could not manage their own affairs and should not be considered as nations at all, and that the advanced European nations thus had a duty to police and manage the internal affairs of these backward peoples for their own welfare. The debate was bitter. Finally, 45 percent of the membership voted to condemn English imperialism, and 55 percent opted to approve of or ignore imperialism. Immediately, 18 members of the society, including several of its most prominent personalities, handed in their resignations.

The sentiments of the German Revisionists were similar to those of the Fabians, the majority either approving of European imperialism or not considering it a proper issue on which to take a stand. Bernstein, for example, wrote, "Only a conditional right of savages to the land occupied by them can be recognized. The higher civilization ultimately can claim a higher right."[10] Orthodox Marxists, however, were virtually unanimous in condemning imperialism, which they analyzed as only the latest stage in the historical development of capitalism: Capitalists were forced by the mounting contradictions of the economic system to turn frantically to economic exploitation of more backward areas.

ROSA LUXEMBURG'S ANALYSIS OF IMPERIALISM

Rosa Luxemburg was one of the most important political leaders and exponents of orthodox Marxism. Her book *The Accumulation of Capital* contained a description and analysis of imperialism that was to exert a strong influence on subsequent generations of socialists.

Luxemburg began her analysis by a review of Marx's analysis of the process of *capitalist commodity production* discussed in Chapter 7, the process

---

[9]Ibid., pp. 88–89.
[10]Eduard Bernstein, *Evolutionary Socialism* (New York: Schocken Books, 1961 [first published in 1899]), p. xii.

in which capitalists started with some given amount of money and purchased one commodity—labor power—and then sold a different commodity—that produced by labor in the production process. From the sales of the products of labor, they received a greater value than they laid out in expenses for raw materials, goods in process, and labor; that is, they received surplus value, or profits. The money they received in sales, however, had to be spent by purchasers of their commodities.

These purchasers of their commodities could be the laborers spending their wages for the means of subsistence, or other capitalists buying the raw materials and goods in process necessary for production. But we have already said that in order for surplus value to exist the proceeds from sales of commodities must exceed wages and expenditures on raw materials and goods in process. Part of the difference might be made up by capitalists' expenditures on consumption. Luxemburg observed, however, that capitalists' consumption expenditures typically make up only a small part of the surplus value they receive.

Another part of the deficiency in expenditures could be made up by capitalists purchasing capital goods that were not necessary to maintain the current level of production but were desired so that future production could be expanded. But the desire to expand production would have to be predicated on the expectation of greater demand for consumption goods, and it was the insufficiency of this demand for consumption goods that represented the crux of the problem. Capitalists would accumulate capital goods not for their own sake but only in the expectation that this accumulation would increase their profits. The inescapable conclusion, for Luxemburg, was that from within the internal sphere of a capitalist economy the expenditures of capitalists and workers could not for any lengthy period be sufficient to permit continuous realization of the surplus value generated from expanding commodity production.

Yet capitalism had been more or less continually expanding for well over a century, and Luxemburg sought to discover the source of the necessary additional expenditures that made this expansion possible. This source she found in the historical tendency of the capitalist mode of production to continually expand into noncapitalist areas, bring these areas under its control, and incorporate them within the domain of capitalist relations. The expenditures of these noncapitalist areas in the purchase of commodities produced in capitalist areas would represent the additional necessary demand:

> From the aspect both of realizing the surplus value and of procuring the material elements of constant capital, international trade is a prime necessity for the historical existence of capitalism—an international trade which under actual conditions is essentially an exchange between capitalistic and noncapitalistic modes.[11]

[11]Rosa Luxemburg, *The Accumulation of Capital* (New York: Monthly Review Press, 1964), p. 359.

Luxemburg therefore believed that "imperialism is the political expression of the accumulation of capital in its competitive struggle for what remains still open of the non-capitalist environment."[12] The continuous diminution of the size of the unexploited noncapitalist areas of the world had led to a situation in which "imperialism grows in lawlessness and violence, both in aggression against the noncapitalist world and in ever more serious conflicts among the competing capitalist countries."[13]

Within this theoretical framework Luxemburg wrote penetrating and insightful descriptions of the way in which the development of capitalism necessitated the growth of nationalism, militarism, and racism. In her analysis of military spending, for example, she understood the dual function such spending served in protecting capitalist empires around the world while providing the necessary stimulation of aggregate demand at home:

> The multitude of individual and insignificant demands for a whole range of commodities . . . is now replaced by a comprehensive and homogeneous demand of the state. And the satisfaction of this demand presupposes a big industry of the highest order. It requires the most favorable conditions for the production of surplus value and for accumulation. In the form of government contracts for army supplies the scattered purchasing power of the consumers is concentrated in large quantities and, free of the vagaries and subjective fluctuations of personal consumption, it achieves an almost automatic regularity and rhythmic growth. Capital itself ultimately controls this automatic and rhythmic movement of militarist production through the legislature and a press whose function is to mould so-called "public opinion." That is why this particular province of capitalist accumulation at first seems capable of infinite expansion. All other attempts to expand markets and set up operational bases for capital largely depend on historical, social and political factors beyond the control of capital, whereas production for militarism represents a province whose regular and progressive expansion seems primarily determined by capital itself.
>
> In this way capital turns historical necessity into a virtue.[14]

This passage was written in 1913. This level of clear understanding of the role of military expenditures was not widely achieved among economists until about a half-century later, when the forces Luxemburg was describing had developed well beyond what they had been on the eve of World War I.[15]

Despite such brilliant insights, Luxemburg's analysis of imperialism rested on a faulty theoretical structure. Noncapitalist consumers are not automatically a source of increased demand. If products are to be sold to them, products must also be purchased from them—otherwise they would have no foreign currency with which to make the purchases. The net result on aggregate demand from this buying and selling cannot be determined in advance.

---

[12]Ibid., p. 446.
[13]Ibid.
[14]Ibid., p. 466.
[15]For a further discussion of the importance of military expenditures in increasing domestic aggregate demand, see Chapter 12.

Moreover, in less developed countries capitalist investments are soon yielding surplus value of their own. This tends to worsen rather than solve the problem of adequate demand.

Luxemberg's problem was that she focused on the wrong problem—underconsumption. The real driving force of imperialism was the search for profitable investment outlets to which the advanced capitalist countries could export capital. These deficiencies in the Marxist analysis of imperialism were corrected by Lenin.

LENIN'S ANALYSIS OF IMPERIALISM

The most famous and influential socialist analysis was contained in Lenin's pamphlet *Imperialism: The Highest Stage of Capitalism,* published in 1916. Lenin attempted "to show, as briefly and as popularly as possible, the principal economic characteristics of imperialism."[16] The most important was that in the imperialistic phase of capitalist development the capitalist economies were thoroughly dominated by monopolies, a development Marx had correctly foreseen. By monopolies Lenin did not mean industries consisting of only one firm (the modern economic definition of monopoly); rather, he referred to industries dominated by trusts, cartels, combinations, or a few large firms.

Drawing heavily on the German experience, Lenin argued that the development of monopolies was closely related to important changes in the banking system. Banks had assumed a position of central importance in the drive toward cartelization and had come to exercise considerable control over many of the most important industrial cartels. This control was so extensive that Lenin spoke of the imperialistic phase of capitalism as the age of "finance capital."

Banks were able to mobilize huge sums of money for investment, but persistent downward pressures on domestic profit rates dictated that investment outlets be sought outside the home country. Lenin, unlike Hobson, did not believe the necessity to export commodities was the most important economic cause of imperialism. Rather, it was the necessity to export capital. Backward areas offered a large and inexpensive labor force and lucrative investment prospects.

In the imperialist phase of capitalism the various governments fought to gain access to privileged and protected markets for the combines and cartels within their own political boundaries. At the same time, these national combines and cartels sought to partition the world markets through international cartels. Deep-seated rivalry and competition, however, were more important than opportunistic short-run collaborations. Persistent national conflicts and wars were the inevitable result. In Lenin's words:

> The epoch of the newest capitalism shows us that certain relations are being established between capitalist combines, *based* on the economic division of

[16]V. I. Lenin, *Imperialism: The Highest Stage of Capitalism* (London: Lawrence & Wishart, 1939), p. 1.

the world; while parallel with this and in connection with it, certain relations are being established between political alliances, between states, on the basis of the territorial division of the world, of the struggle for colonies, of the "struggle for economic territory."[17]

Such a situation was, Lenin believed, inherently unstable. Imperialism would lead to wars among the advanced capitalist countries and to rebellions and revolutions in the exploited areas. As long as the capitalist system could support its imperialistic thrust, however, it would prolong its existence by providing outlets for excess investment funds. The extra profits that imperialism secured for the home country meant that the wages paid its workers could be raised. Thus, because it shared in the spoils, labor would be at least temporarily sapped of its revolutionary potential and controlled by right-wing labor leaders, "justly called social imperialists."[18]

If imperialism expanded the domain of capitalism and in doing so prolonged the system's existence, the tensions and conflicts it engendered were, Lenin believed, more severe than those of the competitive capitalism about which Marx wrote. Capitalism was still doomed, and socialism was still the wave of the future.

SUMMARY

The late nineteenth and early twentieth centuries witnessed the imperialistic carving up of most of the world's economically underdeveloped areas. The inhabitants of these areas were harshly and cruelly exploited for the profits of large corporations in the advanced capitalist countries.

The issue of imperialism split the evolutionary socialist movement. Many of the reform socialists, such as George Bernard Shaw and Eduard Bernstein, were strongly pro-imperialist. Others, among them J. A. Hobson, were strongly anti-imperialist. Hobson's analysis of imperialism stressed the maldistribution of wealth and income as the causes of this socioeconomic phenomenon. He advocated reforms to redistribute income and wealth within the capitalist framework.

Virtually all Marxist socialists opposed imperialism. Rosa Luxemburg saw the root problem as inadequate aggregate demand. Although her theoretical framework had some weaknesses, she had brilliant insights into the nature of imperialism, nationalism, racism, and militarism. Her weaknesses were corrected in Lenin's *Imperialism: The Highest Stage of Capitalism.* He stressed the importance of investment outlets and the capitalists' need to export capital. His analysis has remained the most influential Marxist critique of imperialism.

[17]Ibid., p. 69.
[18]Ibid., p. 99.

CHAPTER *12*

Keynesian Economics and the Great Depression

Although the period from the Civil War to 1900 was one of rapid economic expansion in the United States, these accomplishments were dwarfed by the growth that occurred between 1900 and 1929. The following figures show the percentage increase in manufacturing production in several key industries between 1899 and 1927.[1]

Chemicals, etc.	239%
Leather and products	321%
Textiles and products	449%
Food products	551%
Machinery	562%
Paper and printing	614%
Steel and products	780%
Transportation and equipment	969%

It has been estimated that U.S. wealth (the market values of all economic assets) reached $86 billion by 1900; in 1929, it stood at $361 billion.

This spectacular growth gave the United States a huge edge over all other countries in manufacturing output. The American prosperity of the 1920s was based on high and rising levels of output—though there were recessions in

[1]Figures taken from Leo Hubertman, *We the People* (New York: Monthly Review Press, 1964), p. 254.

1923 and 1927. The gross national product, the value of all goods and services produced, increased by 62 percent from 1914 to 1929. Only 3.2 percent of the labor force was unemployed in 1929, and labor productivity rose during that decade at least as fast as wages. Between 1921 and 1929, total automobile registrations increased from less than 11 million to more than 26 million; consumers spent tens of millions of dollars on radios, refrigerators, and other electric appliances that had not been available before. American manufacturing seemed to most people a permanent cornucopia destined to create affluence for all.

This leadership in manufacturing was associated with financial leadership in the world economy. The American economic empire began to rival that of England. By 1930 American businessmen owned large investments around the world. The following figures give the values of these investments in 1930:[2]

Canada	$3,942,000,000
Europe	4,929,000,000
Mexico and Central America	1,000,000,000
South America	3,042,000,000
West Indies	1,233,000,000
Africa	118,000,000
Asia	1,023,000,000
Oceania	419,000,000

THE GREAT DEPRESSION

This era of rapid growth and economic abundance came to a halt on October 24, 1929. On that "Black Thursday" the New York stock market saw security values begin a downward fall that was to destroy all faith in business. Their confidence undermined, businessmen cut back production and investment. This decreased national income and employment, which, in turn, worsened business confidence even more. Before the process came to an end, thousands of corporations had gone bankrupt, millions were unemployed, and one of the worst national catastrophes in history was under way.

Between 1929 and 1932 there were over 85,000 business failures; more than 5,000 banks suspended operations; stock values on the New York Exchange fell from $87 billion to $19 billion; unemployment rose to 12 million, with nearly one-fourth of the population having no means of sustaining themselves; farm income fell by more than half; and manufacturing output decreased by almost 50 percent.[3]

America had plunged from the world's most prosperous country to one in which tens of millions lived in desperate, abject poverty. Particularly hard hit were the blacks and other minority groups. The proportion of blacks among the unemployed was from 60 to 400 percent higher than the proportion of

[2]Ibid., p. 251.
[3]Figures taken from Louis M. Hacker, *The Course of American Economic Growth and Development* (New York: Wiley, 1970), pp. 300–301.

blacks in the general population.[4] Certain geographic areas suffered more than others. Congressman George Huddleston of Alabama reported in January 1932:

> We have about 108,000 wage and salary workers in my district. Of that number, it is my belief that not exceeding 8,000 have their normal incomes. At least 25,000 men are altogether without work. Some of them have not had a stroke of work for more than 12 months, maybe 60,000 or 75,000 are working one to five days a week, and practically all have had serious cuts in their wages and many of them do not average over $1.50 a day.[5]

Many cities reported that they could give relief payments for only a very short time, often one week, before people were forced to their own devices to subsist. The executive director of the Welfare Council of New York City described the plight of the unemployed:

> When the breadwinner is out of a job he usually exhausts his savings if he has any. Then, if he has an insurance policy, he probably borrows to the limit of its cash value. He borrows from his friends and from his relatives until they can stand the burden no longer. He gets credit from the corner grocery store and the butcher shop, and the landlord forgoes collecting the rent until interest and taxes have to be paid and something has to be done. All of these resources are finally exhausted over a period of time, and it becomes necessary for these people, who have never before been in want, to ask for assistance. The specter of starvation faces millions of people who have never before known what it was to be out of a job for any considerable period of time and who certainly have never known what it was to be absolutely up against it.[6]

The abject despair of these millions of people is at best suggested by a 1932 report describing the unloading of garbage in the Chicago city garbage dumps: "Around the truck which was unloading garbage and other refuse were about 35 men, women and children. As soon as the truck pulled away from the pile all of them started digging with sticks, some with their hands, grabbing bits of food and vegetables."[7]

What had happened to reduce the output of goods and services so drastically? Natural resources were still as plentiful as ever. The nation still had as many factories, tools, and machines. The people had the same skills and wanted to put them to work. Yet millions of workers and their families begged, borrowed, stole, and lined up for a pittance from charity, while thousands of factories stood idle or operated far below capacity. The explanation lay within

[4]See Lester V. Chandler, *America's Greatest Depression* (New York: Harper & Row, 1970), pp. 40–41.

[5]U.S. Congress, Senate, Hearings before a subcommittee of the Committee of Manufactures, 72d Cong., 1st sess., p. 239.

[6]Quoted in Chandler, *America's Greatest Depression,* pp. 41–42.

[7]Quoted in Huberman, *We the People,* p. 260.

the institutions of the capitalist market system. Factories could have been opened and people put to work, but they were not because it was not profitable for businessmen to do this. And in a capitalist economy production decisions are based primarily on the criterion of profits, not on people's needs.

THE ECONOMICS OF KEYNES

The socialist cause gained many enthusiasts in the 1930s. While the capitalist world was suffering what was perhaps its most severe depression, the Soviet economy was experiencing rapid growth. When the depression struck, it was a traumatic shock to many Americans, who had come to believe their country was destined to achieve unparalleled and unending increases in material prosperity.

The capitalist economic system seemed to be on the verge of total collapse. Drastic countermeasures were essential, but before the system could be saved the malady had to be better understood. To that task came one of the most brilliant economists of this century: John Maynard Keynes (1883–1946). In his famous book *The General Theory of Employment, Interest and Money,* Keynes attempted to show what had happened to capitalism so that it could be preserved.

Keynes began his analysis by looking at the process of production. In a given production period a firm produces a certain dollar volume of goods. From the proceeds of the sale of these goods, it pays its costs of production, which include wages, salaries, rent, supplies and raw materials, and interest on borrowed funds. What remains after these costs are paid is profit.

The important point to remember is this: What is a cost of production to the business firm represents income to an individual or another firm. The profit is also income—the income going to the owners of the firm. Because the value of production is exhausted by the costs of production and profits, and all these are income, it follows that the value of what has been produced must be equal to the incomes generated in producing it.

In terms of the entire economy the aggregate picture is the same as that for the individual firm: The value of everything produced in the economy during any period is equal to the total of all incomes received in that period. Therefore, in order for businesses to sell all that they have produced, people must spend in the aggregate all their incomes. If an amount equal to the total income in society is spent on goods and services, then the value of production is realized in sales. In that case profits remain high, and businessmen are willing to produce the same amount or more in the succeeding period.

Keynes called this a *circular flow:* Money flows from business to the public in the form of wages, salaries, rents, interests, and profits; this money then flows back to the businesses when the public buys goods and services from them. *As long as businesses sell all they have produced and make satisfactory profits,* the process continues.

This does not happen automatically, however. When money flows from businesses to the public, some of it does not flow directly back to businesses. The circular flow has leakages. To begin with, all people do not spend all their incomes. A percentage is saved, usually in banks, and therefore withdrawn from the spending stream. This saving may be offset by other people, who borrow money from banks and spend more than their income. Keynes, however, pointed out that at the peak of prosperity saving is usually greater than consumer borrowing: thus there is usually net saving, or a net leakage, from the circular income-expenditure flow.

Keynes also identified two other leakages: (1) People buy goods and services from foreign businesses, but the money spent on these imports cannot be spent on domestically produced goods. (2) The taxes people pay are also withdrawn from the income-expenditure flow.

These three leakages (savings, imports, and taxes) may be offset by three spending injections into the income-expenditure flow: (1) Imports can be offset by exports. They are exactly offset when foreigners buy goods produced in the United States in amounts equal to foreign imports purchased by Americans. (2) The government uses taxes to finance the purchase of goods and services. If it uses all taxes for this purpose and balances the budget, then government expenditures will exactly offset taxes in the spending stream. (3) If businessmen wish to expand their capital, they can finance investment in capital goods by borrowing the funds that were saved. Investment, then, may exactly offset the saving leakage.

If these three injections into the income-expenditure flow are just as large as the three leakages, then spending equals the value of production. Everything that has been produced can be sold, and prosperity reigns.

Keynes, however, believed it was unlikely that the process could continue uninterrupted for very long. Investment, which is necessary to absorb savings, enlarges the capital stock and hence increases the economy's productive capacity. In order to utilize the new productive capacity fully, production and income must increase in the next period. But with the higher income there will be more saving, which necessitates more investment, and this investment is by no means automatically forthcoming.

Keynes saw that individuals with higher incomes saved a higher percentage of their incomes than those with low incomes. He concluded that this pattern would hold for the whole society. As the aggregate income of society increases, total savings increase more than proportionately. In other words, at each new higher level of income a larger percentage of income is saved.

Thus investment would have to increase at a faster rate than income if it were to continually offset saving. Only this rapid increase would permit businesses to sell everything they produced; but the faster investment grows, the more rapid is the increase in productive capacity. Because of this, the economy must invest ever-greater amounts (both absolutely and relatively) in each successive period if the balance is to be maintained. However, according to Keynes, in any mature private enterprise economy the number of profitable investment outlets is limited. Hence, as the process of economic growth continues, the difficulty of finding sufficient investment outlets becomes more and more acute.

If it becomes impossible to find enough investment outlets, then investment falls short of saving and total expenditures for goods and services fall short of the value of those produced. Businesses, unable to sell all they have produced, find that their inventories of unsold goods are increasing. Each business sees only its own problem: that it has produced more than it can sell. It therefore reduces production in the next period. Most businesses, being in the same situation, do the same thing. The results are a large reduction in production, a decrease in employment, and a decline in income. With the decline in income, however, even less will be spent on goods and services in the next period. So businessmen find that even at the lower level of production they are unable to sell all they have produced. Again they cut back production, and the downward spiral continues.

Under these circumstances businesses have little or no incentive to expand their capital goods (because excess capacity already exists), and therefore investment falls drastically. Expenditures of all types plummet. As income declines, saving declines more than proportionately. This process continues until the declines in income have reduced saving to the point where it no longer exceeds the reduced level of investment. At this low level of income equilibrium is restored. Leakages from the income-expenditure flow are again equal to the injections into it. The economy is stabilized, but at a level where high unemployment and considerable unused productive capacity exist.

Keynes's analysis was not, in its essentials, drastically different from those offered by Marx (Chapter 7) and Hobson (Chapter 11). The principal cause of a depression was, in the opinion of all three thinkers, the inability of capitalists to find sufficient investment opportunities to offset the increasing levels of saving generated by economic growth. Keynes's unique contribution was to show how the relation of saving to income could lead to a stable but depressed level of income with widespread unemployment.

Marx (and Lenin) had believed the disease incurable under capitalism. Hobson had prescribed measures to equalize the distribution of income and thereby reduce saving as a cure. Could Hobson's prescription work? This probably is not a very meaningful question. In most industrial capitalist countries wealth and economic power determine political power, and those who wield power have never been willing to sacrifice it to save the economic system.

In the United States, for example, of the 300,000 nonfinancial corporations existing in 1925 the largest 200 made considerably more profit than the other 299,800 combined. The wealthiest 5 percent of the population owned virtually all of the stocks and bonds and received more than 30 percent of the income. Needless to say, this 5 percent dominated American politics. In these circumstances speculating about what would happen if the income and wealth were radically redistributed amounts to mere fanciful daydreaming.

Keynes's answer to the problem was more realistic. Government could step in when saving exceeded investment, borrow the excess saving, then spend the money on socially useful projects. These projects would be chosen in order not to increase the economy's productive capacity or decrease the investment opportunities of the future. This government spending would increase the injections into the spending stream and create a full-employment equilibrium. In doing so, it would not add to the capital stock. Therefore, unlike investment spending, it would not make a full-employment level of production more difficult to attain in the next period. Keynes summarized his position thus:

> Ancient Egypt was doubly fortunate, and doubtless owed to this its fabled wealth, in that it possessed *two* activities, namely, pyramid-building as well as the search for precious metals, the fruits of which, since they could not serve the needs of many by being consumed, did not stale with abundance. The Middle Ages built cathedrals and sang dirges. Two pyramids, two masses for the dead, are twice as good as one; but not so two railways from London to York.[8]

What types of expenditures ought the government make? Keynes himself had a predilection toward useful public works such as the construction of schools, hospitals, parks, and other public conveniences. He realized, however, that this would probably benefit middle- and lower-income recipients much more than the wealthy. And because the wealthy have political power, they would probably insist on policies that would not redistribute income away from them. He saw that it might be politically necessary to channel this spending into the hands of the large corporations, even though little that was beneficial to society would be accomplished directly. He wrote:

> If the Treasury were to fill old bottles with banknotes, bury them at suitable depths in disused coalmines which are then filled up to the surface with town rubbish, and leave it to private enterprise on well-tried principles of laissez-faire to dig the notes up again . . . there need be no unemployment. . . . It would indeed be more sensible to build houses and the like; but if there are political and practical difficulties in the way of this, the above would be better than nothing.[9]

The depression of the 1930s dragged on until the outbreak of World War II. From 1936 (the year Keynes's *General Theory* was published) to 1940, economists hotly debated the merits of his theory and policy prescriptions. When the various governments began to increase armament production rapidly, however, unemployment began to melt away. During the war years, under the stimulus of enormous government expenditures, conditions in most capitalist economies were rapidly transformed from a situation of severe unemployment to one of acute labor shortage.

[8]J. M. Keynes, *The General Theory of Employment, Interest and Money* (New York: Harcourt Brace Jovanovich, 1936), p. 131.
[9]Ibid., p. 129.

The American armed forces mobilized 14 million people, who had to be armed, quartered, and fed. Between 1939 and 1944 the output of the manufacturing, mining, and construction industries doubled, and productive capacity increased by 50 percent. The American economy produced 296,000 planes, 5400 cargo ships, 6500 naval vessels, 64,500 landing craft, 86,000 tanks, and 2,500,000 trucks.[10] During the war period the most pressing problem was a *shortage* of labor, as contrasted with the 19 percent unemployment that existed as late as the beginning of 1939.

KEYNESIAN ECONOMICS AND IDEOLOGY

Most economists believed this wartime experience had proved the basic correctness of Keynes's ideas. Capitalism could be saved, they proclaimed, by wise use of the government's powers to tax, borrow, and spend money. Capitalism was again a viable social and economic system.

Viability alone was insufficient as an ideology for capitalism, however. The USSR did not have unemployment in the 1930s, and its spectacular rate of growth during this period had proved the viability of the Soviet economic system. This challenge elicited a resurgence of the older neoclassical economic ideology. These older theories were cast in an esoteric and highly elaborate mathematical framework. Typical of the new economists was Paul A. Samuelson, whose book *The Foundations of Economic Analysis* is among the technically most formidable treatments of economics.[11] In 1947 The American Economic Association awarded him the first John Bates Clark Medal for the most outstanding contribution to economics made by an economist under 40 years of age. The book was also instrumental in securing the Nobel Prize in economics for Samuelson in 1970.

Samuelson has made an even more significant contribution in terms of his influence on the dominant economic ideology of capitalism in the past 25 years. His introductory text, *Economics,* has undergone ten editions, has been translated into almost every major language, and has sold millions of copies.[12] The first edition set out mainly to explain and simplify Keynes's ideas. Each subsequent edition has tended to bring in more of the traditional neoclassical ideology of capitalism. In 1955 Samuelson offered his "grand neoclassical synthesis," an integration of Keynesian with neoclassical economics. The Keynesian theory would provide the knowledge necessary to maintain a full-employment economy, and the market system could operate within this Keynesian framework to allocate resources according to the time-honored principles of the neoclassical ideology. Almost every student of economics in the past 25 years has learned his or her elementary economics from Samuelson's textbook or from one of the many others that have attempted to copy his approach and content.

[10]All figures taken from Hacker, *Course of American Economic Growth,* p. 325.
[11]Paul A. Samuelson, *The Foundations of Economic Analysis* (Cambridge, Mass.: Harvard University Press, 1947).
[12]Paul A. Samuelson, *Economics* (New York: McGraw-Hill, 1948).

THE EFFICACY OF KEYNESIAN ECONOMIC POLICIES

After 1945, Keynesian economics became orthodoxy for both economists and the majority of politicians. Almost 3 million veterans were demobilized in that year. In 1946 another 11 million joined the civilian labor force. Congress and many economists feared a new depression and immediately took steps to apply the new Keynesian ideas. Passage of the Employment Act of 1946 legally obligated the government to use its taxing, borrowing, and spending powers to maintain full employment. The act declared that "it is the continuing policy and responsibility of the Federal government to use all practicable means . . . for the purpose of creating and maintaining . . . conditions under which there will be afforded useful employment opportunities, including self-employment, for those able, willing, and seeking to work, and to promote maximum employment, production and purchasing power." This was the first time the U.S. government ever acknowledged responsibility for employment, and it is still not really committed to full employment for all people.

Have Keynesian economic policies worked? The answer to this question is very complex. Since World War II there have been no major depressions in the United States, but there have been eight recessions (the modern euphemism for a mild depression). In 1948–1949, a recession lasted for 11 months; in 1953–1954, for 13 months; in 1957–1958, for 9 months; and in 1960–1961, for 9 months. The 1969–1971 recession went on for more than two years. The 1974–1975 recession was more severe than those that preceded it. In 1979 and 1980 there was another recession. After a very brief recovery the recession of 1981–1982 incurred levels of unemployment higher than at any time since the Great Depression of the 1930s.

Because of these recessions, the economy's performance in the 1950s left much to be desired. The real rate of growth of GNP was 2.9 percent, which does not compare very favorably with the 4.7 percent for 1920–1929 or the 3.7 percent for 1879–1919. The brightest spot in the American economy's performance has been the growth rate in the 1960s, which averaged around 5 percent. In the 1970s the growth rate fell and the economy experienced mild stagnation together with steadily worsening inflation.

Unemployment for the 1950s and early 1960s averaged 4.5 percent, although it dipped to 3.5 percent in the mid-1960s. Moreover, inflation has been a persistent problem since World War II. From 1945 through 1968 the average annual increase in wholesale prices was 3.8 percent (most of which occurred in the late 1940s); the rate of increase from 1968 to 1970 was nearly 5 percent. The 1969–1971 inflation was accompanied by an economic recession in which unemployment soared to rates in excess of 6 percent. The simultaneous occurrence of both high unemployment and a high rate of inflation led to President Nixon's attempt to freeze wages and prices in late 1971, followed by government control over increases in wages and prices. By the late 1970s inflation rose to levels well in excess of 12 percent. In early 1980 an inflation rate of 18 percent worsened the soaring rate of unemployment that signaled another recession. After the 1981–1982 recession the inflation rate was reduced significantly, but only at the cost of persistently high unemployment and general economic stagnation.

Economists like Samuelson argued that Keynesian policies, reflected in enormous government spending, resulted in the impressive growth performance of the 1960s; but they find the accompanying inflation quite mysterious. Before judging this performance, however, it is necessary to see what the American government substituted for the pyramids of Egypt and the cathedrals of the Middle Ages. In 1960 one observer wrote: "A central aspect of our growth experience of the past two decades is one which few spokesmen for the future candidly discuss. This is the fact that our great boom did not begin until the onset of World War II, and that its continuance since then has consistently been tied to a military rather than to a purely civilian economic demand."[13] Twenty-five years later the statement remains as true as ever.

THE WARFARE ECONOMY

In 1940 military-related expenditures were $3.2 billion, or 3.2 percent of GNP. In 1943, at the height of World War II, military spending consumed almost 40 percent of GNP, while profits rose to unprecedented heights. The war provided capitalists with a clear example of how government military spending can end a depression and guarantee large returns to capital.

By 1947 military spending was back to only $9.1 billion, or 3.9 percent of GNP. During the rapid growth of the 1960s, military expenditures grew at approximately the same rate as GNP. If other expenses that are related to militarism but not included in the "defense" budget are taken into account, the total has been close to 15 percent in recent years.[14] The United States has spent and continues to spend more on militarism than any other country— more in absolute terms, relative terms, and per capita.

The result of these enormous expenditures has been growth of the *military-industrial complex* as a necessary adjunct to economic prosperity. Its essential features have been described as follows:

> The warfare state we have constructed over the last two generations has a large clientele. At the top of the pyramid is the so-called military-industrial complex. It comprises, first, the Defense Department of the Federal Government, along with such satellites as the CIA and NASA. The admirals and generals, the space scientists and the intelligence men, like all government bureaucrats, are busily engaged in strengthening their influence. To this end they cultivate congressmen and senators, locate military establishments in politically strategic districts, and provide legislators with special favors. Former military men are drawn into the net of influence through the Army and Navy associations and through veterans' organizations. The military are supported by the industrial side of the complex. These are the large corpora-

---

[13] Robert Heilbroner, *The Future as History* (New York: Harper & Row, 1960), p. 133.

[14] See, for example, Daniel R. Fusfeld, "Fascist Democracy in the United States," *Conference Papers of the Union for Radical Economics,* December 1968, pp. 11, 34–35.

tions on whom the military depend for the hardware of modern war. Some sell the bulk of their output to the military, like North American Aviation, Lockheed Aircraft, General Dynamics, McDonnell-Douglas, and Thiokol Chemical. Others are important military suppliers but make the bulk of their sales in civilian markets, such as Western Electric, Sperry Rand, General Electric or IBM. Others, such as Dupont and General Motors, are only occasionally military contractors.[15]

The extent to which military production dominates the American economy is indicated by a recent survey showing that the five key military-related industries accounted for 7.9 percent of all employment in New York, 12.3 percent in New Jersey, 13 percent in Texas, 14.6 percent in Massachusetts, 15.7 percent in Maryland, 20.9 percent in Florida, 23.4 percent in Connecticut, 30 percent in Kansas, 31.4 percent in California, and 34.8 percent in Washington.[16]

Military expenditures operate in exactly the way Keynes believed pyramid building operated in the ancient Egyptian economy. For generals and most politicians, a tenfold overkill potential is twice as good as a fivefold overkill; two ABM (antiballistic missile) systems are twice as good as one but only half as good as four. And if the public cannot be easily convinced of this, the immense amount of research financed by the military-industrial complex comes to the fore. Weapons and delivery systems are rapidly superseded by new models. Horror stories convince the public that a further escalation of the arms race is necessary and that "obsolete" (and often unused) models must be scrapped.

Military spending keeps the capital goods industry operating near full capacity without raising the economy's productive capacity as rapidly as would be the case if they provided capital goods for industry. Demand does not tend to drop below supply as persistently as it formerly did; military spending increases demand without increasing productivity.

The neglect of these effects of the Keynesian military-induced prosperity is perhaps "the most important abdication of any by the economists."[17] This type of economic theory has led to "an ahistorical, a technical or mechanical, a nonpolitical view of what the economy is and how it works."[18]

Very few Keynesian economists have been willing to come to grips with the implication of militarism as a tool of economic policy.

The arms economy has been the major Keynesian instrument of our times. But its use has been cloaked as "national interest," its effects have been largely undermined, its international consequences largely deleterious and destabilizing, its importance making for uncritical acceptance and dependence by large segments of the society, its long-run effects hardly glanced

[15]Ibid., p. 13.
[16]Ibid., p. 15.
[17]Sumner M. Rosen, "Keynes Without Gadflies," in T. Roszak, ed., *The Dissenting Academy* (New York: Random House, Vintage Books, 1968), p. 83.
[18]Ibid., p. 85.

at. The arms economy has done much more than distort the use of scarce creative scientific and engineering talent. . . . It has forced us to neglect a whole range of urgent social priorities, the consequences of which threaten the fabric of our society.[19]

SUMMARY

The severity of the Great Depression of the 1930s caused many economists to become dissatisfied with the orthodox neoclassical economists' view that unemployment was merely a short-run, ephemeral "adjustment" to a temporary disequilibrium situation. Keynes's new ideas were rapidly accepted by most important economists. World War II proved that massive government intervention in the market economy could create full employment; indeed, Hitler's Germany had already established this in the 1930s.

Since the war the United States had not had a major depression. Most economists agree that massive government spending is largely responsible for this improved performance of American capitalism. Critics have argued, however, that the social price of this prolonged prosperity has been the creation of a military-industrial complex that currently threatens the entire fabric of American society.

If this view is correct, then it is possible to conclude that Keynes's theories enabled the neoclassical ideology to come to grips with the most important economic problem of the 1930s but have obscured if not worsened other problems. Some of these problems and some contemporary ideologies of capitalism are examined in Chapter 13.

[19]Ibid., pp. 86–87.

Contemporary American Capitalism and Its Defenders

During the 25 years following World War II the American economy experienced five mild recessions, although by historical standards its growth was fairly satisfactory. Gross national product, in constant (1958) dollars, grew from $355 billion in 1950 to $727 billion in 1969. Disposable personal income grew at an equally impressive rate.[1] While the growth rate was slightly below the historical average in the 1950s, it was well above average in the 1960s. Although the late 1970s and early 1980s was a period of general stagnation in the American economy, the period from World War II to the present has been, generally, a period of relative prosperity.

The technological advances of American capitalism were particularly impressive during this period. For several decades before World War I, the increases in output per man-hour in American industry had been about 22 percent per decade. In the quarter century following World War II, output per man-hour increased by 34–40 percent per decade.[2] This growth was made possible by huge expenditures on research and development, which increased from $3.4 billion in 1950 to $12 billion in 1960; fully half of these funds came from the federal government. With the advent of the pervasive use of comput-

---

[1]Figures taken from *Federal Reserve Bulletin,* August 1970, pp. A68–A69.

[2]Louis M. Hacker, *The Course of American Economic Growth and Development* (New York: Wiley, 1970), p. 326. The increases in productivity in the 1920s had been even more impressive, however.

Table 13.1   LARGE MERGERS AND ACQUISITIONS, 1966–1968

	1966	1967	1968
Total number of acquisitions	1,746	2,384	4,003
Number of acquired manufacturing and mining companies with more than $10 million in assets	101	169	192
Value of assets of acquired companies with more than $10 million in assets (in billions)	$4.1	$8.2	$12.6
Number of acquisitions made by 200 largest companies	33	67	74
Value of assets of companies acquired by 200 largest companies (in billions)	$2.4	$5.4	$6.9

ers in the 1980s the rapid increase in technological innovation continued at an even accelerated pace.

These improvements in technology and increases in production led to a greater concentration of economic power in the hands of a very small number of corporations. In 1929, the 100 largest manufacturing corporations had legal control (actual control being far greater) of 44 percent of the net capital assets of all manufacturing corporations. By 1962, this figure had increased to 58 percent.[3]

In 1962 there were 420,000 manufacturing enterprises. A mere 5 of these enterprises owned 12.3 percent of all manufacturing assets; 20 owned 25 percent of the total. The total assets of the 20 largest firms were approximately as large as those of the 419,000 smallest companies combined. These 20 giants took a whopping 38 percent of all after-tax profits, leaving the smallest 419,980 to divide 62 percent. Furthermore, among the 180,000 corporations involved in manufacturing, the net profits of the five largest were nearly twice as large as those of the 178,000 smallest corporations.[4]

During the 1960s, the rate of concentration quickened. In every year of that decade there were at least 60 mergers involving the acquisition of companies with over $10 million in assets. Table 13.1 illustrates this trend.[5] From 1968 to 1970 the evidence points to an ever-faster rate of acquisition. The process of increasing economic concentration, which began about 100 years ago, continues unabated today.

Although the rate of mergers and acquisitions slowed somewhat during the 1970s, the size of the corporate giants increased steadily. In 1978, five industrial corporations had total sales of over $229 billion, total assets of over $137 billion, and net profits of nearly $11 billion. The magnitude of these numbers is staggering. Most of us would consider a business to be very big if it received net profits of $1 million. It would take 11,000 businesses, each receiving net profits of $1 million, to equal the profits of these five giants. A

[3]Gardiner C. Means, "Economic Concentration," in *Hearings Before the Subcommittee on Antitrust and Monopoly of the Committee of the Judiciary, United States Senate* (Washington, D.C.: U.S. GPO, July 1964), pp. 9–19.

[4]Willard F. Mueller, "Economic Concentration," in *Hearings,* pp. 111–129.

[5]Table 13.1 is constructed from data of the Federal Trade Commission, derived by Paul Sweezy and Harry Magdoff, in "The Merger Movement: A Study in Power," *The Monthly Review,* June 1969, pp. 1–5.

mere five industrial corporations employed 2,451,048 workers. Since on average somewhat over two people live on the salary of each worker, these five companies directly controlled the destiny and well-being of about 6 million Americans. Indirectly, through their social, political, and economic power, they have enormous control over all of us.[6]

The post–World War II prosperity has not reduced the extremes of inequality in the United States. In the most complete study of the distribution of ownership of wealth ever undertaken,[7] it has been shown that the wealthiest 1.6 percent of the population own over 80 percent of all corporate stock and virtually all state and local government bonds. Moreover, the ownership of these income-yielding assets has become steadily more concentrated since the early 1920s.

The distribution of income reflects the same extreme inequality. Despite the economy's impressive growth over the past decades—and the much-publicized war on poverty of the early 1960s, which proved to be a half-hearted minor skirmish—poverty has remained an acute problem in the United States. In 1981, for example, nearly 32 million Americans lived in families that had an annual income of less than $9287, the officially designated "poverty level" for an average family of four persons.[8] This "poverty" level is inherently misleading, however. It is so unrealistically low that most families that live on welfare are not even considered to be poor. For example, in 1977, of the more than 20 million families whose incomes before taxes or welfare payments would have been classified as living in poverty *more than two-thirds* are removed from the poverty category when welfare payments are included. In other words most of the people who are so poor that they must live on the meager welfare dole are not listed as living in poverty by the government's conservative definition of poverty.[9] More realistic definitions of the poverty level for an urban family of four in 1981 have involved calculations showing that at the inflated prices of that year it would require a before-tax income of at least $11,600 dollars for an urban family of four to live at a minimal level of subsistence.[10] Nearly 44 million people lived in families that had less income than this minimal figure. In 1981 an adequate, comfortable life-style for an urban family of four required an income of about $20,000. Well over one-half of Americans received less than this level of family income. Thus extreme poverty remains the plight of tens of millions of Americans and more than half of all Americans do not receive sufficient income for an adequate, comfortable life-style.

In stark contrast to this widespread poverty, the wealthiest 5 percent of the American population received nearly 20 percent of all income. At the top of this 5 percent was the elite 1.6 percent that owns most of the income-yielding stocks and bonds in the United States. The richest of the elite had incomes

[6]Data reported in *Fortune,* May 1979, pp. 270–271.
[7]Robert J. Lampman, *The Share of Top Wealth-holders in National Wealth, 1922–1956* (Princeton, N.J.: Princeton University Press, 1962).
[8]Bureau of the Census, *Statistical Abstract of the United States for 1982* (Washington, D.C.: U.S. GPO, 1983), p. 440.
[9]Bureau of the Census, *Statistical Abstract of the United States for 1977* (Washington, D.C.: U.S. GPO, 1978), p. 468.
[10]Bureau of the Census, *Statistical Abstract for 1983,* p. 440.

estimated between $50 million and $100 million per year (the latter amounts to about $275,000 per day). According to *Forbes* magazine, in 1983 the 400 families with the most wealth ranged in wealth from a net worth of $125 million to $2.2 billion dollars.[11]

Furthermore, taxes do little, if anything, to reduce the inequities in the distribution of income. It is commonly assumed that the U.S. tax system reduces inequality by taking a higher percentage of the income of the wealthy than is taken from the poor. The personal income tax does tend to reduce income inequalities, but the effect is much smaller than most people imagine. And when economists analyze the total tax burden, they find that taxes actually increase inequality in the distribution of income because sales taxes, excise taxes, property taxes, and social security taxes all take a much larger percentage of the poor person's income than of the rich person's.

One economist, a recognized authority on taxes, has analyzed the total tax burden on incomes along the entire distribution spectrum. He found in a study published in 1964 that families with incomes below $2000 per year—certainly a level of abject poverty—paid out one-third of their income in taxes. For example, families making between $10,000 and $15,000 paid out a proportion of their income that was nearly one-third lower than that paid by families with incomes below $2000. Only among the wealthiest 5 percent of families did the total tax bite exceed that exacted from the poorest. The wealthy elite actually paid out, on the average, 36.3 percent of their income for taxes—a mere 3 percent higher than the poorest segment of society paid.[12] Although this study is now 15 years old and the income figures have changed dramatically in the inflation-plagued 1970s, there is no evidence that the tax structure is any less regressive today. In fact, some economists argue that it is worse because the rich still have all their tax loopholes, whereas the poor are being taxed in much higher tax brackets even though their income buys no more than it did then.

The rapid economic growth experienced during the quarter century following World War II imparted a conservatism to millions of Americans. They acquiesced in the growing inequalities of wealth and power as long as their income grew slowly but steadily. During the 1970s this began to change. The economy suffered two more recessions, and in the recessions of the 1970s inflation was combined with high unemployment, and wage earners' purchasing power began to stagnate or decline. With inflation pushing them into higher tax brackets, many participated in the "taxpayer revolts" of the late 1970s. The corporations and the wealthy were successful in dominating these revolts, with the consequences being greater inequality. It is estimated, for example, that two-thirds of the benefits from Proposition 13 in California (which, in 1978, decreased and set limits on property taxes) went to large corporations. After his election in 1980, President Reagan succeeded in persuading Congress to enact an income tax reduction together with a number of increases in other taxes such as social security taxes. The net effect of these

---

[11]*Forbes,* Fall 1983, pp. 71–144.
[12]B.A. Musgrave, "Estimating the Distribution of the Tax Burden," in *Income and Wealth,* ser. 10 (Cambridge, England: Bowers & Bowers, 1964), p. 192.

tax changes has been a significant worsening of the distribution of wealth, income, and power. Therefore, the issue of the believability of conservative capitalist ideologies is becoming more and more important.

CONTEMPORARY CLASSICAL LIBERAL IDEOLOGY

Neoclassical economics was the principal purveyor of the classical liberal ideology of capitalism during the late nineteenth and early twentieth centuries. Since the 1930s neoclassical economics has become more and more complex mathematically, which has enabled modern economists to gain many new theoretical and scientific insights. Its most important assumptions, however, those on which the entire theory rests, are still metaphysical in character. They have not been established on a scientific basis, either empirically or theoretically.

The finest summary of contemporary neoclassical economics is C. E. Ferguson's *The Neoclassical Theory of Production and Distribution.* [13] The mathematical reasoning in this book is so complex that very few people other than professional economists who are thoroughly competent in higher mathematics can understand it. Professor Ferguson is aware, however, of the tenuous nature of many of the assumptions of this ideology, which, like the medieval religious ideology of feudalism, ultimately must be accepted on faith alone. He admits this and asserts his personal faith: "Placing reliance upon neoclassical economic theory is a matter of faith. I personally have the faith; but at present the best I can do to convince others is to invoke the weight of Samuelson's authority." [14]

When the thrust toward esoterica removed classical liberal ideology from the level at which it could be widely understood, however, it also substantially reduced its effectiveness as a popular ideology of capitalism. To promote widespread popular acceptance of the ideology has been the task of numerous organizations. The best-known American organizations that propagate a simplified, more popular version of the classical ideology are the National Association of Manufacturers (NAM), the Foundation for Economic Education, the Committee for Constitutional Government, the U.S. Chamber of Commerce, and the American Enterprise Association.

A congressional committee found that out of $33.4 million spent "to influence legislation" $32.1 million was spent by large corporations. Of this $32.1 million about $27 million went to such organizations as these. [15] The

[13]C. E. Ferguson, *The Neoclassical Theory of Production and Distribution* (London: Cambridge University Press, 1969).
[14]Ibid., pp. xvii–xviii. Professor Ferguson's candid admission was prompted by a rather esoteric debate among academic economists. The debate proved conclusively that some of the most fundamental tenets of neoclassical orthodoxy were untenable. For a summary of the conclusions of the debate, see E. K. Hunt, "Religious Parable Versus Economic Logic: An Analysis of the Recent Controversy in Value, Capital and Distribution Theory," *Inter-Mountain Economic Review,* Fall 1971; also see E. K. Hunt and Jesse Schwartz, *Critique of the Economic Theory,* sec. III (London: Penguin, 1972).
[15]R. Joseph Monsen, Jr., *Modern American Capitalism* (Boston: Houghton Mifflin, 1963), p. 19.

NAM uses this money to publish a large amount of probusiness propaganda, including "an educational literature series, labor and industrial relations bulletins, news bulletins, a magazine of American affairs, and numerous studies on legislation, education, anti-trust laws, tariffs and unions."[16]

The Foundation for Economic Education reviews and distributes books that reflect the classical liberal ideology of capitalism, as well as publishing and distributing, free of charge, a monthly journal, *The Freeman,* that propagates this ideology. The other organizations engage in numerous publishing and promotional activities designed to inculcate the same ideology as widely as possible.

The popularized statement of the classical ideology emphasizes the benefits of the free market. It is argued that the forces of supply and demand in a free market will always lead to results that are preferable to anything that could be achieved by the government or a central planning agency. The NAM, for example, asserts that the proper function of the government is to strengthen and "make more effective the regulation by competition."[17] Almost none of its literature, however, suggests a concern with the concentration of corporate power. Rather, the main economic problems are the powers of big labor unions and the "socialistic" welfare measures of the government.

In essence, most of this literature uses a drastically simplified version of some of the classical and neoclassical economists' analyses. It supports the view that any conceivable threat to the operation of the free market, whether real or potential, is an evil to be avoided at any cost. These organizations have had considerable success in propagating this point of view, particularly among small businessmen. (Big business, however, generally continues to look with favor on government intervention because it usually benefits from such actions.)

After the election of President Reagan in 1980 one heard a great deal about "supply-side" economics. This "new" theory was really just an old ideology given a new name. Supply-side economics represented a renewed popularity for the old classical liberal arguments for a very restricted role for the government. There were no new arguments in supply-side economics— only a new name.

CONTEMPORARY VARIANTS
OF THE CLASSICAL LIBERAL IDEOLOGY

Most critics of the classical liberal ideology emphasize its failure to come to grips with the realities of the concentration of immense power in the hands of considerably less than 1 percent of all corporations. Several attempts have been made to construct an ideology that retains the competitive, private enterprise flavor of classical liberalism while recognizing the existence of concentrated

---

[16]Ibid.

[17]National Association of Manufacturers, Economic Principles Commission, *The American Individual Enterprise System, Its Nature and Future* (New York: McGraw-Hill, 1946), p. 57.

corporate power. Two of these will be discussed: the *countervailing power* ideology, associated primarily with the economist John Kenneth Galbraith, and the *people's capitalism* ideology, associated primarily with Professor Massimo Salvadori.

In his famous book *American Capitalism, the Concept of Countervailing Power*, Professor Galbraith recognized the existence of large, special-interest power blocks in the American economy, but argued that they should not be of much concern because "private economic power begets the countervailing power of those who are subject to it."[18] The result of this newly created countervailing power is "the neutralization of one position of power by another."[19]

Thus strong unions neutralize strong business firms in the field of labor relations, and strong buyers' associations neutralize the monopolistic or oligopolistic powers of the strong sellers. The result, then, is a kind of market equilibrium or invisible hand that harmonizes the interests of all. The harmonious whole is now simply made up of a few neutralized giants rather than numerous, atomistically competitive small firms.[20]

Another influential attempt to show the innocuous (or even beneficial) nature of corporate concentration was made by Professor Salvadori, who used the slogan "people's capitalism" to characterize what he believed to be the most essential feature of contemporary American capitalism: diffusion of ownership. The widespread diffusion of ownership of corporate stock, as well as other types of assets, means to Salvadori that capitalism is no longer a system where a tiny minority reaps most of the privileges, but one in which the majority are rapidly becoming capitalists and getting a share of the privileges.[21] Salvadori has conveniently summarized his people's capitalism ideology:

> At present in the United States there are nearly half a million corporations; stockholders total about ten million (1959). Their numbers have increased rapidly in the post-war period. Standard Oil of New Jersey, for instance, had about 160,000 stockholders in 1946; twelve years later there were three times as many, close to half a million. As a rule, the larger the corporation the more widely spread the ownership. Large corporations in which a majority of shares are owned by an individual or by a family are fewer and fewer. It is already exceptional for a single individual to own more than four or five per cent of the stock of a given corporation. Unincorporated non-farm businesses number about four million; they belong to one or more individuals and this means millions of "capitalists." Nearly four million farmers (three-fourths

---

[18]John Kenneth Galbraith, *American Capitalism, the Concepts of Countervailing Power* (Boston: Houghton Mifflin, 1956), p. 4.

[19]Ibid., p. 1.

[20]It should be mentioned that Professor Galbraith has published several books since *American Capitalism, the Concept of Countervailing Power* appeared. Even a cursory reading of these books shows that he has altered his opinions fundamentally. Nevertheless, because the ideology of countervailing power has been very influential, and because most of this influence flows from his book, we are justified in associating this ideology with his name.

[21]This is curiously similar to socialist Eduard Bernstein's idea, discussed in Chapter 10.

of the total) are full owners or part owners of the farms they cultivate. Even considering that there is a good deal of overlapping among the three groups (shareholders, individual non-farm owners, farmers) one can say that at least one-fourth to one-third of all American families share the ownership of natural and artificial capital. There are also half a million independent professional people—lawyers, doctors, architects, engineers, accountants, etc.— whose other means of production are not only equipment of one kind or another but also skill and training, and whose income is related to the capital invested in acquiring professional efficiency; they are "capitalists" just as much as owners of natural and artificial capital. Most other families own durable consumer goods (houses, summer cottages, furniture, cars, electrical appliances, etc.), federal, state, and municipal bonds, insurance policies and savings to the extent that they can consider themselves "capitalists."[22]

Thus the large size of corporations does not, for Salvadori, appear to be an issue. Ownership is becoming more equitably distributed because most people are becoming "capitalists," and hence, by implication, none is powerful enough to exploit another. Disciples point out that by 1970 there were approximately 30 million stockholders. In this view the United States is becoming a nation where the majority are capitalists.

Even many defenders of capitalism concede that Salvadori's analysis serves only to obscure the nature of the concentration of economic power in the United States and that it neither eliminates nor justifies this concentration. A. A. Berle, Jr., a distinguished scholar of American capitalism as well as a corporate executive, has written:

In terms of power, without regard to asset positions, not only do 500 corporations control two-thirds of the non-farm economy, but within each of that 500 a still smaller group has the ultimate decision-making power. That is, I think, the highest concentration of economic power in recorded history. . . . Since the United States carries on not quite half of the manufacturing production of the entire world today, these 500 groupings—each with its own little dominating pyramid within it—represents a concentration of power over economies which makes the medieval feudal system look like a Sunday school party.[23]

Contrary to the tone of this quotation, Berle is not a critic of American capitalism but one of the most important developers of a contemporary corporate, or collective, ideology of capitalism. Other conservatives have admitted that a very small percentage of all the millions of stockholders hold most of the corporate stock.

[22]Massimo Salvadori, *The Economics of Freedom* (Garden City, N.Y.: Doubleday, 1959), pp. 70–71.
[23]A. A. Berle, Jr., "Economic Power and the Free Society," in Andrew Hacker, ed., *The Corporation Take-Over* (Garden City, N.Y.: Doubleday, 1965), p. 97.

THE CONTEMPORARY CORPORATE ETHIC
AND CAPITALIST IDEOLOGY

The tactics of the late nineteenth-century robber barons led to a widespread rejection of the corporate ideology (discussed in Chapter 8). Their destructive competition and financial wheeling and dealing hardly supported the conclusion that they were becoming socialized stewards of the public welfare. Yet the classical liberal ideology had no real defense for the existing concentration of economic and political power. The Christian paternalist ethic, with its emphasis on the benevolence of the powerful, was still the only successful ideological defense of great inequalities of wealth and power.

It was simply not possible to cast the nineteenth-century capitalist in a kindly, paternalistic role. Some twentieth-century ideologists of capitalism have argued that capitalism has changed so drastically that capitalists have lost their importance in the system and have been replaced by a new class of professional managers. These theories envision this "new man," the professional manager, as the paternalistic steward of public welfare.

In 1932 A. A. Berle and G. C. Means published an important and influential book, *The Modern Corporation and Private Property.* [24] In it they argued that ownership of most of the colossal corporate giants had become so widely diffused that the owners of stock had lost or were rapidly losing control of these corporations. With no single owner holding more than 1 or 2 percent of the stock and with no effective means of collusion, the owners were left with only the formal voting function when selecting the board of directors. Candidates for whom they could vote were selected by the existing board of directors. Thus the boards chose their own replacements and were essentially a self-perpetuating oligarchy. They wielded power but had no necessary connection with the owners of stock. They were not capitalists in the usual sense of the term.

In 1955 Berle wrote another book, *The Twentieth Century Capitalist Revolution,* in which he argued that corporations had developed a quasi-political status. Managers were motivated primarily by the desire to promote the general public interest in their decision making, and any who were not so motivated could be brought into line by public opinion and the threat of government intervention. This view has been widely accepted. Another economist, for example, wrote:

> No longer the agent of proprietorship seeking to maximize return on investment, management sees itself as responsible to stockholders, employees, customers, the general public, and, perhaps most important, the firm as an institution. . . . There is no display of greed or graspingness; there is no attempt to push off onto workers or the community a large part of the

---

[24] A. A. Berle, Jr., and G. C. Means, *The Modern Corporation and Private Property* (New York: Macmillan, 1932).

social costs of the enterprise. The modern corporation is a soulful corporation.[25]

The corporation was "soulful," of course, because in this economist's opinion
its managers were conscientious, paternalistic stewards of society's welfare.

The managerial ideology was spelled out in some detail in a series of
lectures delivered by prominent corporate managers at Columbia University
in 1956. According to the chairman of General Electric, the lectures were
intended "to coax us businessmen out of our offices and into the arena of public
thought where our managerial philosophies can be put to the test of examination by men trained in other disciplines."[26]

One of the dominant themes in these lectures was that because American
capitalism has undergone a transformation the complaints people may once
have had against capitalism are no longer justified. Thus the chairman of Sears
Roebuck asserted, "The historic complaint that big business, as the producing
arm of capitalism, exploited the many for the profit of the few and deprived
workers of the products of their own labor had a valid basis in the facts of
European capitalism, but lacks substance when applied to American capitalism today."[27]

Another theme was the justification of bigness on the grounds of better
efficiency and higher quality. "The American public," asserted the chairman
of U.S. Steel, "has gradually become accustomed to larger and larger groups
and has become convinced that big production groups are outstanding in
reliability and in the quality of their products and services and are necessary
to perform America's larger production tasks in research, in production, and
in the procurement of raw materials."[28]

Finally, the businessmen all saw managers as "professionals" who are as
much concerned with "customers, share owners, employees, suppliers, educational institutions, charitable activities, government and the general public" as
with sales and profits. They believed that managers "all know that special
power imposes special responsibilities on those who hold it." Most managers,
they asserted, fully accept "their responsibilities for the broader public welfare."[29]

Since 1942 this corporate managerial ideology has been assiduously
disseminated by the Committee for Economic Development (CED). The CED
has been one of the most effective institutional purveyors of pro-business
propaganda. It readily accepted big business and also "the fact that government was big and was constantly growing bigger and that there was no return-
ing to a simpler, happier past in this respect. It believed that the question was

[25]Carl Kaysen, "The Social Significance of the Modern Corporation," *American Economic
Review,* May 1957, pp. 313–314.
[26]Quoted in Robert L. Heilbroner, *The Limits of American Capitalism* (New York: Harper
& Row, 1966), p. 30.
[27]Ibid., pp. 31–32.
[28]Ibid., p. 32.
[29]Quotations in this paragraph are all from ibid., pp. 32–33.

not *how much* the government should do, but *what* it should do."[30] Government should not only accept all the duties assigned to it by the classical liberal ideology but also follow Keynesian policies to ensure stable full employment. Further, government should cooperate with corporate management in resolving conflicts and maintaining the tranquil, stable atmosphere within which management can effectively perform its public-spirited, paternalistic function of promoting the public welfare.[31]

Big business and big government are accepted by this ideology as not only inevitable but also necessary for maximum efficiency. Big labor unions are also accepted as long as they recognize that most of their legitimate interests are in harmony with those of business and management.

Another important propagator of the managerial ideology has been the U.S. Information Agency (USIA), the official government agency charged with the worldwide propagandizing of the "American point of view." The USIA operates on a grand scale. Its Voice of America broadcasts are heard around the world daily in scores of languages, and it publishes dozens of newspapers and magazines, maintains libraries, shows motion pictures, and engages in countless other propaganda operations.

Arthur Larson, who as head of the U.S. Information Agency "was a semi-official ideologist to the Eisenhower Administration,"[32] published a book, *What We Are for,*[33] in which he explained the philosophy of USIA propaganda. In the modern capitalist economy, Larson argued, the government should do only what "needs to be done" and cannot be done "as well" by private businesses.[34] Modern capitalism has a multitude of powerful interest groups, such as big business, big unions, big government, and so forth, that have no major or basic conflicts. Rather, their interests harmonize, and they mutually support each other. Larson assumed both that business managers are motivated primarily by the desire to promote social welfare to meet the "basic political and economic needs of all people"[35] and that businesses operate more efficiently than government. There is therefore a built-in preference for a minimal role for government in the economy.[36]

In our discussion of the contemporary corporate ethic, the reader may have noticed that most of the ideas on which it is based are rather old. The same holds for the contemporary variants of the classical liberal ideology in the previous section of this chapter. The fact is that very little new or innovative thinking has emerged in the conservatism of the 1960s and 1970s. When one combines this fact with the fact that the Vietnam War and the Watergate scandals have created widespread suspicion and distrust of the American

[30]Karl Schriftgiesser, *Business Comes of Age* (New York: Harper & Row, 1960), p. 224.
[31]See Monsen, *Modern American Capitalism,* pp. 25–29.
[32]Ibid., p. 42.
[33]Arthur Larsen, *What We Are for* (New York: Harper & Row, 1959).
[34]Ibid., pp. 16–17.
[35]Monsen, *Modern American Capitalism,* p. 45.
[36]Larsen, *What We Are for,* p. 17.

capitalist government, it would appear that if new variations on our old ideologies are not forthcoming in the 1980s, we face the distinct possibility of a grave crisis of authority in the American capitalism of the 1980s.

CRITICISMS OF CONTEMPORARY CAPITALIST IDEOLOGIES

Criticisms of capitalism have often gone hand in hand with criticisms of capitalist ideologies. In the remainder of this chapter criticisms of the ideologies of capitalism are examined. Some of the principal criticisms of contemporary American capitalism are discussed in Chapter 14.

Criticisms of Neoclassical Ideology

Neoclassical economics completely dominated orthodox academic economics in the late nineteenth and early twentieth centuries. From the 1930s on, however, it came increasingly under attack. In 1938 Oscar Lange and Fred M. Taylor published their significant book, *On the Economic Theory of Socialism.* [37] Lange and Taylor accepted the neoclassical argument that a "purely" and "perfectly" competitive economy will lead to an "optimum allocation of resources," but they also showed that such an economy need not be a capitalist one. They demonstrated that a socialist economy, in which the means of production were collectively owned, could also operate (through perfect planning or decentralized decision making) in a state of "optimal economic efficiency." Private ownership had absolutely no formal or theoretical importance in the neoclassical theory. Furthermore, under socialist ownership, they argued, the inequities of income distribution under a capitalist system would disappear.

The conclusion that many people drew from this book was that the neoclassical liberal ideology could be equally well (if not better) used as an ideology of socialism. This was, indeed, a radical undermining of neoclassical economics as an ideology defending capitalism.

The classical liberal ideology was rejected by many, however, because it seemed to present a severely distorted picture of the realities of twentieth-century capitalism. Its basic assumption of pure competition—no buyers or sellers large enough to affect prices—was patently ridiculous. Moreover, it had little or nothing to say about the important problem of pollution of the environment. Economists also established that simple countercyclical policies of the Keynesian variety are insufficient to obviate the problems of capitalism's cyclical instability [38] and cannot cope with inflation.

[37] Oscar Lange and Fred M. Taylor, *On the Economic Theory of Socialism* (Minneapolis, Minn.: University of Minnesota Press, 1938). Lange had published his essay two years earlier in *Review of Economic Studies,* October 1936, pp. 53–71, and February 1937, pp. 123–142.

[38] On this last point see Milton Friedman, "The Effects of a Full Employment Policy of Economic Stability: A Formal Analysis," in *Essays in Positive Economics* (Chicago, Ill.: University of Chicago Press, 1953); and William J. Baumol, "Pitfalls in Counter-Cyclical Policies: Some Tools and Results," *The Review of Economics and Statistics,* February 1961, pp. 21–26.

The coup de grace came with J. De V. Graaff's tightly reasoned *Theoretical Welfare Economics.* [39] Graaff showed that economists had not really appreciated the long and restrictive list of assumptions necessary for the optimally efficient allocation of resources envisioned in the model of a competitive, free-market capitalism to be realized. He cited 17 such assumptions, [40] many of which were so restrictive and unrealistic that Graaff concluded that "the measure of acceptance . . . [this theory] has won among professional economists would be astonishing were not its pedigree so long and respectable."[41]

A few of Graaff's 17 conditions will suffice to illustrate his point. Neoclassical ideology requires that any individual's welfare be identical with his preference ordering. In other words, children, dope addicts, fiends, criminals, and lunatics, as well as all other people, always prefer that which is best for them. Neoclassical theory also requires that neither risk nor uncertainty is ever present. Graaff's book devastatingly attacked the very basis for the economic analysis on which the classical liberal ideology was constructed.

Criticisms of the Managerial Ideology

The managerial ideology has also come under extensive criticism. Many economists (including several in the neoclassical tradition) argue that the scale of American big business cannot be shown to be related to efficiency or better service. Giant corporations are much larger than would be required for maximum productive efficiency.[42] Such examples as the electric power industry's competition with the Tennessee Valley Authority (TVA), the oligopolistic airlines' struggle with small, unscheduled competitors, and the challenge to the American steel industry from foreign competition are used to point out that private profits and monopoly power, not social welfare or social efficiency, are the prime motivations of big business.[43]

Critics also argue that managers have exactly the same motives as owner-capitalists. They cite an extensive study of the behavior of "management-controlled" giant corporations that showed managers to be as profit-oriented as owner-capitalists. The author of the study concluded that "it would appear that the proponents of theories of managerial discretion have expended considerable time and effort in describing a phenomenon of relatively minor importance. The large management-controlled corporations seem to be just as profit-oriented as the large owner-controlled corporation."[44]

Many critics assert that modern managers have no more social conscience or "soul" than the nineteenth-century robber barons. The late Profes-

[39]J. De V. Graaff, *Theoretical Welfare Economics* (London: Cambridge University Press, 1967).

[40]Ibid., pp. 142–154.

[41]Ibid., p. 142.

[42]See, for example, Walter Adams, "Competition, Monopoly, and Planning," in M. Zeitlin, ed., *American Society, Inc.* (Chicago, Ill.: Markham, 1970), pp. 240–248.

[43]Ibid.

[44]Robert J. Larner, "The Effect of Management-Control on the Profits of Larger Corporations," in Zeitlin, *American Society, Inc.,* p. 258.

sor Edwin H. Sutherland, once known as the dean of American criminologists and former president of the American Sociological Association, conducted a thorough and scholarly investigation of the extent to which corporate executives were involved in criminal behavior. He took the 70 largest nonfinancial corporations, with only a few additions and deletions (due to special circumstances), and traced their criminal histories through official histories and official records.[45] There were 980 court decisions against these corporations. One corporation had 50 decisions against it, and the average per corporation was 14. Sixty of the corporations had been found guilty of restraining trade, 53 of infringements, 44 of unfair labor practices, 28 of misrepresentation in advertising, 26 of giving illegal rebates, and 43 of a variety of other offenses. There was a total of 307 individual cases of illegal restraint of trade, 97 of illegal misrepresentation, 222 of infringement, 158 of unfair labor practices, 66 of illegal rebates, and 130 of other offenses.[46] Not all of those cases were outright criminal cases. Yet 60 percent of the corporations had been found guilty of criminal offenses an average of four times each.

From May 10, 1950, to May 1, 1951, a U.S. Senate Special Committee to Investigate Crime in Interstate Commerce, under the chairmanship of Senator Estes Kefauver, probed the connections of business and organized crime. Senator Kefauver, Democratic vice-presidential candidate in 1956, later wrote a book based on those hearings. Although he emphasized that there was no evidence to link most big corporations with organized crime, he was nevertheless greatly alarmed at the extent of such connections.

> I cannot overemphasize the danger that can lie in the muscling into legitimate fields by hoodlums. . . . There was too much evidence before us of unreformed hoodlums gaining control of a legitimate business; then utilizing all his old mob tricks—strong-arm methods, bombs, even murder—to secure advantages over legitimate competition. All too often such competition either ruins legitimate businessmen or drives them into emulating or merging with the gangsters. The hoodlums are also clever at concealing ownership of their investments in legitimate fields—sometimes . . . through "trustees" and sometimes by bamboozling respectable businessmen into "fronting" for them.[47]

In 1960 Robert Kennedy, who later became attorney general of the United States, published *The Enemy Within.* He gathered the material for this book while serving as chief counsel of the U.S. Senate Select Committee on Improper Activities in the Labor or Management Field. Kennedy, like Kefauver, stressed the fact that he was not condemning all or even most businessmen. He wrote:

[45]Edwin H. Sutherland, *White Collar Crime* (New York: Holt, Rinehart and Winston, 1961).

[46]These data are summarized by F. Lundberg in *The Rich and the Super Rich* (New York: Bantam, 1968), pp. 131–132.

[47]Estes Kefauver, *Crime in America* (Garden City, N.Y.: Doubleday, 1951), pp. 139–140.

We found that with the present-day emphasis on money and material goods many businessmen were willing to make corrupt "deals" with dishonest union officials in order to gain competitive advantage or to make a few extra dollars. . . . We came across more than fifty companies and corporations that had acted improperly—and in many cases illegally—in dealings with labor unions . . . in the companies and corporations to which I am referring the improprieties and illegalities were occasioned solely by a desire for monetary gain. Furthermore we found that we could expect very little assistance from management groups. Disturbing as it may sound, more often the business people with whom we came in contact—and this includes some representatives of our largest corporations—were uncooperative.[48]

Kennedy's list of the names of offending companies included many of the largest and most powerful corporations in the United States.

Ferdinand Lundberg has described the extent to which corporate leaders and management receive either very light punishment or no punishment at all when they become involved in improprieties or illegalities. Among the many cases he cites is that of

the bribe of $750,000 by four insurance companies that sent Boss Pendergast of Missouri to jail, later to be pardoned by President Truman . . . It was almost ten years before the insurance executives went to jail. There was, too, the case of Federal Judge Martin Manton who was convicted of accepting a bribe of $250,000 from agents of the defendant when he presided over a case charging exorbitant salaries were improperly paid to officers of the American Tobacco Company. While the attorney for the company was disbarred from federal courts, the assistant to the company president (who made the arrangements) was soon thereafter promoted to vice president: a good boy.[49]

In recent years the situation has grown worse. In 1978 more businessmen received jail sentences for illegal business practices than during the previous 89 years.[50] In the January 1980 issue of *Harper's* magazine, there is a two-page table listing 25 of the largest and most powerful corporations in America. In these 25 corporations at least one or more of the top executives had been convicted of a major crime connected to the conduct of the business corporation. In the July 23, 1979, issue of *U.S. News & World Report* an article on "Business Criminals" estimated that managerial and other white collar business crime added as much as 15 percent to the retail price of U.S.-manufactured merchandise. In the December 17, 1979, issue of *Fortune* magazine, that conservative, business-oriented periodical published a lengthy article complaining that "too many executives are going to jail." On November 14, 1980, Mr. Herchell Britton, Executive Vice President of Burns International Security Services, Inc., delivered a speech in Chicago, Illinois, to a number of top

[48]Robert Kennedy, *The Enemy Within* (New York: Harper & Row, 1960), p. 216.
[49]Lundberg, *Rich and Super Rich,* p. 135.
[50]*Forbes,* February 5, 1979, p. 61.

executives from America's most powerful corporations. Among his remarks were the following:

> The security of corporations is seriously threatened by the growing incidence of white collar crime. It is a major national problem. Right now, at this moment while you're listening to me some 60 to 65 percent of the companies you represent are being ripped off.... White collar crime, excluding computer and industrial espionage crimes currently costs this country nearly $70 billion a year. ... The Assistant Director of the FBI's Criminal Investigative Division recently reported that there are almost 16,000 white collar crimes—including 1,100 cases of public corruption—now pending nationwide.[51]

Critics of the managerial ideology do not cite such studies and examples to show all businessmen to be criminals. Obviously most of them are not. The point they wish to make is that the power of monetary incentives and the quest for profits are no less pronounced among managers than among owner-capitalists. In fact, the pressure to acquire ever-increasing profits is so strong on many businessmen and managers that some persistently resort to illegal or improper means. With such pressures, the critics argue, society can ill afford to turn to the managerial class for paternalistic stewardship of the social and economic welfare.

SUMMARY

Since World War II the concentration of corporate power has become more extreme, and inequalities of income distribution have been reduced very little, if at all. Despite these facts, many contemporary ideologies continue to rely on the classical liberal defense of capitalism. Other ideologists continue to place the corporate ethic at the base of their defense of capitalism. The latter group stresses the "efficient, farsighted policies" of the large corporations, and the "professionalism" as well as "broad, humanistic concerns" of corporate managers. Critics of this point of view argue that corporate managers are motivated by the same force that motivated nineteenth-century capitalists— the quest for maximum profits.

[51] *Vital Speeches,* January 1, 1981, p. 485.

CHAPTER 14

Contemporary American Capitalism and Its Radical Critics

Radical criticism of American capitalism was widespread during the depression of the 1930s. During the late 1940s and early 1950s, however, pervasive repression of dissent, combined with a relatively prosperous economy, effectively stifled most radical criticism.[1]

THE CIVIL RIGHTS MOVEMENT

The struggle for equality for blacks in America began in 1619, when the first black slaves were brought to the colonies. Since that time the struggle has been nearly continuous. In the 1950s, however, the blacks' quest for their basic human rights entered a new phase.

On May 17, 1954, in the case *Brown* v. *Board of Education of Topeka,* the U.S. Supreme Court unanimously concluded "that in the field of public education the doctrine of 'separate but equal' has no place!" and declared that "separate educational facilities are inherently unequal."

In 1954 and 1955, the few black individuals who applied for admission to white schools were rebuffed and very often suffered severe reprisals. It began to appear that the Court decision would have little effect on the patterns of

[1]For a thorough description of the repression of this period, see Fred J. Cook, *The Nightmare Decade: The Life and Times of Senator Joe McCarthy* (New York: Random House, 1971); also see Cedric Belfrage, *The American Inquisition, 1945–1960* (New York: Bobbs-Merrill, 1973).

segregation that then existed. In December 1955, however, a black woman in Montgomery, Alabama, refused to give up her bus seat to a white man. She was immediately arrested. Within days the blacks of Montgomery had organized a boycott of the bus company.

After a year of intense and bitter conflict, the protest ended in victory. The 50,000 blacks of Montgomery succeeded in getting the local bus segregation law nullified. The symbolic significance of this victory extended far beyond the particular issue of bus segregation. Blacks everywhere vicariously shared a new sense of dignity, freedom, and power. They began to organize actively to fight white racism.

Their attempts were met with fanatical resistance. In the fall of 1957, Arkansas Governor Orville Faubus used armed troops to bar the entrance of nine black students into Central High School in Little Rock. The federal government interpreted this as a blatant challenge to its authority and sent in paratroopers to enforce the federal court orders. Many southern communities chose to close their public schools rather than allow them to be integrated.

In 1957 and 1960 Congress passed civil rights acts designed to extend voting rights to blacks. The Kennedy administration urged young people, black and white, to concentrate on a massive registration drive to get southern blacks on voting lists. Attracting both radical critics of capitalism and liberal young people who generally did not seriously question the basic social and economic system of capitalism, a civil rights movement emerged nationwide. In the early 1960s the liberals dominated the movement numerically. They believed that a massive protest against racism would open the public's eyes and that an aroused population would demand new laws that would improve, if not completely cure, the situation.

During this period civil rights activists organized sit-ins at segregated lunch counters and bus depots, pray-ins at segregated churches, and wade-ins at segregated beaches. Massive nonviolent demonstrations or nonviolent civil disobedience would, they hoped, reach the consciences of enough people to achieve integration.

Despite some successes in terms of new civil rights legislation, disillusionment began to affect large numbers of blacks as well as white civil rights workers. They began to realize that political enfranchisement had little effect on the vast economic inequalities that blacks suffered. Of what use was the vote if a black man or woman could not secure a job, or if he or she was paid a salary that kept the family in a condition of poverty and degradation? Whereas in 1950 the average salary earned by a black was 61 percent of that earned by a white, by 1962 it had fallen to 55 percent. In the face of a massive civil rights movement, the relative economic position of the blacks had actually deteriorated. Furthermore, in 1950 the rate of unemployment among blacks had been slightly less than twice as high as that for whites, but by 1964 it was, significantly, more than twice as high. In 1947 blacks constituted 18 percent of the poorest segment of the population in America; by 1962 they accounted for 22 percent of this segment.

Many civil rights advocates became convinced that the most significant barriers to black equality were economic. They turned their attention to a critical analysis of American capitalism as a means of understanding the perpetuation, indeed the worsening, of the inequalities suffered by blacks.

THE WAR IN VIETNAM

The other major force that helped spark the resurgence of radical criticism was the war in Vietnam. Throughout the 1950s the U.S. government consistently fought against fundamental social and political change in less developed countries. In the guise of "protecting the world from communism" the United States had intervened in the internal affairs of at least a score of countries. In some, like Guatemala and Iran, U.S. agents actually engineered the overthrow of the legitimate governments and replaced them with regimes more to American liking.[2]

Most criticism was muted by the political repression of McCarthyism. The college students of the 1950s, the "silent generation," generally acquiesced in the national mood of anticommunism that provided the justification for political repression at home and extensive intervention in other nations' internal affairs. During the 1950s American intervention in Vietnam attracted little attention. It was merely one of many countries that, it was claimed, were being saved from communism. In the 1960s, however, this was to change drastically. The Vietnam War became a powerful force in regenerating radical criticism of American capitalism. For this reason, a brief examination of the origins of the Vietnam War is useful here.

During the World War II occupation of Vietnam, the French colonial regime collaborated with the Japanese. Toward the end of the war the Japanese locked up the colonial administrators and established a puppet regime under the Annamite Emperor Bao Dai. Throughout this period the Americans and the French had supported a resistance movement, the Vietminh, headed by Ho Chi Minh. When Japan surrendered, there was a peaceful transfer of political power to the Vietminh.

The French did not want to lose this part of their colonial empire but realized that they were too weak to inflict a quick military defeat on the new government. On March 6, 1946, they signed an agreement with the Ho Chi Minh government that read in part, "The government of France recognizes the Republic of Vietnam as a free state having its government and its parliament, its army and its finances, forming part of the Indo-Chinese federation and of the French Union."[3] This agreement clearly meant that the Ho Chi Minh government would enjoy status similar to the governments of the members of the British Commonwealth. It legally established Ho Chi Minh's regime as the legitimate government of *all* Vietnam. Nothing that subsequently occurred changed this essential fact.

---

[2]For a popular account of these interventions, see David Wise and Thomas B. Ross, *The Invisible Government* (New York: Random House, 1964).

[3]Quoted in Leo Huberman and Paul M. Sweezy, "The Road to Ruin," *Monthly Review,* April 1965, p. 787.

The French were confident that they could make a subservient puppet of Ho Chi Minh. They failed completely in this task. Unable to reduce Ho Chi Minh to this role, they brought back Emperor Bao Dai, even though he had voluntarily abdicated his throne, changed his name, and retired to Hong Kong. They "installed" him as "chief of state" and declared the Vietminh to be outlaws. There followed 6 years of intense, bitter warfare. Finally, in 1954, the Vietminh decisively defeated the French. The Geneva Accords of July 1954, which arranged for the French surrender, called for a cease-fire and a *temporary* separation of opposing forces. Ho Chi Minh's followers were to move north of the seventeenth parallel, and Emperor Bao Dai's were to move to the south. This arrangement was to end within 2 years with a national election to choose the leader of Vietnam. Shortly after these negotiations American-backed Ngo Dinh Diem ousted Bao Dai, proclaimed the existence of a "Republic of Vietnam," and appointed himself its first president.

There were no elections. The Americans and Diem simply asserted that there were now two Vietnams. The reason for refusing to have the election was candidly admitted by President Eisenhower in his book *Mandate for Change:*

> I am convinced that the French could not win the war because the internal political situation in Vietnam, weak and confused, badly weakened their military position. I have never talked or corresponded with a person knowledgeable in Indochinese affairs who did not agree that had elections been held as of the time of the fighting, possibly 80 percent of the population would have voted for Communist Ho Chi Minh as their leader rather than chief of state Bao Dai.[4]

Obviously the substitution of Diem for Bao Dai did not change the situation.

This American-imposed solution was rejected not only by Ho Chi Minh and his followers in the North but also by people in the South. So the war of national liberation, which had been previously fought against the Japanese and the French, was continued against the United States.

Americans were repeatedly told that their government was fighting a war to protect the South Vietnamese from the armed aggression of North Vietnam. The North Vietnamese were pictured as violators of the Geneva agreements, determined to enslave the South Vietnamese.

Critics of American policy challenged this official version of the nature of the war. Their assessment of what was happening in Vietnam received widespread support in academic circles, and college campuses became centers of antiwar sentiment. From the early 1960s through about 1966, opposition to the war was largely confined to the campuses. During the last years of the decade, however, people from all segments of society actively opposed the war. The antiwar movement had become a mass movement.

Finally, in 1968, U.S. Secretary of Defense Robert S. McNamara, himself becoming disillusioned with the official rationale for the war, ordered the

[4]Quoted in ibid., p. 789.

U.S. Department of Defense to prepare an in-depth account of how the United States became involved. In early 1971 the report was completed. The 7000-page document was obtained by the *New York Times*, which paid researchers to determine whether new facts had been brought to light. The Defense Department admitted that (1) the Eisenhower administration had played a "direct role in the ultimate breakdown of the Geneva settlement";[5] (2) from 1954 onward, the United States engaged in "acts of sabotage and terror warfare against North Vietnam";[6] (3) the United States "encouraged and abetted the overthrow of President Ngo Dinh Diem" when he was no longer considered to be of use; and (4) for many years before 1965 the U.S. government undertook "the careful preparation of public opinion for the years of open warfare that were to follow."[7]

American involvement increased steadily until by 1968 the United States had an army of over 500,000 men on Vietnamese soil and were spending nearly $3 billion per month ($100 million per day!) in the attempt to impose a "suitable political solution" on the Vietnamese. American battle casualties rose until hundreds of thousands of Americans were wounded and well over 50,000 Americans were killed.

Young people everywhere began to question the morality of the war. Beginning in 1964, teach-ins protesting the war were mounted on college campuses around the United States. Most organizers and participants were convinced that American involvement in the war was a tragic mistake that would be rectified if the public could be made aware of the facts of the situation.

The antiwar movement grew rapidly. President Johnson's landslide victory in 1964 and his decision not to seek another term in 1968 are often attributed, at least in part, to the powerful, widespread opposition to the war. After a few years of debate, antiwar critics were convinced that most Americans did know the basic facts of Vietnam and wanted a hasty end to the war. Yet the American government, without giving any convincing reasons for its actions, continued to seek military victory.

Critics began to ask whether there was not some deeper motive than simple anticommunist sentiment propelling the American government. In particular, they began to search for an economic motive or rationale for the war. They began seriously to reexamine the older radical theories of capitalist imperialism.

THE WOMEN'S LIBERATION MOVEMENT

The women's movement, like the black movement, did not suddenly spring into being in the 1960s out of thin air. The earliest political activity of a significant number of U.S. women came in the 1820s and 1830s in the abolitionist movement to end slavery. Experience in the abolitionist movement

---

[5]Quoted in Neil Sheehan, "The Story Behind the Vietnam War, Based on a Pentagon Study," *New York Times News Service*, June 13, 1971.
[6]Ibid.
[7]Ibid.

made women aware of their own oppression and gave them the confidence to build a movement of their own, especially because they were ignored or dismissed by some of the abolitionists. The women's movement before the Civil War fought not only for the abolition of slavery, but also for ending laws that made the man the sole controller of all property and all decisions in marriage (even giving men guardianship of the children in event of separation), as well as for the right to vote.

The aftermath of the Civil War gave the vote to blacks—or, rather, it gave the formal right to black *men,* but with no mechanism of enforcement in the South. Women, both black and white, were not given the vote. The women's movement fought a long, hard battle until women were finally given the vote in 1920. The early movement had concerned itself with a broad range of issues, from poverty and divorce laws to working conditions, but after about 1890 the movement concentrated solely on the narrow issue of voting. By 1920 some 2 million women were members of the leading women's suffrage organizations. Yet when the vote was given, most of these women thought the battle was won—so the women's movement collapsed and did not recover until the late 1960s.

A brief upsurge in the fight for women's rights occurred during World War II, when millions of women were drawn into war work. The symbol of Rosie the Riveter replaced that of Hedda the Housewife. Overnight it became fashionable for women to work in a war factory or a war office, and there was even discussion of child care to help working mothers. Moreover, the two political parties made considerable sympathetic noises in favor of the idea of an equal rights amendment for women in the federal constitution.

Unfortunately for women, the late 1940s and 1950s was a period of general repression on the American scene. People were happy to see the war's end and wanted nothing but simple private lives devoted to money making, with no discussion or recognition of continuing social problems. Radicals and liberals who advocated any social change were hounded by Senator McCarthy and a huge number of publicity-seeking inquisitors; one of those who made a successful career of "witch-hunting" was Richard Nixon. Women were told to leave their war jobs and return to kitchens, children, and churches (just as Hitler had told German women). The media—and even conservative psychologists—painted a picture in which every woman was a happy housewife surrounded by hordes of smiling children and shiny gadgets.

Yet reality was quite different. Later studies have shown that most women who are nothing but housewives are dreadfully unfulfilled and unhappy. Moreover, even in the 1950s the number of women at work kept increasing, despite all the propaganda. By 1985 more than four out of every ten workers were women—and a majority of all women between 16 and 64 now work. Yet they work in the poorest jobs, such as domestic servant or secretary, and are paid less than men even for the same job. The average full-time woman worker only makes 59 percent of what a full-time male worker is paid. Furthermore, in every area women who are fully qualified are denied promotions. Only a few of the thousands of corporate executives are women, only 9 percent of full professors are women, in 1985 only 24 of the 535 members of the U.S.

House and Senate are women; and no woman has ever been president or vice-president.

In the 1960s women began to protest these conditions. The first result of protest was the Equal Pay Act of 1963. Then, in 1964, a provision for women was added to the Civil Rights Act that prohibited discrimination in employment against minority groups. The addition was made by a southern congressman who wanted to defeat the whole act by amending it to add the ban on sex discrimination, and its final passage was a political miracle. Even after it was passed, the agencies who were responsible for enforcing it treated the sex discrimination ban as a joke and made little attempt to enforce it.

As a result, in 1966 the National Organization of Women was formed. It is a moderate organization that wishes to see the laws against sex discrimination fully enforced and has worked to get other laws—like the Equal Rights Amendment—passed in order to give women fully equal rights at last.

In the meantime, radical women gained a great deal of experience in the civil rights movement and the antiwar movement. Once again, recognition of the oppression of blacks made women conscious of their own oppression. They therefore began to work to direct the Left toward the fight for equality for women as well as for minorities. In this, however, they were rebuffed by many male radicals who were unenlightened on the subject of women. When the subject of women's rights was broached by black women in the civil rights organization called the Student Nonviolent Coordinating Committee, its leader Stokely Carmichael said, "The only position for women in SNCC is prone."[8] By 1968 many radical women were fed up with most leftist organizations, so they organized their own separate movement.

The women's movement, however, has never been intellectually or politically homogeneous. The National Organization of Women has always been its largest and best-organized component. This group advocates reforms that would not seriously alter the more fundamental economic, social, or political institutions of the United States. It seems implicitly to accept the view that sexism is primarily the result of ignorance and that through education and political pressures applied to the Democratic and Republican parties most of the inequities suffered by women can be eliminated by legislative reform.

The most extreme segment of the women's movement is the separatists. They see all men as the enemy and believe that women's liberation cannot be achieved within a society of both men and women. They advocate a radically new society (or new enclaves in society) composed solely of women—they have a variety of plans or schemes by which to assure conception and biological propagation of the women. They see all oppression as merely so many aspects of "male institutions" and all oppressive behavior as "male behavior" (whether the behavior is on the part of a man or a woman).

Marxist feminists form a third component of the women's movement. They see sexism as resulting from social institutions and systematically inculcated subjective attitudes about women, which in both cases serve to

---

[8]Quoted in Judith Hole and Ellen Levine, *Rebirth of Feminism* (New York: Quadrangle, 1971), p. 110.

strengthen and perpetuate the capitalist system of power and privilege. All Marxist feminists agree that sexism is related to the class oppression that has existed for many centuries, and that sexism will never be eliminated until all class oppression is eliminated. There were and are, nevertheless, continuing disagreements among Marxists concerning the exact relationships between class struggles—in slavery, feudalism, capitalism, and other class-divided societies—and the psychological attitudes and prejudices relating to sexist discrimination.

Some Marxist feminists—probably a minority, but including several influential writers—stress that some form of sexual oppression may be a necessary prerequisite for the creation of the subjective attitudes necessary to create and maintain *any* form of class-divided society. They emphasize that any form of class domination requires authoritarian personalities in the dominant groups and repressed psychological attitudes for most people in the society. Therefore, they argue that sexism can be seen in some ways prior to, and more fundamental than, the class oppression that Marx showed to be one of the defining features of any class-divided mode of production, including capitalism.

The majority of Marxist feminists would agree that sexism has existed in many class-divided societies before capitalism, and they would agree that the authoritarian and paternalistic psychology of sexism is a vital and important feature of all known class societies. Both groups of Marxist feminists would stress that the oppression of women helps to increase capitalist profits and to divide men from women workers, which ultimately weakens the working class both politically and economically. According to the majority of Marxist opinion, however, because sexism performs such a necessary function for capitalism, it will always be the prevailing ideology under capitalism, regardless of how many laws are passed against it. Therefore, these Marxist feminists contend that the struggle to abolish capitalism is the most important and fundamental way to fight sex oppression.

A minority of Marxist feminists insists that unless the fight to abolish both sexist institutions and attitudes is made coequal with the fight to abolish the class division of society, it is probable that the society that results from a socialist revolution will itself become a class-divided, exploitative society. In the majority view, all class oppression must be abolished and socialism established as the *necessary prerequisite* for the liberation of women and all human beings. The majority of Marxist feminists would agree with the minority (as against some vulgar Marxists) that a socialist revolution is not a sufficient guarantee of women's liberation, that a continuing movement for women's liberation is needed both *before* and *after* the socialist revolution.

CONTEMPORARY CRITIQUES OF AMERICAN CAPITALISM

The civil rights, antiwar, and women's liberation movements led to a burgeoning literature critical of the basic institutions of American capitalism. Like earlier critiques, this literature censured the grossly unequal distribution of income, wealth, and power in the United States. These critics, like the leftist Keynesians, deplored the extent to which post–World War II economic stability had been purchased at a cost of thoroughgoing militarism (discussed in Chapter 12).

On these points radical and liberal critics have been in agreement. Liberal critics, however, believe that political reform and electoral politics are sufficient to correct these perversions of the American economy. Radical critics believe inequality and militarism are inherent in a capitalist economy and that it also necessarily involves (1) imperialistic exploitation of underdeveloped countries as a means of maintaining high output and large profits in the United States, (2) endemic discrimination against minority groups and women, (3) inability to control pollution and resource exhaustion, and (4) a degrading commercialism and social alienation. In the remainder of this chapter some of the literature in these four general areas is described. Much of this literature has appeared in the *Review of Radical Political Economics,* published by the Union for Radical Political Economics (URPE). Its address is 41 Union Square West (Room 901), New York, New York, 10003. URPE is the main organization of U.S. radical economists.

American Imperialism

One of the first and most influential of these critics was Paul A. Baran. His book *The Political Economy of Growth,*[9] first published in 1957, has been translated into several languages; it has sold very well in the United States and even better in most less developed countries. Baran argued that, before a less developed country could industrialize, it would have to mobilize its *economic surplus,* or the difference between what is produced and what has to be consumed in order to maintain the economy's productivity. It is the source of investment capital with which the country can industrialize. Under present institutional arrangements, most less developed countries either waste their surpluses or lose them to imperialistic capitalist countries.

"Far from serving as an engine of economic expansion, of technological progress and of social change, the capitalist order in . . . [underdeveloped] countries has represented a framework for economic stagnation, for archaic technology, and for social backwardness."[10] The peasant agriculture usually produces a sufficiently large surplus in these countries. In fact, Baran pointed out that the surplus is frequently as high as 50 percent of the total amount produced. "The subsistence peasant's obligations on account of rent, taxes, and interest in all underdeveloped countries are very high. They frequently absorb more than half of his meager net product."[11]

The problem is in the disposition of this surplus. Part goes to middlemen, speculators, moneylenders, and merchants—petty capitalists who have neither

[9]Paul A. Baran, *The Political Economy of Growth* (New York: Monthly Review Press, 1962).

[10]Ibid., pp. 164–165.

[11]Ibid., p. 165.

the interest nor the wherewithal to finance industrialization. A much larger part goes to the landowning ruling class, which uses its "share" to purchase luxury consumption goods, usually imported from capitalist countries, and to the extensive military establishments needed to maintain their internal power.

Importing luxuries and military hardware necessitates sending exports to the industrialized countries; exports usually consist of one or two primary agricultural products or mineral resources. The capitalist countries with which they trade have a great deal of monopsonistic buying power (that is, there are many sellers and only a few collusive buyers), and thus can set the terms of trade in their own interest. The large multinational corporations that purchase the raw materials are not interested in the industrialization of these countries. Thus foreign capitalist investment is limited to that necessary for the profitable extraction of resources.

An alliance between the reactionary landowning class and foreign capitalists protects the interests of both by suppressing all opposition and keeping the masses at a subsistence standard of living. Thus landowners can maintain their position, and capitalists are guaranteed cheap labor and large profits.

> Small wonder that under such circumstances Western big business heavily engaged in raw materials exploitation leaves no stone unturned to obstruct the evolution of social and political conditions in underdeveloped countries that might be conducive to their economic development. It uses its tremendous power to prop up the backward areas' comprador administrations, to disrupt and corrupt the social and political movements that oppose them, and to overthrow whatever progressive governments may rise to power and refuse to do the bidding of their imperialistic overlords.[12]

Baran believed the American government works hand in hand with American big business. Most U.S. economic and military aid provided to less developed countries is given, in his opinion, in order to prop up client governments. Often such governments are not strong enough to survive on their own, even with this aid. Under these circumstances the United States intervenes, either clandestinely (through CIA sabotage and intrigue) or directly (through the use of military force).

Baran and like-minded critics see the interventions in Guatemala, Iran, Korea, Cuba, the Dominican Republic, Vietnam, Nicaragua, and El Salvador as examples of American endeavors to protect business interests, both current and potential, against threats from more progressive social and political movements. They point to 53 different "U.S. defense commitments and assurances" that commit the United States to the use of military force to maintain existing governments, very often against their own people.[13]

The dependence of less developed countries on a small number of export commodities is documented in a study based on International Monetary Fund

---

[12]Ibid., p. 198.
[13]See Harry Magdoff, *The Age of Imperialism, The Economics of U.S. Foreign Policy* (New York: Monthly Review Press, Modern Reader Paperbacks, 1969), pp. 203–206.

data. Each of the 37 countries considered earns 58 to 99 percent of its export receipts from one to six commodities.[14] Furthermore, the United States depends on imports as the principal source for most of the 62 types of materials the Defense Department classifies as strategic and critical. For 38 of these, 80 to 100 percent of the new supplies are imported; for 14 more, 40 to 79 percent are imported.[15]

A large and increasing percentage of U.S. corporate sales and profits result from exports and sales of foreign subsidiaries (many of which, of course, are in less developed countries).[16] Moreover, detailed examination reveals that the foreign trade of the less developed countries is very lopsided. Raw materials and metals in their first state of smelting constitute 85 percent of exports and manufactured goods (mostly textiles) only 10 percent, but about 60 percent of imports are manufactured goods.[17] Because most manufactured imports are consumer goods, such a pattern of trade cannot lead to development but only to continued economic dependence.

Critics of this point of view (that is, defenders of American economic foreign policy) argue that although foreign trade and foreign investments are important to American corporations, they also benefit the less developed countries. The orthodox argument is expressed in a widely used textbook:

In general, a restrained optimism as to the future prospects for underdeveloped countries in their trading relations with the developed countries seems to be warranted. The most encouraging sign is the growing recognition on the part of developed countries that opening their markets to the export products of underdeveloped areas is an essential part of their accepted program to assist underdeveloped countries to grow.[18]

Yet this position does not deal directly with radical critiques of American economic foreign policy. It simply assumes that all the less developed countries need is *more* trade and more private investment. Another orthodox scholar who has studied the problem more thoroughly admits that "increasing the flow of private capital to underdeveloped countries will probably require a *recasting of economic policies* in both underdeveloped and advanced countries."[19] He does not go on to analyze what obstacles prevent this "recasting of economic policies."

Conservative defenders of American policies grant that developed capitalist countries have had immense economic, political, and military power, which they have used to influence and control peoples around the world. They

[14]Magdoff, ibid., pp. 99–100.
[15]Percy W. Bidwell, *Raw Materials* (New York: Harper & Row, 1958), p. 12.
[16]Magdoff, *Age of Imperialism,* p. 57.
[17]Pierre Jalee, *The Pillage of the Third World* (New York: Monthly Review Press, 1969), p. 8.
[18]Delbert A. Snider, *Introduction to International Economics* (Homewood, Ill.: Irwin, 1963), p. 548.
[19]Benjamin Higgins, *Economic Development* (New York: Norton, 1959), p. 593; italics added.

deny, however, that this "imperialism" is basically economic in nature. Thus the widely respected economic historian Professor David S. Landes writes:

> It seems to me that one has to look at imperialism as a multifarious response to a common opportunity that consists simply in disparity of power. Whenever and wherever such disparity has existed, people and groups have been ready to take advantage of it. It is, one notes with regret, in the nature of the human beast to push other people around—or to save their souls or "civilize" them as the case may be.[20]

One radical critic has answered this assertion by noting that the modern capitalist drive to save people's souls from communism and to civilize them is perfectly compatible with economic motives. He cites the following quotation from an officer of the General Electric Company: "Thus, our search for profits places us squarely in line with the national policy of stepping up international trade as a means of strengthening the free world in the Cold War confrontation with Communism." The critic, Harry Magdoff, summarizes his position: "Just as the fight against Communism helps the search for profits, so the search for profits helps the fight against Communism. What more perfect harmony of interests could be imagined?"[21]

Many books written in the 1960s attempted to explain contemporary American foreign policy—and the cold war between the United States and the Soviet Union—in terms of American economic imperialism.[22]

Racism and Sexism

Radical critics also point to the pervasive effects of discrimination based on race and sex that exist in capitalist countries, particularly in the United States. Virtually everyone agrees that racism and sexism create severe discrimination. Defenders of American capitalism explain this discrimination in one of two ways. The more reactionary argue that job discrimination merely reflects the innate inferiority of women and blacks. Few, if any, intellectuals embrace this position, but it apparently is accepted by a large minority in the United States. The other contention is that racism and sexism are products of a fairly universal human bigotry and are not related to capitalism or any other economic system.

Critics of capitalism point out that the wages of blacks and women make up a significant part of capitalists' wage costs. In 1970, for example, the wages of American women averaged only about 50 percent of the wages of men doing

[20]David S. Landes, "The Nature of Economic Imperialism," *The Journal of Economic History,* December 1961, p. 510.

[21]Magdoff, *Age of Imperialism,* pp. 200–201.

[22]See Magdoff, ibid.; D. F. Fleming, *The Cold War and Its Origins* (Garden City, N.Y.: Doubleday, 1961); Gar Alperowitz, *Atomic Diplomacy: Hiroshima and Potsdam* (New York: Simon & Schuster, 1965); David Horowitz, ed., *Corporations and the Cold War* (New York: Monthly Review Press, 1969); and David Horowitz, *Empire and Revolution* (New York: Random House, 1969).

the same jobs. On that basis it would appear that approximately 23 percent of all manufacturing profits is attributable to the lower wages paid to women. Profits made as a result of racial discrimination are smaller, but they are still significant.

In one of the most influential socialist critiques, Paul A. Baran and Paul M. Sweezy have argued that it is necessary to

> consider first the private interests which benefit from the existence of a Negro subproletariat. (a) Employers benefit from divisions in the labor force which enable them to play one group off against another, thus weakening all. . . . (b) Owners of ghetto real estate are able to overcrowd and overcharge. (c) Middle and upper income groups benefit from having at their disposal a large supply of cheap domestic labor. (d) Many small marginal businesses, especially in the service trades, can operate profitably only if cheap labor is available to them. (e) White workers benefit by being protected from Negro competition for the more desirable and higher paying jobs.[23]

They also assert that, in addition to increasing profits, discrimination increases social stability in a capitalist economy. The class structure of capitalism, they hold, leads to a situation in which

> each status group has a deep-rooted psychological need to compensate for feelings of inferiority and envy toward those above by feelings of superiority and contempt for those below. It thus happens that a special pariah group at the bottom acts as a kind of lightning rod for the frustrations and hostilities of all the higher groups, the more so the nearer they are to the bottom. It may even be said that the very existence of the pariah group is a kind of harmonizer and stabilizer of the social structure.[24]

Although Baran and Sweezy's assertions pertain to racism, many critics argue that sexism performs a similar function in a capitalist society. These critics generally do not believe that capitalism is the original creator of racism and sexism, but they do argue that capitalism perpetuates and intensifies racism and sexism because these serve valuable functions.

> Today, transferring the locus of whites' perceptions of the source of many of their problems from capitalism and toward blacks, racism continues to serve the needs of the capitalist system. Although an individual employer might gain by refusing to discriminate and agreeing to hire blacks at above the going black wage rate, it is not true that the capitalist class as a whole would profit if racism were eliminated and labor were more efficiently allocated without regard to skin color. . . . The divisiveness of racism weakens workers' strength when bargaining with employers; the economic conse-

[23]Paul A. Baran and Paul M. Sweezy, *Monopoly Capital* (New York: Monthly Review Press, 1966), pp. 263–264.
[24]Ibid., pp. 265–266.

quences of racism are not only lower incomes for blacks but also higher incomes for the capitalist class coupled with lower incomes for white workers. Although capitalists may not have conspired consciously to create racism, and although capitalists may not be its principal perpetuators, nevertheless racism does support the continued well-being of the American capitalist system.[25]

Similarly, the critics argue that sex prejudice helps divide the labor, civil rights, and radical movements to the benefit of American capitalists.

Alienation

Many contemporary radical critics have refined and elaborated on Marx's theory of the human alienation inherent in the capitalist economic system.[26] Baran and Sweezy, for example, maintain that total alienation pervades and dominates contemporary American capitalism:

> Disorientation, apathy, and often despair, haunting Americans in all walks of life, have assumed in our time the dimensions of a prolonged crisis. This crisis affects every aspect of national life, and ravages both its social-political and its individual spheres—everyman's everyday existence. A heavy strangulating sense of the emptiness and futility of life permeates the country's moral and intellectual climate. High level committees are entrusted with the discovery and specification of "national goals" while gloom pervades the printed matter (fiction and non-fiction, alike) appearing daily in the literary market place. The malaise deprives work of meaning and purpose; turns leisure into joyless, debilitating laziness; fatally impairs the education system and the conditions of healthy growth in the young; transforms religion and church into commercialized vehicles of "togetherness"; and destroys the very foundation of bourgeois society, the family.[27]

The fact of alienation, like the facts of racism and sexism, is explained by many defenders of capitalism as an unfortunate but inevitable by-product of industrial civilization. They point to all the boring and dangerous work that must be done, as well as to the narrow and fragmented personalities of the enormous number of bureaucrats. An industrialized socialist economy would, they assert, create the same type of alienation. Few people, regardless of political and economic views, would be willing to forgo the advantages of industrialization in order to combat alienation. Moreover, even if people did want to return to preindustrial society, there is simply no practical way of turning back time to some imagined golden age.

[25]Michael Reich, "The Economics of Racism," in David M. Gordon, ed., *Problems in Political Economy: An Urban Perspective* (Lexington, Mass.: Raytheon/Heath, 1971), pp. 109–110.

[26]See Chapter 7.

[27]Baran and Sweezy, *Monopoly Capital*, p. 281.

Socialist critics reply that although some amount of alienation will surely exist in any industrialized society, capitalism significantly intensifies alienation and makes it more pervasive. Erich Fromm, the psychoanalyst, social philosopher, and author, argues that the most important single cause of alienation is the fact that the individual feels no sense of participation in the forces that determine social policy. Individuals see these forces as anonymous and totally beyond their sphere of influence. "The anonymity of the social forces," writes Fromm, "is inherent in the structure of the capitalist mode of production."[28]

Fromm identifies several types of alienation created by the capitalist mode of production. Conditions of employment alienate workers. Their livelihoods depend on whether capitalists and managers are able to make a profit by hiring them, and thus they are viewed as means only, never as ends. The individual worker is "an economic atom that dances to the tune of atomistic management." Managers "strip the worker of his right to think and move freely. Life is being denied; need to control, creativeness, curiosity, and independent thought are being balked, and the result, the inevitable result, is flight or fight on the part of the worker, apathy or destructiveness, psychic regression."[29] The worker feels that the capitalist controls his or her whole life; both workers and consumers (and voters) feel weak and insignificant compared to the colossal power of the corporations over working conditions, prices, and even government policy.

Yet Fromm argues that the "role of the manager is also one of alienation," for managers too are coerced by the ineluctable forces of capitalism and have very little freedom. They must deal "with impersonal giants; with the giant competitive enterprise; with giant impersonal markets; with giant unions; and the giant government."[30] Their position, status, and income—in short, their very social existence—all depend on the generation of ever-increasing levels of profits. Yet managers must do this in a world in which they have little personal influence on the giants surrounding them.

Fromm also maintains that the process of consumption in a capitalist society "is as alienated as the process of production." The truly human way of acquiring commodities, according to Fromm, would be through need and the desire to use: "The acquisition of bread and clothing [should] depend on no other premise than that of being alive; the acquisition of books and paintings on my effort to understand them and my ability to use them."[31] In capitalist societies, however, the income with which to purchase these commodities can come only through sales in the impersonal market.

As a consequence, those who have money are subjected to a constant barrage of propaganda designed to create consuming automata. Capitalist

[28]Erich Fromm, *The Sane Society* (New York: Fawcett World Library, Premier Books, 1965), p. 125.

[29]Quoted in ibid., p. 115.

[30]Ibid., pp. 115–116.

[31]Ibid., p. 120.

socialization processes make consumption-hungry, irrational, compulsive buying machines of us all. Acts of buying and consuming have become ends in
themselves, with little or no relation to the uses or pleasures derived from the
commodities.

> Man today is fascinated by the possibility of buying more, better, and espe-
> cially, new things. He is consumption-hungry. The act of buying and consum-
> ing has become a compulsive, irrational aim, because it is an end in itself,
> with little relation to the use or pleasure in the things bought and consumed.
> To buy the latest gadget, the latest model of anything that is on the market,
> is a dream of everybody in comparison to which the real pleasure in use is
> quite secondary. Modern man, if he dared to be articulate about his concept
> of heaven, would describe a vision which would look like the biggest depart-
> ment store in the world, showing new things and gadgets, and himself having
> plenty of money with which to buy them. He would wander around open-
> mouthed in his heaven of gadgets and commodities, provided only that there
> were ever more and newer things to buy, and perhaps that his neighbors
> were just a little less privileged than he.[32]

Finally, the most severe alienation is the alienation of a person from his
or her "self." A person's "worth" in a capitalist market economy is determined
in the same way as the "worth" of anything else: by sales in the marketplace.
In this situation,

> man experiences himself as a thing to be employed successfully on the
> market. He does not experience himself as an active agent, as the bearer of
> human powers. He is alienated from these powers. His aim is to sell himself
> successfully on the market. His sense of self does not stem from his activity
> as a loving and thinking individual, but from his socio-economic role. . . . If
> you ask a man "Who are you?", he answers "I am a manufacturer," "I am
> a clerk," "I am a doctor." That is the way he experiences himself, not as a
> man, with love, fear, convictions, doubts, but as that abstraction, alienated
> from his real nature, which fulfills a certain function in the social system. His
> sense of value depends on his success: on whether he can sell himself
> favorably, whether he can make more of himself than he started out with,
> whether he is a success. His body, his mind and his soul are his capital, and
> his task in life is to invest it favorably, to make a *profit* of himself. Human
> qualities like friendliness, courtesy, kindness, are transformed into commodi-
> ties, into assets of the "personality package," conducive to a higher price
> on the personality market. If the individual fails in a profitable investment of
> himself, he feels that he is a failure; if he succeeds, he is a success. Clearly,
> his sense of his own value always depends on factors extraneous to himself,
> on the fickle judgment of the market, which decides about his value as it
> decides about the value of commodities. He, like all commodities that cannot
> be sold profitably on the market, is worthless as far as his exchange value
> is concerned, even though his use value may be considerable.[33]

[32]Ibid., p. 123.
[33]Ibid., pp. 129–130.

Thus, socialist critics argue that the impersonal nexus of the capitalist market mediates all human relationships. It makes profit and loss the ultimate and pervasive evaluative criteria of human worth. This means that human alienation must inevitably be extremely severe in a capitalist market economy.

Environmental Destruction

Capitalism must either experience economic growth or else suffer depression, unemployment, stagnation, and their attendant social problems. Yet economic growth can also create situations in which the pursuit of profits comes into direct conflict with the public welfare. Critics of capitalism have argued that corporate profit seeking is generally accompanied by very little concern for conservation or the maintenance of a clean, livable environment.

Pollution is of concern to defenders of capitalism as well as to its critics. Defenders argue that it is a problem common to all industrialized economies. Critics maintain, however, that the problem is worse in a capitalist economy. Furthermore, they point out that it is virtually impossible to control pollution effectively in a capitalist system because the basic economic cause of pollution in a capitalist economy is that business firms do not have to pay for *all* the costs incurred in the production process. They pay for labor, raw materials, and capital used up in production. Generally, however, they pay little or nothing for the use of the land, air, and water for the disposal of waste products that are created in the process of production. Thus the environment is treated as a garbage disposal.

It has been estimated[34] that each year businesses are responsible for over 25 billion tons of pollutants being spewed into the air and dumped into the water and on the land. This is about 125 tons of waste per year for every man, woman, and child in the United States. Included in this figure are about 150 million tons of smoke and fumes that blacken the skies and poison the air, 22 million tons of waste paper products, 3 million tons of mill tailings, and 50 trillion gallons of heated and polluted liquids that are dumped into streams, rivers, and lakes each year. Critics argue that it is extremely difficult if not impossible for a capitalist economy to deal with these problems because those who receive the profits from production do not pay these social costs, and those who do pay the social costs have little or no voice in the operation of the business.

In response to the widespread public demand for control of pollution and polluters, the government has given contracts to many corporations to devise new methods of combating pollution. In effect, the government is asking private corporations to act as the controllers of other private corporations. Critics are convinced that this corporate integration of polluters and controllers will never lead to any substantial improvement. Most of the important

[34]These estimates are taken from an important and impressive study on pollution: R. C. D'Arge, A. V. Kneese, and R. V. Ayres, *Economics of the Environment: A Materials Balance Approach* (Baltimore: Johns Hopkins Press, 1970).

pollution control companies have become subsidiaries of the giant corporations that do most of the polluting.

One radical critic has analyzed the effects of this corporate control as follows:

> It is the chemical industry . . . that best illustrates the consequences of the incest between the pollution control business and the industrial polluters. First, the chemical industry is in the enviable position of reaping sizable profits by attempting to clean up rivers and lakes (at public expense) which they have profitably polluted in the first place. To facilitate this practically every major chemical company in the U.S. has established a pollution abatement division or is in the process of doing so. . . . A second consequence of placing the "control" of pollution in the hands of big business is that the official abatement levels will inevitably be set low enough to protect industry's power to pollute and therefore its ability to keep costs down and revenues high. According to a recent study by the FWPCA (Federal Water Pollution Control Administration) if the chemical industry were to reduce its pollution of water to zero, the costs involved would amount to almost $2.7 billion per year. This would cut profits almost by half.[35]

Under such circumstances the critics do not expect much progress in cleaning up the environment unless fundamental social, political, and economic changes occur first.

The Energy Crisis

In 1973 the American public suddenly found that there had developed a shortage of gasoline. They were told that it was because the Arab countries, where much of the world's crude oil is extracted, had formed a cartel called the Organization of Petroleum Exporting Countries (OPEC), and that the cartel was cutting back on production and charging higher prices.

Very shortly thereafter the shortage led to long lines at gas stations and much higher prices. Once the shortage forced prices up approximately 50 percent, however, it mysteriously disappeared. The giant, oligopolistic oil companies realized a colossal increase in profits; for some of these massive corporations profits increased in excess of 200 percent. Higher profits having been achieved, there was suddenly plenty of gasoline (at the higher prices) for everyone.

So that Americans would not see themselves simply as victims of a hoax perpetrated by greedy, profit-hungry oil companies, however, they were told that there was a general "energy crisis." The speed limit on major highways was reduced from 70 to 55 miles per hour. People were exhorted to use lights, appliances, and air conditioners very sparingly. They were repeatedly told that it was patriotic to pay much more to the energy-supplying corporations for the use of less energy.

[35]Martin Gellen, "The Making of a Pollution-Industrial Complex," in Gordon, *Problems in Political Economy,* pp. 469–470.

Again in 1979 there developed another gasoline shortage. The results were, once again, long lines and soaring prices. Again Americans were told that the OPEC countries were to blame for not extracting and exporting enough crude oil and for charging higher prices. Yet this time Americans were not as gullible as the big oil companies and the government thought. They realized that the official explanation left facts unexplained. First, for a period of over 15 years the oil companies had purposely refrained from expanding their productive capacity as fast as demand was expanding and thereby had purposely created a situation in which at some point a shortage would become inevitable (and would be very profitable for them). Second, during the winter months of 1979 the oil companies cut back on the percentage of their refining capacity they were utilizing, thereby purposely creating the immediate acute shortage. Third, the higher prices the oil companies paid to the OPEC countries came nowhere near accounting for all of the increases in the price of gasoline that Americans were paying, and once again the profits of the oil companies soared.

Radical critics pointed out that there was absolutely nothing "unnatural" or even unusual about all of this. The energy crisis perfectly reflects how private enterprise capitalism works. Capitalists have always tried to create oligopolies and monopolies that can "corner a market." Once they have control of a market, then they increase the price to whatever level the "traffic will bear" in order to maximize profit. Maximizing profits is what private enterprise is all about.

The more the general public needs the product in question the higher the price that can be charged and the profit that can be made. In the case of petroleum, our entire society is an automobile culture in which driving a car is absolutely necessary for most working-class people to get to work and to shopping centers. Hence gasoline is an absolute necessity of life. Therefore, both the wealthy Arab kings who own the crude oil and the giant oil companies who refine it and sell it have behaved exactly as one would have expected them to behave. Depending on values and intellectual perspective, one can call it gouging and robbing the public through monopoly power over a necessary commodity—or one can call it ingeniously successful free enterprise at work.

Radicals point out that it is a form of gross social stupidity to allow a few greedy individuals to engage in what is tantamount to blackmail simply because they have monopolized ownership of things that are daily necessities. They further point out that the oil companies dominate the ownership of such alternative energy sources as coal, shale oil, and tar sands oil, so we have no choice but to submit to their blackmail.

Radicals insist that only when the production of all necessities is owned and controlled by the general public, that is, only with socialism, can this grip of blackmailing giants be broken. Only then can a rational energy policy be built around a program of low-cost, efficient public transportation for everyone. In the meantime, we all wait for the next crisis with its long lines, soaring prices, and mushrooming profits for the oil companies.

Inflation

As a result of prolonged massive military expenditures, financed in part through deficit spending, together with the steadily increasing debt levels of individuals, businesses, and government, there has not been a depression of the magnitude of the Great Depression during the years since World War II. This form of stimulating expenditures, however, creates difficulties of its own. Each year levels of debt must be increased to service past borrowing and to stimulate new expenditures. This means that the amount of debt as well as the money supply have increased much faster than any increases in productivity and output. The result has been prolonged chronic inflation. By early 1980 the rate of inflation was 18 percent per year. During the early 1980s the effort to decrease the rate of inflation severely increased the rate of unemployment. Because there were 7 million or more unemployed workers since the early 1970s, decreasing the rate of inflation by increasing unemployment risked precipitating a major depression.

Inflation, however, does not harm everyone. It merely *redistributes* wealth and income. The hardest hit by inflation are people on fixed incomes and pensions. Their buying power continuously shrinks. Next hardest hit are workers. According to the government index of labor productivity, productivity between 1967 and 1978 increased by 16.5 percent, whereas during those same years real wages (that is, wages after adjustment for inflation) increased by only 2.4 percent. Thus more than 80 percent of the workers' increased productivity was taken from them by higher prices. The beneficiaries of inflation are the capitalists. They own the commodities that are going up in price and realize windfall gains. Bankers are the most significant beneficiaries of the current inflation. They have managed to keep the interest rate above the rate of inflation and have continuously expanded their loans. Throughout the 1970s bank profits soared to all-time highs.

The general benefits of inflation for capitalists can be seen in the profits of the largest 500 industrial corporations for 1978 as reported in *Fortune* magazine. The editors of *Fortune* wrote that in 1978, when most people were reeling under the blows of inflation, "profits were absolutely sensational . . . and median profit margins reached . . . the highest level in a decade. The median return on stockholders equity . . . was the highest on record."[36]

Radicals point out that even the massive expansion of credit cannot eliminate the boom-bust cycle of capitalism. To the degree that this credit expansion has mitigated the severity of depressions it has involved two significant social costs. First, it has redistributed income and wealth from the old, the poor, and the working class to capitalists. Second, it has created a worldwide superstructure of credit in which A owes B, B owes C, C owes D, and so forth, so that solvency at any level depends on ever-increasing borrowing. Thus, the possibility now exists for a chain reaction of default that could precipitate a crisis potentially worse than the depression of the 1930s. The underlying problem of the inherent instability of capitalism always remains. At present (1985), the economy is expanding in the wake of the recession of 1981–1983. Economists are, nevertheless, already talking about the timing of the next recession. The next recession may, of course, be short and relatively mild. It is also always possible that any recession can bring about the chain reaction that will lead to a socially disastrous depression.

LIBERAL VERSUS RADICAL CRITIQUES OF CAPITALISM

The glaringly unequal distribution of wealth, income, and political power and the facts of militarism, imperialism, vicious discrimination, social alienation, environmental destruction, irrational use of resources and energy sources, and severe inflation are all recognized and decried by both liberal and radical critics of capitalism. There is, however, an immensely important difference between the positions of liberals and radicals.

Liberals tend to see each of these social and economic problems as separate and distinct. The problems, they believe, are the results of past mistakes or random cases of individual perversity. Liberals also tend to consider the government as disinterested, as motivated by a desire to maximize the welfare of all its citizens. Hence, they generally favor government-sponsored reforms designed to mitigate the many evils of capitalism. These reforms never threaten the two most important features of capitalism—private ownership of the means of production and the free market.

Radicals, however, see each of the social and economic problems we have discussed as the direct consequence of private ownership of capital and the process of social decision making within the impersonal cash nexus of the market. The problems cannot be solved until their underlying causes are eliminated, but this means a fundamental, radical economic reorganization. If private ownership of capital is eliminated and if significant restrictions are placed on the areas in which the market determines social decision, the resulting system would no longer be a capitalist economic system. It would of necessity be some type of socialist society.

RADICAL POLITICAL MOVEMENTS
IN THE 1960s, 1970s, AND 1980s

In the 1930s and 1940s the "old left" political movements had gained substantially in both numbers and influence. The old left was almost entirely socialist, and its growth had been a consequence of the Great Depression of the 1930s, which had convinced many people that capitalism was an irrational, dying system. The principal organizations of the left were the Communist party, the Socialist party, and the Socialist Workers party. Although their memberships constituted only a tiny percentage of the American population, they had an influence in labor organizations and in American social and political life that was far greater than their numbers would indicate.

The economic recovery of the late 1940s and 1950s, combined with the harsh intellectual and political repression of McCarthyism, had almost destroyed the leftist movement by the late 1950s and early 1960s. The civil rights and antiwar movements led to a widespread rebirth of the belief that many of the worst evils of American society were the inevitable outcomes of the structure and organization of capitalism. These movements thus led to a rebirth of the socialist movement.

Yet the radicals of the 1960s were generally very different from their counterparts in the 1930s. These differences—which resulted in their being called the "new left," in contrast to the "old left" of the 1930s and its surviving organizations—can be categorized under three headings. First, many believed that moral and emotional contempt were more important than the old left's intellectual dogmas as potential sources for transforming American society. Often their own emotional intensity and moral fervor led them to believe a new American revolution was just around the corner. Second, many were so contemptuous of intellectual dogmatism and old left sloganeering that they refused for several years to accept very many of the theoretical and empirical insights of the Marxist tradition. Third, their dislike of authority, authoritarian structures, and the suppression of the individual was so great that they were unable to create any effective organizations through which to further their aims.

The organization most typical of, and influential among, the new left was the Students for a Democratic Society (SDS). Organized in the early 1960s, it was most instrumental in disseminating the facts about the Vietnam War and in mobilizing massive student resistance against the war. By 1968, however, two things had become obvious. First, its aversion to leftist dogma was so great as to degenerate at times into anti-intellectualism. As a result, there was amazing diversity in its members' opinions about the nature of American society and the best tactics to use in attempting to restructure that society. Second, the aversion to authority (euphemistically extolled as "participatory democracy") had resulted in an organization so loosely and ineffectively structured that it was hardly capable of any well-coordinated mass action at all.

It is not surprising that in 1969, shortly after President Nixon was elected, relatively little effort was required on the part of government agents and provocateurs to precipitate the immediate and almost total disintegration of SDS. By this time, however, the antiwar movement had a momentum of its own and was able to survive the demise of SDS. Many moderate and liberal leaders had joined the bandwagon, and the Socialist Workers party and the Communist party had become active in the leadership of the radical wing of the antiwar movement.

By early 1973 several things became apparent. With the end of the Vietnam War, hundreds of thousands of Americans who had opposed the war and had sometimes been thought to be a part of the movement lapsed into a mood of relief and what appeared to be social and political indifference. People were weary of social conflict and hopeful that a peaceful, tranquil mood would come to prevail in the United States. The Watergate revelations and subsequent disclosures of widespread, illegal operations of the American CIA and

FBI showed Americans how far their government would go to crush political criticism at home and to maintain the worldwide American empire.

The result of these revelations was not, as leftists hoped, a widespread indignation and determination for radical social change. The more usual response was apathy and a naive hope and faith that these abuses and excesses had simply been the result of a few corrupt and unscrupulous politicians. Both the Republican and Democratic parties chose presidential candidates for the 1976 election who could be portrayed as simple and honest—"just plain folks." Jimmy Carter was widely seen as uncorrupted by national office. He was elected president.

The 1970s saw several important changes in the radical movement. Many new left radicals of the 1960s came to see that their hopes for radical social change in the near future were unrealistic. They saw that promoting such change would require a more adequate knowledge of the structure and functioning of capitalist society. It would also require a much more effectively organized movement.

The first of these requirements led to a widespread tendency to study Marx and the ideas of Marxist theoreticians of the last 100 years. Radical students of the 1960s became radical professors in the 1970s. Organizations, such as the Union for Radical Political Economics (URPE), devoted themselves to the promotion and propagation of radical understanding of American capitalism. The URPE currently has about 2000 members and publishes analyses of the current economic and political trends in the United States as well as studies aimed at increasing radicals' understanding of the nature and functioning of capitalism. These are published regularly in two journals—*The Review of Radical Political Economics* and *Dollars and Sense*—and a newsletter. Informal study groups have sprung up around the United States. Several universities have academic departments where radical professors now regularly teach Marxist views on history and the social sciences.

The widely felt need for better organization affected members of the new left in very diverse ways. A large part of them felt that no satisfactory nationwide socialist organization existed, so they concentrated their efforts solely on local organizing. Another major segment joined the various old left organizations. During the 1970s several Maoist organizations (political organizations that base many of their ideas on the writings of Mao Tse Tung and the Chinese Communists), the Communist party, the Socialist Workers party, the Progressive Labor party, the International Socialists, the Socialist party, and other old left organizations have grown more rapidly than at any time since World War II.

A sizable number of former SDS members as well as many other members of the new left retained their dissatisfaction with the old left organizations, but they still hoped to reorganize on a nationwide basis. The most important organization to come out of this group was the New American Movement (NAM), which was formed in 1973 with approximately 50 chapters in various cities across the United States. The NAM aimed to create a democratic socialist society in the United States, in which racism, sexism, imperialism, and all other forms of human oppression were to be eradicated. It believed that the old left socialist organizations were too thoroughly affected by mistakes and outworn attitudes to be effective means for the economic, social, and political alterations that it believed were ultimately necessary to create a humane, moral society in the United States.

In the early 1970s, as a result of a number of internal conflicts, the Socialist party broke into three separate factions. One group remained the Socialist party. Another group, calling themselves Social Democrats U.S.A., abandoned socialism as a goal. A third group, calling themselves The Democratic Socialist Organizing Committee, was the largest of the three. In 1982 the Democratic Socialist Organizing Committee and The New American Movement merged to form the Democratic Socialists of America (DSA). In 1985 the DSA is the largest American socialist organization since the 1930s and is growing rapidly. The Socialist party, while small, continues to maintain the traditions of Eugene V. Debs, perhaps the greatest socialist in American history.

By 1980 very little of the civil rights, or black, movement remained as a separate movement. Most of their more moderate demands for economic reform have been taken up by the liberal wing of the Democratic party. Their more radical demands for fundamental change in the social, political, and economic institutions as a means of achieving human equality have been taken up by most of the socialist organizations (which have always fought for racial equality). The black separatist movement of the 1960s, which advocated a separate all-black nation, appears virtually to have disappeared.

The women's movement also changed in the 1970s and 1980s. The women's separatist movement appears to be following in the footsteps of the black separatist movement. Its members, like the members of the SDS in the 1960s, have an aversion to nearly all organizational forms and, consequently, have never been able to create a nationwide organization. Generally, their dislike of authority renders their political organizations ineffective.

The National Organization of Women advocates few, if any, fundamental changes in social, political, or economic structures of capitalism. Consequently, although they do have a large and effective nationwide organization, they are definitely not socialist—though their rhetoric has recently become very radical on a number of important issues.

The Marxist feminist movement has had a considerable impact on several socialist organizations. This component of the women's movement has no effective national organization with an all-women membership, nor is it devoted solely to feminist issues. Marxist feminists, however, constitute a significant portion of the Democratic Socialists of America (whose leadership bodies have always had more than 50 percent women), and feminist issues are very prominent in the program and activities of the Democratic Socialists of America.

The socialist movement in the United States is much smaller and less effective than its counterparts in most advanced capitalist countries. In several western European countries, coalitions of communists and socialists regularly receive somewhere near a majority of votes in national elections. Socialist and communist parties in these countries have memberships in the millions. Because the United States is the most powerful of all capitalist countries, it is not surprising that its socialist movement is the weakest.

As we have seen in earlier chapters, socialist ideas and movements came into being with the Industrial Revolution, and socialists have always fought to eradicate the worst effects of capitalism. Socialists have also always fought and will continue to fight for the complete abolition of capitalism and its replacement by a democratic socialist society. As long as capitalism involves poverty, inequality, imperialism, unemployment and economic crises, environmental pollution, racism, sexism, and alienation, there will undoubtedly be socialists speaking, writing, organizing, and acting in their efforts to create a better society.

SUMMARY

From the late 1950s to the early 1970s, the civil rights movement, the women's liberation movement, and the antiwar movement generated a resurgence of radical criticism of American capitalism. The radicals argue that inequality, discrimination, alienation, environmental destruction, militarism, irrational use of resources, instability, inflation, and imperialism are integral parts of a capitalist economy. Unlike liberals, who believe that these evils are accidental and that the system can be reformed, radicals contend that these evils cannot be overcome until the basic structure of capitalism is fundamentally changed.

The principal obstacle to the achievement of such reforms is the fact that political power is derived from economic power. Radicals see capitalist governments as plutocracies hidden behind phony facades of democracy. Both political parties, they point out, spend millions of dollars on each election. As a consequence, both political parties are almost completely controlled by the wealthiest 2 percent of the population, who own most of the income-producing capital.[37] In this situation one would not expect the wealthy elite to support any government that threatened to destroy the basis of their wealth, privileges, and power. Therefore fundamental reform seems unlikely unless a reform movement can establish a base of power independent of wealth. In the 1960s at radical gatherings one often heard the slogan "Power to the People!" A strategic plan to peacefully and legally transfer power from this elite to the democratic control of common people remains the most difficult task of the left.

[37]For detailed evidence for this point of view, see G. William Domhoff, *Who Rules America?* (Englewood Cliffs, N.J.: Prentice-Hall, 1967), and *The Higher Circles: The Governing Class in America* (New York: Random House, 1970).

Index